# The Grand Old Duke of York

# The Grand Old Duke of York

A Life of Prince Frederick,
Duke of York and Albany,
1763–1827

Derek Winterbottom

Pen & Sword
**MILITARY**

First published in Great Britain in 2016 by
Pen & Sword Military
an imprint of
Pen & Sword Books Ltd
47 Church Street
Barnsley
South Yorkshire
S70 2AS

ISBN 9781473845770

Typeset in Ehrhardt by
Replika Press Pvt Ltd, India
Printed and bound in England
By CPI Group (UK) Ltd, Croydon, CR0 4YY

Pen & Sword Books Ltd incorporates the imprints of Pen & Sword Archaeology, Atlas, Aviation, Battleground, Discovery, Family History, History, Maritime, Military, Naval, Politics, Railways, Select, Social History, Transport, True Crime, and Claymore Press, Frontline Books, Leo Cooper, Praetorian Press, Remember When, Seaforth Publishing and Wharncliffe.

For a complete list of Pen & Sword titles please contact
PEN & SWORD BOOKS LIMITED
47 Church Street, Barnsley, South Yorkshire, S70 2AS, England
E-mail: enquiries@pen-and-sword.co.uk
Website: www.pen-and-sword.co.uk

# Contents

# List of Illustrations

# Preface

I decided to write this book because, as a part-time Londoner, I had for long admired the Duke of York's column. Having walked past it one sunny day on the way to have lunch at my Club in Mayfair, I happened to mention it to those at the table, very few of whom – though aware of the column – knew much about the man it honoured. The duke has not had many biographers: two rushed into print in the year of his death, itself a testament to his popularity at the time, but one of them, Robert Huish, has not enjoyed a good reputation for reliability. The other, John Watkins, produced a work packed with information, much of it very detailed, but of a selective nature and full of lengthy digressions.

It was more than a hundred years before anyone else attempted to relate the duke's story and during that time the Victorians had passed a stern verdict on the scandals of the Regency and the loose morality of George IV and his circle. Sir Roger Fulford, himself a politician as well as an historian, edited the diaries of Charles Greville and then, in 1933, published a brilliant book, *Royal Dukes*, a witty, irreverent but also scholarly account of the lives of George IV's brothers, fifty pages of which are devoted to the Duke of York. Finally, in 1949, Lieutenant Colonel Alfred Burne DSO, soldier and military historian, published his carefully researched military study. This was prompted by the fact that Burne had found himself, in the closing years of the First World War, fighting over terrain that would have been familiar to the duke in 1793 and 1794, and wondering whether he deserved his reputation of being, as he put it, 'an amiable dolt, a dull dunderhead, or an incompetent nincompoop'.

Without whitewashing York in any way, Burne produced a balanced judgement on his military career and I could not have written this biography without frequent reference to his book – which has been validated and amplified by subsequent military historians, especially Professor Richard Glover, to whose work I am also indebted. However, I have attempted to present the duke 'in the round' and to set his life story against the eventful times, military, political and social, in which he lived. In addition, I have tried to produce a theory about the source of the famous 'Grand Old Duke of York' nursery rhyme which I think is far more realistic than the long-held assumption – based on no sure evidence – that it was a critical joke at York's expense.

My thanks to friends at the Savile Club whom I have bored from time to time about the duke, and especially to Robert Harding, who made available to me a fine contemporary caricature in his private collection. Andrew Murray found time, despite being in the middle of moving house, to walk across to the Esplanade at Edinburgh Castle and photograph the duke's fine statue there, and Don Oliver provided information about his home town of Woodbridge. Anthony and Lorna Hamilton made visits to Oatlands and Weybridge possible, and I am grateful to the London Library, the Institute of Directors and the National Portrait Gallery for their help and co-operation.

Derek Winterbottom
Isle of Man, 2016

# Chapter One

## Family

Frederick, Duke of York and Albany, was the second son of King George III of Great Britain. His elder brother, later King George IV, lived a life of great debauchery and was often in seriously bad health and although he had one legitimate child, a daughter, she died tragically young. This alone made Frederick a person of great political importance in his day, courted by both the Whigs and the Tories as heir presumptive to the throne. He was his father's favourite son and (most of the time) his elder brother's best friend, so he had a lot of influence over the two men who reigned in his lifetime. In two separate campaigns he commanded British forces overseas and he was Commander-in-Chief of the Army for twenty-nine years. During this time he introduced vitally important reforms and presided over the defeat of Napoleonic France. He founded the military academy that became Sandhurst and in London he was connected with fine buildings such as Lancaster House, the Albany and the Duke of York's former barracks in Chelsea. Alone among British royalty, his statue stands high on a pillar in central London that predates Nelson's column and is only slightly shorter. In folklore he is commemorated by a world-famous jingle and in his lifetime he lost huge sums on the turf and through playing cards badly; he also found himself at the centre of a corruption scandal so great that the case was tried by the House of Commons.

Frederick never became king but British history has been radically affected on many occasions by the accession to the throne of a second son. In modern times (i.e. since 1485) Henry VIII would not have become king without the early death of his elder brother Arthur, while Charles I succeeded to the throne, to the dismay of most people who knew him, on the death of his very popular elder brother Henry, who caught a fatal chill after swimming in the Thames. Charles II, despite having innumerable illegitimate children, had none by his lawful wife and was succeeded by his younger brother as James II. Charles feared that what he termed 'the stupidity of my brother' might cost James his crown and he was right. Not content with being a Roman Catholic convert at a time when Catholics were deeply mistrusted in Britain, James insisted that his subjects should be Roman Catholics also and this triggered the 'Glorious Revolution' of 1688, after which Parliament declared that he had abdicated the throne. Acts of Parliament established that his Protestant daughter Mary should be queen and that her husband William, Prince of Orange, should be king jointly: should they have no children, the throne would pass to Mary's younger sister Anne. This in fact occurred but Anne and her husband, Prince George of Denmark, suffered over the years the appalling tragedy that all seventeen of their children died young, so that when Anne herself died in 1714 her successor, according to the Act of Settlement of 1701, was George, generally known as the Elector of Hanover. His branch of the ancient Guelph family had ruled territories in North Germany since the early Middle Ages and his father Ernest Augustus, Duke of Brunswick-Lüneburg, had supported the Holy Roman Emperor, the titular sovereign of most Germanic lands, in a war against the Turks. For this he had been rewarded in 1692 with the promise of promotion to the status of *Kurfürst*, or Electoral Prince of the Empire, although this was not officially confirmed by the Imperial Diet until 1708. His son George succeeded to his lands in 1698 and inherited more territory from his uncle in 1705. What came to be known as the Electorate of Hanover, after its chief city, was about the size of Wales, with a population of three-quarters of a million people. Although not a king, George was a sovereign ruler, and together with the eight other imperial electors was empowered to choose a new emperor whenever the imperial throne fell vacant.

On top of all this steady advancement, George was also the heir to the kingdoms of Great Britain (i.e. England and Scotland) and Ireland, because the Act of Settlement had barred the Roman Catholic heirs of James II from the succession. It declared that George's mother Sophia, who was the grand-daughter of King James I and the nearest Protestant heir to the throne, should succeed Queen Anne. Sophia died in June 1714, aged eighty-three, only a few weeks before Anne died, aged only forty-nine, on 1 August. Somewhat reluctantly, George said farewell to his beloved palace at Herrenhausen, near Hanover, and arrived in London. Within a few months this 'Hanoverian Succession' was tested in 1715 by a rebellion in favour of James Edward Stuart, the son of James II, but the Whig party defended the Act of Settlement and the 'Jacobites', whose support was largely in Scotland, were defeated. The party names 'Whig' and 'Tory', both denoting thieves and villains, had emerged in the reign of Charles II as terms of abuse used by one political group against the other. Broadly speaking, the Whigs supported the Protestant, Anglican Church and the concept of a monarchy whose powers were limited by parliamentary statute. The Tories included many with Roman Catholic or 'High Church' sympathies and many of them took the view that kings ruled by 'divine right', not by the will of the people. The abdication of James II in 1688 and the Hanoverian Succession in 1714 were therefore both triumphs for the Whigs, whose aim was that the new king should govern with the advice of his Whig ministers. Although George could speak some English, he was by no means fluent and he was, in the main, prepared to allow the business of government to be undertaken by able ministers. Chief among these was Sir Robert Walpole, whose ascendancy was so great that he is often thought of as Britain's first prime minister, although this title did not become official until the twentieth century.

George's marriage to Sophia Dorothea of Celle had been made for dynastic and financial reasons and it was a very unhappy one, leading to violence between them. They both took lovers and he divorced her in 1694 and kept her a prisoner in the electorate. This may have been one of the underlying reasons for the unnatural detestation George felt for his only son George Augustus, who succeeded him as George II in 1727. The new king contemplated sacking his father's minister, Walpole, until he came to realize that he was indispensable. His wife, Queen Caroline, was a shrewd politician who, until her death in 1737, helped her husband to work closely with the Whigs, ensuring a stability that was not seriously disrupted, even by a second 'Jacobite' rebellion in 1745.

Unfortunately, relations between George II and his heir Frederick, Prince of Wales, were as bad as those between himself and his own father. The king was in many ways an unattractive and unsympathetic character but his wife was a sensible woman, much respected by contemporaries. Yet she, too, had a violent dislike of the heir to the throne. A courtier, Lord Hervey, recorded in his memoirs that she had said of him that he was 'the greatest ass and the greatest liar and the greatest *canaille* [trash] and the greatest beast in the whole world and I most heartily wish he was out of it'. Even on her (early) deathbed she apparently said that she was comforted by the thought that she 'would never see that monster again'.[1] This hatred was vigorously returned by the prince, who attempted to make life as difficult as possible for his father and mother. One of the ways he could do this was by using his considerable patronage as Duke of Cornwall to build up a political party dedicated to the thwarting of the king's ministers in Parliament.

It may be that Lord Hervey, a supporter of the queen, was prejudiced against Prince Frederick but other commentators were also very critical. Horace Walpole found that Frederick could be generous but was insincere, dishonest and childish, while Lord Chesterfield described him as 'more beloved for his affability and good nature than esteemed for his steadiness and conduct'. Unlike his father, whose main leisure pursuits were stag hunting and playing cards, Frederick had intellectual interests, notably music – he played the violoncello – and art, as well as landscape gardening.[2]

The quarrel between Frederick and his parents came to a head over his marriage. In 1736 he agreed to marry Augusta, a daughter of the Duke of Saxe-Gotha, a bride chosen for him by the king. He then demanded that his allowance of £50,000 a year should be doubled and pursued this aim with great determination, to the fury of his father. When Augusta soon became pregnant, the king and queen wished her child to be born at their country residence, Hampton Court, but even while she was in labour Frederick had her conveyed to St James's Palace in London, where the child, a daughter named Augusta, was born. After this flagrant disobedience there was a complete break between the prince and his parents and Frederick was banished from the Court and the royal residences. In June 1738 Frederick's eldest son George was born, two months premature, in a rented house in London and over the next few years he was provided with four younger brothers and three younger sisters.

Frederick never became king. He died in March 1751, suddenly and unexpectedly, from complications after catching a cold, leaving George, aged twelve, as heir to the throne. He was created Prince of Wales a month later and his mother was given charge of his education and upbringing. She never remarried but fell much under the influence of the Earl of Bute, who became her main adviser and tutor to Prince George and her other children. Gossip at the time assumed they were lovers but he was a happily married man with a large family and his constant advice to George, who liked and respected him, was that a king must live a morally upright life, free from all taint of scandal. Bute was a man of considerable learning with an unfashionable interest in science but he was not a man with great political experience. However, his influence on George was very considerable and between the two of them Bute and George's mother brought the boy up to believe that his grandfather had fallen under the spell of Whig ministers who had usurped the rightful powers of the Crown.

As George became older, he became critical of the king's methods of government, as Hanoverian heirs before him had done. The first major disagreement came in 1755, when George II was keen that his grandson should marry a young princess of the related House of Brunswick but, prompted by his mother, the prince showed no interest. When he came of age in 1756 George was given his own household and at the head of it stood Bute, his revered tutor and adviser, a first minister in waiting. When Britain went to war against France in 1757 the prince asked for a high military appointment, but was refused, to his great annoyance. Then, after living longer than any British monarch up to then, George II suddenly died on 25 October 1760, soon after waking in the morning and drinking a cup of hot chocolate.

## The Young Prince, 1763–1780

George III was twenty-two years old when he succeeded to the throne. Tall, handsome and almost certainly a virgin, the previous year he had fallen in love with Lady Sarah Lennox, a fifteen-year-old whom he met at Court, but he knew that a marriage with her was highly unwise because of her family's political affiliations and Bute warned him off any kind of illicit entanglements. Once king, it became a major priority for George to find a suitable wife whom he could marry before his coronation. He was forbidden by Act of Parliament to marry a Roman Catholic and this drastically reduced the field. No marriage with a French or Spanish or Italian person of royal rank could be contemplated, so Denmark, Sweden and the multiplicity of minor sovereign states in Germany were the most fruitful possibilities. Unknown to his ministers, George sent out emissaries to draw up a list of suitable and available Protestant princesses and the list eventually ran to eight names. All of these were eliminated for one reason or another except Charlotte, the seventeen-year-old daughter of the Duke of Mecklenburg-Strelitz, a small state in the north of Germany.

Basing his choice entirely on reports, George proposed marriage and Charlotte, who brought little to the union by way of finance or prestige, excitedly accepted. She also agreed to forgo Lutheranism in favour of the Anglican Church. Then her mother died and George caught chickenpox, but she arrived at Harwich on 7 September 1761 and the next day met George for the first time in the garden of St James's Palace at about 3.00 pm. She then dined with the king and his family and in a ceremony performed by the Archbishop of Canterbury, she was married to him in the Chapel Royal, just across the road, at 9.00 pm. Supper was served, the new queen played the harpsichord and sang, and the happy couple retired to bed at 2.00 am. For a girl of her age, speaking no English and marrying a man she had never met in a country she had never visited, this must all have been quite an ordeal.[3]

George III's decision to marry Charlotte propelled her out of a relatively modest home environment. She and her sisters had been brought up in her family's unpretentious palace at Milow, which was much smaller than many of the aristocratic mansions to be found in England. She was well educated and proved to be deeply appreciative of art and music and also of botany. She learnt English quickly and was already fluent in French and German, as was her husband. Although at first Charlotte was dominated by her mother-in-law, she gradually bonded with the king and they became devoted to one another.

In the twenty-one years between 1762 and 1783 she bore him fifteen children, of whom nine were boys, two of them dying in infancy. The six girls caused little trouble because they were kept at home until a suitable marriage offer arrived; for three of them, it never did. Charlotte, the eldest daughter and Princess Royal, married the King of Württemburg, Elizabeth married the Landgraf of Hesse-Homburg and Mary married her first cousin, the Duke of Gloucester. Two of the sisters, Augusta and Sophia, lived to be old maids, while the youngest, Amelia, died unmarried, aged only twenty-seven. Even the married ones failed to produce children.

Several of the boys, as we shall see, tended as adults to be troublesome and to some extent rebellious, particularly in the conduct of their private lives. Frederick's elder brother, the Prince of Wales, turned out to be charming and intellectually gifted, but, most people thought, morally bankrupt and professionally incompetent. Of his younger brothers, the dukes of Clarence, Kent, Cumberland, Sussex and Cambridge, most were involved in scandals of one sort or another, though two of them eventually became kings. They were all very fond of each other but were at times an embarrassment to their parents as well as to the British public. Why this was so is an interesting question. Certainly the king and queen were very dutiful parents and they strove to ensure that their sons were provided with suitable tutors and an educational programme that would keep them healthy and happy.

George, Prince of Wales, was born on 12 August 1762 and his younger brother Frederick followed hard on his heels on 16 August the following year. Frederick was born at Buckingham House, or 'the Queen's House', which George III at first rented and later bought from the Duke of Buckingham. He used it as a family home in London, as opposed to his official residence, St James's Palace, only a short distance away, where he held royal *levées* on most days of the week and where he conducted official business. The other favoured royal residences were Richmond Lodge and Kew, where the king's mother lived until her death in 1772 and where there were a number of houses ranged around Kew Green, chief of which was 'the Dutch House', the present Kew Palace. Although Hampton Court Palace was in good order, it brought back unhappy memories to the king of his childhood, so he did not use it, while Windsor Castle was in much need of restoration at this stage and was mostly occupied by junior royals.

On 14 September the baby prince was officially baptised at Buckingham House by the Archbishop of Canterbury, who gave him the single name of Frederick, despite the fact that he is often mistakenly referred to as Frederick Augustus.[4] Many members of the royal family and aristocracy attended this ceremony, which was followed by refreshments, including caudle and cake.

For the king and queen to have provided 'an heir and a spare' so quickly was a welcome development, which seemed to ensure both the future and the stability of the monarchy and there was general satisfaction, although most members of the aristocracy were beginning to be taken aback by the unpretentious lifestyle adopted by George and Charlotte. Both of them disliked unnecessary show and the queen once told her confidante, Fanny Burney, that she only wore elaborate jewels for special occasions. They both ate and drank quite frugally, the king because he had a lifetime's horror of growing fat, as a result of which he undertook an enormous amount of physical exercise. He worked hard, too, rising at 6.00 am and attending dutifully to his public business. He kept no secretary and wrote his letters in his own hand for most of his reign.

When Frederick was seven months old he was chosen to succeed to one of the Holy Roman Empire's many anomalies, the Prince-Bishopric of Osnabrück, a small state, some forty-five miles long by twenty-five miles wide, on the borders of the Electorate of Hanover. The diocese, founded by Charlemagne in 772, became a semi-independent princely state within the Holy Roman Empire in the early thirteenth century and survived many subsequent upheavals. One of the bloodiest of these was the Thirty Years War, essentially a conflict between Roman Catholics and Protestants, which came to an end in 1648 with the Treaty of Westphalia. One of the treaty's detailed provisions was the compromise that the ruler of this territory should in future be alternately a Catholic and a Protestant, and that he should be appointed by the Archbishop of Cologne, if Catholic, and by the Duke of Brunswick-Lüneburg, if Protestant.

The first holder after 1648 was a Catholic and the second was George I's father, then Duke of Brunswick-Lüneburg, who appointed himself as Prince-Bishop in 1662 and set about building a new, medium-sized baroque palace known as Osnabrück Castle. When he died in 1698 the prince-bishopric reverted to a Catholic, who died in 1715, whereupon George I, in his capacity as Duke of Brunswick-Lüneburg, appointed his younger brother Prince Ernest Augustus to the dignity (and indeed died suddenly at Osnabrück Castle while visiting his brother in 1727). Ernest died the following year and on the death of his Catholic successor in 1761 it fell to George III to fill the vacancy. After some delay he made the controversial decision to appoint his infant son Frederick.

The practice had been that when a Catholic held the post, he would be a priest who fulfilled the religious duties of a bishop but a Protestant was the secular ruler of the state and his duties were delegated to the cathedral chapter. Hence it was not so strange, though it seemed so to many people, that a baby of seven months could officially preside over a bishopric. Nevertheless, the appointment of an infant to the post antagonized Catholic opinion and gave rise to a major row. The chapter of Osnabrück cathedral claimed the right to administer the territory during the minority of the prince, while the Archbishop of Cologne appointed a Catholic vicar-general to run its affairs and instructed the citizens to obey him or face excommunication.

George III's ministers in Hanover stoutly refused to accept either of these arrangements. Heated argument persisted for a considerable time until a compromise was brokered by King Frederick II of Prussia, Britain's ally in the Seven Years War which had ended in 1763. One of the many details of the arrangement was a promise made by George III that Prince Frederick would spend a considerable time in Germany as part of his education, so that he could become familiar with his bishopric as well as with the laws and customs of the empire.[5] Once the prince's succession was fully recognized, he was routinely referred to in Britain as 'the Bishop of Osnaburg', which was not a completely accurate translation as *brücke* means bridge in German, whereas *burg* means castle or stronghold.

On 16 August 1764, Frederick's first birthday, a celebration fete was held in his honour at Kew and four thousand special medals were struck in gold and silver to mark his election as prince-bishop. Designed by Thomas Pingo, the medals represented on one side the figure of Hope, resting on a shield, bearing the arms of the prince, with a pedestal supporting the mitre, crozier and sword of the bishopric.[6] Seven days later the queen gave birth to her third son, William Henry, and soon after that George and Charlotte took the brave decision to have their two eldest sons inoculated against smallpox.

This was at the time a dreaded disease, which, if it did not kill its victims, could leave them seriously disfigured. Inoculation consisted of introducing infected material from a smallpox lesion into the skin of a patient, on both arms, using the point of a lancet. Then the child had to stay in bed, preferably in the dark, for ten days. The procedure had met with growing success in England during the eighteenth century and was approved by the Royal College of Physicians in 1754. However, there were many, especially among evangelical churchmen, who strongly opposed it, arguing that physicians were meddling in God's work. The operation was performed by the king's surgeon, Fennel Hawkins, and fortunately proved successful. Subsequently George and Charlotte had all their children inoculated until tragedy struck in May 1783 when their thirteenth child, Prince Octavius, died of smallpox shortly after being inoculated, aged four. An angelic child, he was by then the king's favourite, and George was inconsolable: 'There will be no heaven for me', he lamented, 'if Octavius is not there.'[7]

From the very first the king and queen did their best to ensure that their children received the best possible education. In the early years their governess was the kindly Lady Charlotte Finch ('Lady Cha'), of whom all the royal children were very fond. According to a recent historian of the family, 'Every aspect of their lives, both great and small, came under her all-encompassing control', and she was 'exactly the kind of concerned scholarly mother the queen would have chosen to be if her rank had allowed it'.[8] From about 1771 George and Frederick were given their own households on Kew Green and they were taught together under the general direction of their official governor, the Earl of Holdernesse. Their chief academic tutor was Dr William Markham, who gave up his post as Headmaster of Westminster School at the king's request to take up this duty – for which he was later rewarded with the Bishopric of Chester and then the Archbishopric of York.

The king laid down that the two boys should be kept occupied from early in the morning until 8.00 at night and be given careful instruction in the classics as well as in modern languages, so that by the age of ten Frederick was capable of writing letters in excellent French. The princes received instruction in military sketching and plan-drawing from a talented officer in the Royal Engineers, Leonard Smelt, a versatile man who was also accomplished in literature and art. On 15 June 1772 Frederick was formally installed as a Knight Companion of the Bath in Westminster Abbey and ten days later he was invested with the insignia of a Knight of the Garter at a grand ceremony held at Windsor Castle.[9]

In 1774 Holdernesse fell ill and had to leave his post for a time, during which, he alleged, his enemies poisoned the minds of the princes against him so that when he returned, they failed to treat him with proper respect. He resigned in 1776 and was replaced by the Duke of Montagu, with Richard Hurd, Bishop of Lichfield, taking over the academic duties from Markham and Colonel Hotham the more practical studies from Smelt. George and Frederick were now aged thirteen and twelve respectively and beginning to show signs of a rebellious nature. According to one of their sisters, this was curbed, on the king's express instruction, by the vigorous use of corporal punishment.[10]

It was sensibly recognized that growing boys needed physical exercise and George and Frederick played a good deal of single-wicket cricket on Kew Green, becoming highly proficient, according to observers. The two brothers were already beginning to reveal the differences in their characters and tastes – George more intellectual and theoretical, Frederick more physical and practical. Their father was very interested in agriculture, so a small piece of ground was set aside for them at Kew so that they could grow wheat and reap and thresh it themselves, occasionally helped by the king. In every respect they were encouraged to live frugally and to think soberly but in the case of the Prince of Wales, at least, the result was in the end the opposite of what was intended and as the boys moved into their teenage years their tutors began to express doubts about their progress, not so much in academic terms, but in attitude of mind.

A long letter from Frederick, aged fifteen, has been preserved, which finds him discussing current affairs and the details of a marriage scandal and complaining that he has no time to write letters because 'our time is so exactly parcelled out'. At the same age the king took him, with his elder brother, to Eton College, to hear recitations of famous speeches performed by the senior boys and they were all deeply affected by the young Richard Wellesley's rendering of the Earl of Strafford's eloquent defence of himself at his trial in 1641.[11] When Frederick was sixteen he seems to have had a 'youthful amour' with a dairymaid at Kew and by the age of seventeen he was already about six feet tall and very attractive to women.[12] At about this time he seems to have had an affair with Letitia Smith, described as 'an adventuress who was also believed to have been the mistress of the highwayman John Rann'. After Frederick had left for Hanover, she told the Prince of Wales that she missed him so much that she had been ill, and could not live without him.[13]

There was no doubting Frederick's interest in manly sports and also his enthusiasm for soldiering, which the king encouraged in him, although not in George. For military instruction Frederick was placed in the charge of General Smith, a distinguished engineer, as well as Colonel Lake, and he read important texts on the art of soldiering. Moreover, part of the gardens at Kew were used in order to map out some of the campaigns of the Seven Years War and to reconstruct the military triumphs of King Frederick II ('the Great') of Prussia, who became a hero to his young namesake. As Frederick grew to manhood his father saw in him much that was good, while increasingly he despaired of the heir to the throne.[14]

## Home and International Politics, 1756–1780

While his eldest children had been growing up, George III had faced many crises in the government of the country. When he came to the throne he inherited the Seven Years War, which had begun in 1756. The main enemy was France, with her allies Austria and Russia, while the main British ally was Frederick of Prussia. Under the direction of the brilliant but eccentric minister William Pitt 'the Elder', Britain's navy attacked the French empire with great success in Canada, India, the West Indies and West Africa, while money was poured into the Prussian coffers to keep the French armies busy on land. In the famous 'Year of Victories', 1759, General Wolfe captured Quebec, the French navy was defeated at Lagos and Quiberon Bay, and Hanover was saved by the defeat of the French at Minden.

When George became king in the following year he agreed with Bute that the colonial war had already been won and that peace should now be made, a strategy that infuriated Pitt, who resigned in 1761, followed by his political ally, the Duke of Newcastle, in 1762. This left the king and Bute free to conclude the Peace of Paris in 1763, by which Britain gained the whole of Canada, much of 'Louisiana' and the islands of Tobago, Dominica, St Vincent and the Grenadines, as well as Senegal in West Africa. In India the British East India Company was left the dominant force. Britain made peace without reference to her ally, Prussia, but Frederick arranged a separate peace with Austria by which he was able to hold on to gains already made, especially the rich province of Silesia. So Britain emerged from this war the owner of a worldwide trading empire, while Prussia was established as the dominant military power in Europe.

Bute came under strong criticism from politicians, partly because he was a royal favourite and partly because it was argued that he had given away too many gains. He resigned in 1763, to the king's great regret, and for the next seven years George looked for a 'prime minister' whom he trusted and who could also command a majority in the House of Commons. George Grenville, Lord Rockingham, Pitt himself (as Lord Chatham) and the Duke of Grafton all came and went until in 1770 the king appointed Lord North, with whom he was able to work for the next twelve years. The British Constitution had developed by this time to a stage where the king still retained important executive powers, such as the appointment and dismissal of ministers as well as the formulation of foreign policy, but he could not force legislation through the House of Commons, which had almost complete control over the money supply. So he gradually built up his own party of 'king's friends' in the Commons as well as in the Lords, and used these supporters in coalitions with other political factions. In general this approach to government was acceptable to the Tories, but not to the Whigs, who accused the king of meddling too much in matters that were properly the responsibility of Parliament.

The expulsion of the French from North America in 1763 relieved Britain's thirteen American colonies of the threat of French invasion and encouraged them to agitate for more self-government, especially in the matter of raising taxes. Trouble began with the imposition of a Stamp Tax in 1765, which had to be withdrawn after strong protests of 'No Taxation without Representation'. When Lord North actually reduced the tax on tea in 1773, in order to help the East India Company, which was in financial difficulties, the colonists saw this as a plot to bribe them to drink more tea (which they had largely boycotted) and in the famous Boston Tea Party incident in December that year large amounts of tea were thrown into the harbour by colonists. This resulted in legislation which punished the colonies and led to their Declaration of Independence in 1775, which began a long war with the mother country. Britain had a strong navy but only a small army, so the 10,000 British troops which went out to fight in America were buttressed by 18,000 German mercenaries, many of them from Hanover. In 1777 some 5,000 British troops were defeated and forced to surrender at Saratoga, and this encouraged France and her ally, Spain, to enter the war on the side of the colonists, hoping to win back some of their previous losses. Britain also had to declare war on the Dutch, who insisted on carrying supplies to the rebels.

# Chapter Two

## Frederick in Germany, 1780–1787

As we have seen, the settlement of the dispute over Frederick's appointment as Prince-Bishop of Osnabrück had included a promise by George III that he would be sent to Germany as a young man to become familiar with the bishopric as well as with the Electorate of Hanover and the complexities of German politics. In August 1780 Frederick reached his seventeenth birthday and the king felt that he should now fulfil this pledge. Frederick was so keen to pursue a career as a soldier that he had already asked to travel to America to fight the rebels and he had also offered his services in helping to put down the 'Gordon Riots', which brought the city to a standstill in June that year. Both offers had been refused but it was clear that Frederick was ambitious and full of energy and it was important that he should be saved from going down the same road of carousal, gambling and dissipation that had already begun to dominate the life of the Prince of Wales – lured on by the king's political opponents, who were already flattering and manipulating him for their own purposes. So, on 1 November 1780 Frederick was appointed a colonel in the British army and on the 30th he said farewell to his parents at Buckingham House before setting out for what would ultimately be a six-and-a-half-year absence from his home, his family and friends. It was an emotional scene: the king and queen wept and the Prince of Wales, who was effectively losing a childhood friend as well as a brother, was rendered speechless.[1]

Accompanied by Colonel Richard Grenville and a few servants, Frederick sailed from Harwich to Ostend, where he stayed overnight and was fascinated by a Capuchin monastery he noticed from his window. He asked to see round the monastery the next day and also visited two nunneries. The day after that he set out for Hanover in very bad weather, finding the roads almost impassable in some places. He arrived safely and after some delay while suitable apartments were prepared for him, he was eventually accommodated in the royal palace of Herrenhausen, mostly built by the Electress Sophia in the previous century and a place much beloved of George I and George II, who had both spent many summers there during their reigns. Frederick's father had never seen it: indeed, one of the remarkable things about George III is that in a long life and a long reign he never set foot on a foreign shore and never wanted to see his kingdoms of Scotland and Ireland, or his Electorate of Hanover, for himself.

Probably for this reason the citizens of Hanover gave the son of their absent elector a hearty welcome and we are told that 'members of the government, ministers of foreign countries, deputations from the citizens, flocked to pay their respects to the Prince-Bishop of Osnabrück'.[2] He remained in Hanover for several weeks, probably making his first visit to Osnabrück from there. It seems that the revenues of the bishopric were about £20,000 a year but out of this was paid the maintenance of a military contingent of 2,500 men as well as a number of government officials, headed by a 'Grand Steward of the Household'. According to Frederick's contemporary biographer, John Watkins, the initial dissensions 'produced by the nomination of His ... Royal Highness to this dignity were so vexatious, that little or no benefit ever accrued to him from the revenue, during the whole period of his possessing the title. It gave him, however, some consequence among the Germanic powers and afforded him excellent facilities for improving himself both in military tactics and the direction of civil affairs.'[3]

One of the first tasks Frederick set himself was to learn German and at the end of March he was able to report that his fluency was improving day by day and he could dare to attempt a conversation in the language. He studied gunnery, geometry and trigonometry, and one of his instructors, Captain Hogreve, was able to turn what might have been boring lectures into easy and amusing sessions. Hogreve taught him how to draw maps, plans, gun carriages and mortars, as well as the technicalities of sluices, dams and fortifications, while another instructor, Wessel, showed him how to draw cannon. His favourite tutor seems to have been Herr Falk: 'Part of the time I talk German with him, and the other part we read the history of Germany in German, which I understand without much difficulty. Indeed, by Falk's agreeable manner of teaching I find myself much advanced in the time I had learnt from him than I thought I should.' Falk remained an important influence on Frederick's education and two years later he was still in post, this time instructing him in civil law and the laws of the empire.[4]

In the summer of 1781 Frederick left Hanover and travelled to Brunswick, where he came under the tutelage of his uncle Charles, Duke of Brunswick-Wolfenbüttel, who had married George III's elder sister, Princess Augusta. He was a sovereign prince and also a famous military commander who had served with great distinction in the Prussian army during the Seven Years War, being raised to the rank of field marshal. He welcomed his young nephew to his court, and over the next few months gave him personal instruction in the strategy and tactics of eighteenth-century warfare, in which he was an acknowledged expert. In a letter to his mother, Frederick told her all about the Brunswick family:

> The Duke is exceedingly agreeable, and treated me not only with great politeness but also with great affection. As for the Duchess I say nothing about her because Your Majesty knows her very well, only that I do not see the least likeness between her and Princess Amelia. As for the Princesses, they are exceedingly polite and agreeable. I think I never saw a more beautiful face or figure than Princess Caroline: she is not above thirteen years old, so that she is not allowed to appear in public but of a Sunday evening, and that for only half an hour, so that I could make the least acquaintance with her, but by what I have heard, she is very lively and sensible. I cannot however say much in praise of the Hereditary Prince, [the duke's eldest son] who is a stupid, lubberly boy.[5]

It was perhaps fortunate that Princess Caroline was still a child and that Frederick did no more than admire her from afar. She grew up to be a difficult and eccentric woman and eventually married his brother, the Prince of Wales, with disastrous results.

Brunswick arranged for Frederick to attend military manoeuvres and early in September he visited the battlefield at Minden, where an Anglo-Hanoverian army had defeated the French in 1759. Later in the month he was back in Hanover, where he wrote to tell his father that 'the artillery have been encamped here this fortnight. I have not missed a day attending their exercise, which they have done perfectly well, particularly considering the length of time since they were last assembled together and the badness of their guns . . .'[6] George III registered his satisfaction at Frederick's progress and several of his son's letters begin with thanks for his father's 'gracious letters', while one is grateful to both his parents for the thoughtful gift of a Cheshire cheese.

In October 1781 the British attempt to defeat the American colonists met with disaster when General Cornwallis was forced to surrender with his army of 7,000 men at Yorktown. He had been surrounded on land by the army of George Washington and his escape by sea was prevented by a French squadron under the Comte de Rochambeau, which happened to arrive just at the wrong moment for the British. After this it was clear that George III would be forced to accept the independence of the thirteen colonies, an arrangement that was eventually formalized after negotiations held in Paris in 1783. British loss of naval supremacy as a result of the French and Spanish involvement, together with the problems of waging war so far from home against a very determined enemy, had proved too difficult a task. It was a humiliating personal blow for the king and the recognition of the United States had worldwide repercussions. The success of the rebels in America inspired many in France to demand radical changes to their own autocratic monarchical system, while in Britain the loss of one empire in America eventually led to the development of another one in India and the Caribbean. As a soldier, Prince Frederick no doubt shared his father's sense of personal humiliation, as well as a degree of national shame at the defeat of British and Hanoverian soldiers.

In March 1782, as a mark of his approval at the way Frederick had been conducting himself in Hanover, the king appointed him colonel of the second regiment of Horse Grenadiers (later the Life Guards) and in November the same year he was promoted to the rank of major-general. This favour contrasted strongly with the king's increasing dissatisfaction with the behaviour of the Prince of Wales, and even with his third son, Prince William, who was already showing signs of being lazy and rebellious.

During the same year Frederick visited Lüneburg and Hamburg and he also showed that he had an eye for works of art, as well as a sense of history, because he bought 'a frame filled with antiques and miniature pictures'. According to him there had originally been a set of four frames, dating from Charles I's time, and he had seen three of them in Buckingham House. The fourth had been taken by Charles II into exile in 1646 and sold in Holland, so he was thrilled to have been able to buy it back. He was also having problems with his teeth, and had been visiting

> the dentist here who really is exceedingly good and who has saved my teeth, which though I take all the care I can in the world of them, were in so wretched a plight that in six months more they would have been completely spoilt. I do this the more readily because he is not only very knowing in his trade, but is at the same time a very harmless, inoffensive man, and really has very little to live upon.[7]

In 1783 the Duke of Brunswick introduced Frederick to his hero and namesake, King Frederick 'the Great' of Prussia, widely considered to be a military genius. Very soon after inheriting the Prussian military machine from his father in 1740 he had invaded the Austrian province of Silesia without provocation and retained control of it through two gruelling European wars. The prince told his father:

> He is short and small but wonderfully strong made. . . . on horseback Your Majesty would be astonished to see him. One of the days we were with him,

he was from three o'clock in the morning till past eleven o'clock without ever getting off his horse. . . . He has exceedingly the air of a gentleman and something exceedingly commanding in his look.[8]

The Prussian king evidently approved of Frederick because dinners and balls were held in his honour and he was invited to the annual review of the Prussian troops.

In the autumn of 1783 Frederick set out on a journey round many of the lesser courts of Germany, starting at Cassel, 'exceedingly fine and situated in a most beautiful country', where he was 'very politely' received by the landgraf, whose wife had 'one of the finest faces that can be seen, though she is thirty-eight years old, but her figure does not in the least answer to her face, as she is remarkable fat'. From Cassel he moved on to Gotha, but he felt he 'could not say much in praise of this court. The Duke is by all accounts a very good and learned man, but not much a man of the world, and as for the Duchess, the best thing one can say for her is that she is a little mad.' At Hilbourghausen he took part in a hunt which killed thirty-two stags and a shoot which bagged 132 pheasant and 160 hares. But it was cold: 'Your Majesty can have no idea of the cold in this part of Germany, on account of a large range of mountains called the Thüringerwald.'

It was warmer in Anspach, where the margrave 'begged me particularly to express to Your Majesty how much he is attached to your person and your family'. Mannheim appealed to Frederick, who felt that 'the town is beautiful: it is a perfect square, and the streets are quite straight. The palace is immense, but furnished in a very old style. There is a very fine collection of pictures there.' At 'very old and ugly' Frankfurt, his carriages were put on board a yacht for a three-day sail down the Rhine, where he found the countryside very beautiful and full of vines. He disembarked at Cologne 'and from thence made the best of our way to Osnabrück where we stayed a week, which was employed in settling everything there, though indeed everything was in such good order that there was not much to arrange'.[9]

The king had such confidence in Frederick that he decided to send his two younger brothers, Prince William (later Duke of Clarence and King William IV) and Prince Edward (later Duke of Kent and father of Queen Victoria) out to Hanover so that they might benefit from his knowledge of German politics as well as of military affairs. In the summer of 1784 Frederick informed his father that: 'In obedience to Your Majesty's orders to give you my opinion of William, I think that he is rather improved with regard to swearing, but unluckily he has taken an idea into his head that it does not signify in what manner he behaves here, which has great influence upon the whole of his conduct, and besides, he does not pay sufficient regard to any advice that General Budé gives him, and which I am convinced would be a great service to him.'[10]

By this stage it is clear that Frederick had become a trusted confidant of his father, passing on to him information about German affairs as well as giving advice about appointments to various posts. George also complained to his second son on a number of occasions about the behaviour of the Prince of Wales, in particular the way he had by now become a focus for opposition politicians. In June 1784 Frederick wrote: 'Permit me to return Your Majesty my most humble thanks for your last very gracious letter which I received by the courier. I am exceedingly happy to see by it that the opposition are in so very dejected a state, and I trust in God that everything will now go to Your Majesty's desires. Tomorrow I mean to set out on my tour to Vienna.' He travelled by way of Cassel, Frankfurt and Stuttgart, where he was very impressed by the court of the Duke of Württemburg, which 'in point of magnificence is superior to any which I have seen as yet'. In Munich he was greeted by the Elector of Bavaria, 'exceedingly strong and hale: indeed, I never saw a stronger man for his age'.[11]

Eventually Frederick reached Vienna, the Habsburg capital of the Emperor Joseph II, famous as an 'enlightened despot', and for allegedly telling Mozart that his music contained 'too many notes'. Frederick was not particularly impressed:

His manner is most exceedingly engaging. He has a wonderful deal of conversation and is polite to everybody who are *not under* him. His manner of treating me was certainly flattering to the highest degree and he allowed me to see everything I could possibly wish to see, even things which no person whatsoever before was allowed to take a view of. He is, however, astonishingly uncautious in his conversation; he has told me many things that I am sure ought not to be told to anybody whatsoever, and much less to a stranger, and this at a table of sixty covers, so that any person might have heard who pleased. During the time that I was in his dominions I heard and saw a great many things which made me form a very different idea of him than I had before. He is cruel to those under him to a degree that is hardly to be conceived. He certainly is exceedingly attached to his alliance with France, as he one day told me himself, for he said that it was of the greatest consequence to him to be in alliance with France, because it allowed him whenever he had war to draw away all his troops from Flanders and Italy.

I confess that I found myself wonderfully mistaken in the idea which I had formed of the imperial troops. The men are certainly in general fine, but in their discipline, their march, their firing and their manoeuvres they are indeed very, very far behind the Prussians; indeed, I was astonished to see their inattention. The Emperor, however, appears vastly fond of his troops as well as of meddling with their manoeuvres, though I cannot say that he appears to understand much of the matter. The Austrian cavalry is much worse, however, in proportion than their infantry; they are exceedingly ill mounted, they ride infamously, and their whole accoutrements are in exceedingly bad order ... Their Artillery is certainly very good and their engineers are I believe now the very best in the world, though that is indeed not at all astonishing, as they are at this present moment building eleven large fortresses.[12]

Despite the inadequacies of some aspects of the Austrian military machine, Frederick nevertheless recognized that it was well organized in the matter of magazines and provisions. Indeed, he told the king that, ultimately, he was convinced that 'the Emperor will do everything in his power to augment his German possessions. As yet, he has not had time to finish all his arrangements, but when they are ready he will certainly strike some blow or other and I am certain it will be a very hard one.[13]

On the lighter side, Frederick, by his own account, made the most of the delights offered by the imperial capital. He told his father:

During the time I was at Vienna there was a fete every evening, which lasted so long, particularly at the balls, that I was hardly ever able to get away before six o'clock in the morning. And as I was occupied the whole morning, seeing everything that is remarkable about the town, I was left hardly a moment for repose. One week, particularly, I went to bed on the Monday and never saw my bed again until the Sunday night following. During the camp, however, we had quite a different life, as we always went out with the troops at 4.o'clock in the morning. I cannot say, however, that I am sorry after so very long and boisterous a journey to be at last returned again to my own fireside.[14]

The king was evidently very pleased with the good impression Frederick had made in Vienna and elsewhere, because on 10 December 1784 Frederick wrote to his father from Hanover 'I have this moment received your Majesty's letter of the 30th November in which you are good enough as to communicate to me your having been graciously pleased to create me Duke of York and Albany.' He went on to say that he hoped he would prove worthy of being the holder of two of Britain's most ancient and distinguished royal dukedoms, and apologized for sending a short acknowledgement, as he had to catch the post.[15]

The dukedom of York was first created in 1385 for the fourth son of King Edward III and it merged with the crown when Edward, Duke of York, became King Edward IV in 1461. Edward created Richard, his second son, Duke of York but he is famously presumed to have died (probably murdered) as a boy in the Tower of London. The next holder of the title was Henry VII's second son Henry, who eventually became King Henry VIII after his elder brother (imaginatively named Arthur) died before him. King James I's second son Charles was created both Duke of York and in addition Duke of Albany, a Scottish title first used by the Stuart family in 1398 and denoting the territory north of the river Forth.

Charles's elder brother died before him, so he succeeded as King Charles I; his second son James was created Duke of York and Albany and it was after him that the towns of New York and Albany were named in the American colonies. He succeeded his brother as King James II. George I created his younger brother Ernest Duke of York and Albany but he died without heirs and the next holder of both dukedoms was Edward, the unmarried younger brother of George III, who died in his twenties in 1767. Frederick, as the latest Duke of York and Albany, was also created Earl of Ulster, a title that had accompanied the two dukedoms since 1660. Although, as George III's second son, Frederick might well have expected to receive these honours sooner or later, there was nothing automatic about this and the grant of the dukedoms indicated that he stood high in his father's favour at this point. Moreover, he received a parliamentary grant of £12,000 on his appointment to this new dignity.

He was not, however, the only person alive at the time who called himself 'The Duke of York'. In 1725 a second son was born to James Stuart, the 'Old Pretender', then living in exile in Rome. Named Henry Benedict, he was created by his father Duke of York in the Jacobite peerage and he gave moral support to his elder brother 'Bonnie Prince Charlie' in his attempt to regain the throne of England in the Jacobite rising of 1745. After the defeat of this, Henry decided to enter the Roman Catholic Church and was created a Cardinal in 1747, even before he became fully a priest in the following year. He was appointed titular Archbishop of Corinth and by 1784 was Cardinal-Bishop of Frascati. When his elder brother died in 1788, leaving no children, Henry was recognized by a small minority of Jacobites as 'King Henry IX of England and Ireland and Henry I of Scotland', although this claim was not supported by the Papacy. In 1803 he was appointed Dean of the College of Cardinals and he died four years later at the age of eighty-two. He was the last of the direct descendants of James II and the last Stuart to claim the thrones of England, Ireland and Scotland.

In January 1785 Frederick persuaded his father not to send the seventeen-year-old Prince Edward to the University of Göttingen, which lay about a hundred miles south of Hanover and had been founded by George II. Instead he recommended that he be sent to Lüneburg, where he would receive military, instead of academic, training. He told the king:

One cannot judge of Göttingen or indeed any other German university by an English one, where the young men are confined in colleges and the tutors have a great authority over them. At Göttingen, on the contrary, the young men live all separately and the professors have very little more than a nominal authority over them, so that there does not pass a day without some very great excess or other being committed. We therefore humbly submit it to your Majesty if it would not be very risking to send a young man who has never been in the world before to such a place, where he shall hear every day of these excesses and where he will in a manner be obliged to keep company with the very people who commit them.[16]

Frederick had his way and Edward trained as a soldier, but subsequently became such a stickler for discipline and punishment that he provoked serious unrest in many of his commands, to the great embarrassment of his father as well as Frederick. Perhaps a spell at Göttingen as a carefree student might have countered his martinet tendencies.

The following month Frederick wrote to the king on a far more serious matter: namely, Emperor Joseph II's plans to annex Bavaria to Austria, compensating the Elector of Bavaria with the Austrian Netherlands, a pension, and probably the title of king. Prussia felt threatened by this and took the lead in the establishment of a League of Princes (*Fürstenbund*), which would guarantee the boundaries and rights of existing states. The Duke of York had seen for himself the extent to which the Emperor had been building up his military strength and he feared that Austria would strike first and enter into negotiations afterwards. 'If therefore the Princes of Germany do not beforehand unite and agree together in what manner they will oppose the Emperor's views against the constitution of Germany, there will be no time left, afterward, for negotiation of any sort,' he urged.[17]

In January 1785 Frederick had been appointed one of the Lords of the Regency of Hanover and also a member of the supreme council for managing the affairs of the electorate and in this capacity he played a leading part in the negotiations which led to the establishment of the 'League of Princes' in 1786. Hanover, along with many other German states, became a signatory to this organization, dedicated to the preservation of existing territorial boundaries and rights within the empire. In this matter George III acted very largely on the Duke of York's advice and without consulting his British ministers.[18]

Three letters sent in April 1785, from each of George III's eldest sons, reveal how different were the relations between them and their father. The Duke of York wrote on the first of the month to thank him for 'permitting me to be entrusted in everything belonging to the military here'. As for Prince William, Frederick wrote 'there never can be any real alteration for the better in him till he has been kept for some time under severe discipline, which alone can be done on board a ship, for his natural inclination for all kinds of dissipation will make him, either here, or indeed in any place by land, run into any society where he can form to himself only an idea of pleasure'.

Prince William himself wrote to his father on the same day: 'I was most extremely hurt by the last letter your Majesty thought proper to write to me. It gave me very great uneasiness to find my conduct had been so displeasing to my father.' He ended by 'beseeching your Majesty to change my situation and recall me from Hanover, where everybody is so prejudiced against me, that all my actions will be taken in a bad light if possible'. The third letter was sent to the king by the Prince of Wales, in London, and concerned what had become a very acrimonious dispute between them, namely the prince's exorbitant expenditure and mounting debts, which he considered it the king's duty to pay off. Not surprisingly, his father did not see things that way.[19]

The most exciting event of 1785 for York was Frederick the Great's review of practically the entire Prussian army in Silesia. York had asked to attend this and the Prussian king, in reply, invited him in a letter written in French, describing himself as an old man who sees in York military talents that will cause him to shine one day. York was extremely impressed with the Prussian precision. 'The cavalry is infinitely superior to anything I ever saw,' he wrote. 'One day the King decreed without any previous notice that the thirty-five squadrons of cuirassiers and dragoons should charge in one line. Never was there seen so fine a sight. There was not a single horse out of its place till the word Halt was given.' However, there was heavy rain during a good deal of the review and this had a serious effect on the health of the ageing king. York was present at the last dinner party he ever gave, because the king had a fit later that night and never returned to full health, dying in August the following year, aged seventy-four.[20]

In June 1786 Frederick's senior position within the family was emphasized when his father empowered him to invest his brother Edward with the Order of the Garter, which was carried out with due ceremony in the throne room of the royal palace in Hanover. In July Frederick asked the king whether he could give 'a present' to 'Monsieur de Bussche', who 'has been so good as to assist me in managing the affairs of the bishopric'. This seems to be good evidence that during his time in Germany, although the affairs of the electorate were managed directly by the king through his Hanoverian ministers, Frederick himself was responsible for the administration of the Osnabrück bishopric.[21]

By the time his twenty-third birthday came round in August 1786 Frederick had spent five-and-a-half years in Hanover without once returning to England and he was becoming keen to go home. In the autumn he wrote to the king asking for permission to come back, but received a reply early in October saying that he should stay where he was for the time being. The main reasons the king gave for this were that he was embroiled in a quarrel with the Prince of Wales over financial matters, and the prince was threatening to put his case before Parliament. The king was afraid that if Frederick came home and supported him rather than his brother, this would cause a breach between them, which he wanted to avoid. Second, he would need to find a suitable house and establishment for Frederick, which would take time and be expensive. Frederick, clearly very disappointed, replied in a lengthy letter arguing that these were hardly serious difficulties, and ending: 'I am sure your Majesty is too just not to excuse the eagerness with which I have endeavoured to combat every objection which can be produced towards deferring my return after an absence of very near six years from those whom I have every reason to love and respect.' Still, as well as being his father, George III was his sovereign and, as a serving soldier, his commander-in-chief, so he had no choice but to stay on for another Hanoverian Christmas.

Meanwhile, Frederick was able to send reports of three more of his brothers who had recently been sent by the king to study at the University of Göttingen, despite his misgivings about its loosely disciplined academic regime. These were Prince Ernest, later Duke of Cumberland and King of Hanover, aged fifteen, Prince Augustus, later Duke of Sussex, aged thirteen, and Prince Adolphus, later Duke of Cambridge, aged twelve. According to one royal biographer, the king saw this princely exodus as a means of developing links between Britain and Hanover, which otherwise had little in common other than the same sovereign:

The object with which these Princes went to the University was, on the whole, novel. It was not so much that they should draw from the well of knowledge as that they should fill it. They were to impress the Hanoverians with the superior charms of English gentlemen and to encourage them to adopt English manners and customs. One of George III's ideas ... was that, encouraged by the example of his sons, young Englishmen should flock out to Göttingen and help to anglicize the Hanoverians.[22]

Frederick told his father that the three boys looked 'exceedingly well and very much grown', and that they had made very good progress with their riding lessons. However, the eldest, Ernest, was very short-sighted and had experienced 'some very bad falls from not being able to see where he is going. I am very much afraid this will totally incapacitate him from ever being able to enter into the military line.' Augustus was 'in every thing backwarder than his brothers because . . . he has not been able to attend to his lessons so regularly'. However, 'There is but one voice at Göttingen about Adolphus; they all say they never saw so sensible or so clever a boy for his age, nor a better heart.' Frederick also visited Cassel, where he was not impressed with the new landgrave, 'who has introduced again the same ceremonies, formalities and stiffness for which Germany was so famous about sixty years ago. Besides, he has behaved in so harsh a manner to his subjects that he is everywhere detested.' As for his troops, 'they have not the least idea whatsoever of marching, which is certainly the very first thing for a soldier'.[23]

As can be seen from several of his letters, Frederick was not slow to apportion praise or blame frankly on others and he appeared to disapprove of indiscipline and dissolute behaviour in his brothers. However, according to Robert Huish, who wrote a brief memoir of the duke shortly after his death, he was himself introduced to gambling in Hanover by a certain Baron Seltenheim, 'one of the most finished gentlemen and also one of the most finished scoundrels of his age. To this human shark the young Frederick became the destined victim: not a single florin did Frederick ever lose to him; on the contrary, he was invariably the gainer, but when he left the room he always found himself a considerable loser.'[24] Whether it was Seltenheim's fault or not, Frederick found it almost impossible to resist a gamble, and it was probably his most serious weakness throughout life.

His gambling took many forms besides cards, including bets on games of tennis, which Frederick very much enjoyed. Nor was he a stranger to alcohol, or to the charms of the opposite sex, although neither of these tastes would have seemed unusual in a young, handsome and extremely eligible young soldier. It seems that the dairymaid from his days at Kew wanted to join him in Hanover, but had to be dissuaded. In a constant round of dances, balls and entertainments, he met many young ladies, and it is perhaps surprising that he did not become more seriously entangled in romantic affairs than he actually did. For instance, there is no doubt, as future events were to prove, that during his visits to the Prussian court at Potsdam he was much attracted to Frederick the Great's niece, Princess Frederica, and she to him.[25]

The reality is that during the years Frederick spent in Germany he conducted himself with remarkable restraint and a real sense of responsibility. He studied diligently, both in academic and military matters and he visited many German royal courts, where he was well received as a popular ambassador of his father. He was liked by Frederick the Great and the Duke of Brunswick, both of whom seemed to respect his soldierly qualities. He gave due attention to the military and civil administration of his prince-bishopric, which ran very smoothly during these years. Moreover, he acted as a wise and helpful elder brother to his younger siblings. If he gambled, drank and danced, it was not to a degree which gave rise to unfavourable comment. Indeed, Lord Cornwallis, who met him in 1785, wrote approvingly that he had a 'great deal of good nature and a very good heart ... One cannot help loving him.'[26]

In February 1787 Frederick sent another letter to his father asking if he could come home and this time he got the answer he had been hoping for. The king said that he could return and that he would prepare suitable apartments for him in St James's Palace. Frederick set out from Hanover in May and attended the Prussian military reviews at Potsdam, Berlin and Magdeburg before saying farewell to his uncle in Brunswick. Then he moved to the military camp at Lüneburg, called on his brothers at Göttingen, paid a final visit to Osnabrück and arrived in England early in August.

# Chapter Three

## York and the Regency Crisis, 1787–1789

By 1787 the king and queen had become more fond of Windsor Castle as a residence and, having crossed from Calais to Dover, Frederick drove directly there, where his mother and father and all his sisters received him with the greatest affection. Fanny Burney witnessed the event and wrote of the king's delight in seeing his son again: 'The joy of his excellent father. Oh! That there is no describing. It was the glee of the first youth – nay of ardent and innocent infancy – so pure it seemed, so warm, so open, so unmixed. Might he but escape the contagion of surrounding example.'[1]

By this she meant the Prince of Wales, who was staying in his seaside 'pavilion' at Brighton when the news came through of Frederick's return. We are told that 'without loss of time he threw himself into his carriage and proceeded to salute a brother whom he tenderly loved and from whom he had been so long separated'.[2] During the period that Frederick had been in Hanover, relations between the king and his heir had deteriorated to an alarming degree. Physically, the Prince of Wales was attractive as a young man, although he soon grew to be portly and eventually grossly fat. Georgiana, the dazzling young Duchess of Devonshire – one of innumerable women with whom he eventually had an affair – wrote about him in a private memoir on their first encounter in 1782:

> The Prince of Wales is rather tall and has a figure which, though striking, is not perfect. He is inclined to be too fat and looks too much like a woman in men's clothes, but the gracefulness of his manner and his height certainly make him a pleasing figure. His face is very handsome and he is fond of dress even to a tawdry degree, which young as he is will soon wear off. His person, his dress, and the admiration he has met with . . . take up his thoughts chiefly. He is good-natured and rather extravagant . . . but he certainly does not want for understanding and his jokes sometimes have the appearance of wit. He appears to have an inclination to meddle with politics – he loves being of

consequence, and whether it is in intrigues of state or of gallantry he often thinks more is intended than really is.[3]

Most of these judgements proved to be correct. The prince was intelligent, cultured, possessed of exceptional artistic flair, generous, friendly and good company. Unfortunately he was also seriously lacking in any kind of common sense concerning political decisions, the assessment of other people's characters, moderation in the consumption of food or drink, the expenditure of money in any respect, and the pursuit of women. Despite all the care George III had taken with his education, the prince had turned out to be, as far as his father was concerned, a disaster.

The prince's first serious affair was at the age of sixteen, with Mary, niece of Sir William Hamilton, who did not encourage him, so he turned to Mary Robinson, a married actress with a baby daughter, whom he saw playing the part of 'Perdita' in *The Winter's Tale*. Calling himself 'Florizel' after the prince in the same play, he wrote to her making many promises, including the payment of £20,000 when he should come of age. She kept his letters and when he lost interest in her she blackmailed the king, who paid her £5,000 for them and granted a life annuity of £600 for herself and £200 for her daughter.[4]

George III had two younger brothers, William, Duke of Gloucester, and Henry, Duke of Cumberland, both of whom led their young nephew astray. Cumberland had annoyed the king by marrying a commoner, Anne Horton, and the result of this had been the Royal Marriages Act of 1772 which laid down that no member of the royal family might marry without the sovereign's permission before the age of twenty-five. Cumberland and his wife were ostracized by the king and queen and no doubt he encouraged the prince to drink, swear and whore as a way of striking back.

In 1781 the prince pursued Madame Hardenburg, the wife of a Hanoverian minister in England, who seems to have readily succumbed to his advances. To his dismay she urged him to elope with her and he admitted his dilemma to the queen, who told the king, who quickly despatched Hardenburg, with his wife, on a diplomatic mission to Brussels. George wrote to his brother Frederick in Hanover, asking him not to make love to the baroness when she returned there. Frederick told him that when he had first arrived in Hanover the year before, he had danced with her at a masquerade and she had offered to go alone into another room with him. He went on: 'I desired no better fun ... but unluckily the room was full ... I know also other stories of her still worse than this.' Two months later he told George that 'she has abused you so terribly by all accounts here that I am thoroughly persuaded she is completely cured of her love for you, if she ever had any ... You ought to rejoice at having got rid of her.'[5]

Frederick knew that his brother found the king very short-tempered and grumpy, as a result of his perceived misdemeanours, and he wrote from Hanover, urging that the prince should 'do everything which you can to keep well with him, at least upon decent terms; consider he is vexed enough in public affairs. It is therefore your business not to make that still worse.'[6] George clearly missed the company of his brother because he told the king at Christmas 1781 that Frederick's departure 'was the longest twelvemonth I ever passed', describing him as 'his best and dearest friend'. The feeling was clearly mutual because after he had left home Frederick wrote George twenty-three letters, while George sent only eight letters in reply. Frederick complained in December 1781, 'It is near two months that I have not received the least line from you.'[7] Hearing that George had been ill, Frederick wrote in one of his early letters: 'I hate a sermon as well as you, but my affection for you forces me to entreat you for God's sake to take care of your health. You cannot stand this kind of life, and I am afraid it is the Windsor Lodge Duke [their Uncle Henry of Cumberland] who leads you into it. I have no doubt he means you exceedingly well, but believe me he is not the best adviser you can follow.' The prince replied indignantly that he had not seen Cumberland for ages.[8]

In other letters Frederick boasted, 'I have become one of the best shots here, so much so that I can shoot hare in their full speed with ball at a hundred yards distance.' And again, 'I have practised five or six times with a rifle-barrelled carabine [sic] at a butt, at which I have succeeded better than could have been conceived, as it is very difficult. Grenville and all say that I have the steadiest hand they ever saw.' This was probably true, because he remained an outstanding marksman throughout his life. He also told George that he enjoyed shooting the stag: 'I have often run five or six miles as hard as I could on foot with my gun on my shoulder after a stag.'[9]

George was much too vain to let all this pass without a riposte: 'I am become an exceedingly good shot. ... The first time I ever fired a fowling piece I fired at a sheet of paper at sixty yards distance, and covered it full of shot.' Frederick then switched to his prowess as a dancer: 'When I return to England I must teach you two different kinds of dances from what we have the least idea of, the quadrille and the valtzes.' But everyone agreed that the Prince of Wales was an excellent dancer, and it is doubtful whether Frederick could compete with him on that score.[10]

Another of the young Prince of Wales's mistresses was Elizabeth Armistead, a courtesan who shared her favours with, among others, Charles James Fox. This Eton-educated son of Lord Holland became the dominant force within the Whig party on account of his brilliance and ruthlessness as a political orator and debater. Yet at the same time he was one of the most debauched men in England, intent on the reckless pursuit of gambling, drinking and whoring. At other times in British history this would have made a successful political career impossible but a number of factors combined to make the period from about 1770 to 1830 one in which low standards of public behaviour and morality were in high fashion among the leaders of British society. One of the reasons for this may be that the Anglican Church had become moribund and to some degree corrupt and it had little control over public morality. Another main reason was that many members of the aristocratic and gentry classes had become enormously rich since about 1750 as a result of improved agricultural methods, as well as the mining of coal on their estates, which fed the rapidly developing 'industrial revolution'.

The two most prominent exceptions to the often low standards of aristocratic behaviour were the king and queen, who lived a relatively modest, frugal and godly life, but even though they potentially had enormous social influence, they were not able to quell many of the excesses. The king regarded most of the Whigs as sons of the devil, partly because they were led by debauchees such as Fox and partly because they were opposed to royal methods of government. Lord North, who had been the king's loyal prime minister for twelve years, resigned in 1782 after a major defeat in the House of Commons and the king, to his disgust, was forced to ask the Whigs to form a ministry, which included Fox.

This lasted long enough to negotiate the Treaty of Paris, which ended the War of American Independence, but it collapsed soon afterwards and to the king's further dismay North agreed to form a coalition ministry with Fox. Outraged by this cynical arrangement, the king, in December 1783, took the remarkable step of asking William Pitt 'the Younger' to form an administration. He was a younger son of the famous statesman of the same name but he was only twenty-four years old and at first his appointment was greeted with derision. However, he quickly silenced his critics because he showed that, despite his youth, he was a brilliantly lucid debater in the Commons who had a mastery of detailed exposition that soon commanded the confidence and admiration of the House. Pitt was a bachelor and lived a blameless life, devoted to his work, though even he drank too much.

After 1783, then, the Whigs were firmly in opposition while Pitt commanded the support of the king and a good majority in the House. Since the Whigs were hated by the king, they naturally devoted all their efforts to winning over his heir. The Prince of Wales not only shared a mistress with Fox, but he shared his taste for drinking and wild living and they became firm friends. The year 1783 also marked two very important developments in the life of the Prince of Wales. He became the owner of Carlton House and ruined himself financially by remodelling it on a fabulous and extravagant scale and he genuinely fell in love and subsequently married illegally.

Carlton House, situated on Pall Mall, was a royal residence that had been occupied by George III's mother until her death in 1772, after which it fell into disuse. The king granted it to his heir as his first independent home to mark his twenty-first birthday, imagining that the prince would make a number of necessary improvements and pay for them out of his parliamentary allowance of £50,000 a year plus the £12,000 he received from the Duchy of Cornwall. But George had grand plans for Carlton House and he employed the architect Henry Holland to create a veritable palace, which was decorated in the most lavish and expensive style and was readily compared in magnificence (though not size) with Versailles and St Petersburg. But it cost a huge fortune and by 1786 the prince was in debt to the tune of £269,000, with his programme of refurbishment by no means complete.[11]

Meanwhile George had fallen in love with a young widow, Maria Fitzherbert, who, unfortunately for him, was a Roman Catholic as well as a commoner. He could not marry a Roman Catholic without forfeiting his right to the throne, as laid down by the 1701 Act of Settlement, and he could not marry at all until he was twenty-five, according to the Royal Marriages Act of 1772. Maria fled abroad in 1784 and in July that year George contemplated giving up his right to the throne in favour of Frederick and following her into exile.[12] The king, unaware of the true situation, refused him permission to go, but in 1785 Maria agreed to become the prince's lover, although only if a secret marriage could be formalized. Seeing that this might destroy hopes of the prince's succession to the throne, Fox urged him not to marry, but George went ahead, having persuaded a priest in a debtor's prison to conduct a highly secret ceremony in Maria's house. This marriage was legitimate in the eyes of the Roman Catholic and Anglican Churches (and of the bride) but illegal according to two Acts of Parliament.

As to the impact it might ultimately have on his claim to the throne, the prince swept this aside in the enthusiasm of the moment. When his father, still unaware of the secret marriage, ultimately suggested that he should marry some suitable princess, the prince's stated view was 'I will never marry. My resolution is taken on that subject. I have settled it with Frederick. No, I will never marry ... Frederick will marry, and the crown will descend to his children.'[13] George and Maria had to live separately, both in London and in Brighton, where the prince was also lavishing money on his seaside home, but it was generally accepted that they were together, until the prince eventually left her for a string of mistresses as well as a legitimate wife. The fact that they had been married remained a closely guarded secret until after George's death in 1830.

So the Duke of York, aged twenty-four, returned to England in 1787 to find his brother living at Carlton House, and secretly married, while he himself lived in apartments in St James's Palace, almost next door. Soon after his arrival home, he sat for Sir Joshua Reynolds, who painted a fine full-length portrait of him, which now hangs in Buckingham Palace. It shows him resplendent in his robes as a Knight of the Garter and looking every inch a prince. In Hanover he had been in charge of military affairs and a member of the governing council, as well as being the ruler of his prince-bishopric of Osnabrück. He had been feted at the courts of Frederick the Great and the Emperor Joseph as well as by dozens of lesser sovereigns and treated with almost exaggerated respect as a Prince of Great Britain. He had been influential in the conduct of international diplomacy and instrumental in the setting up of the League of Princes. He had been a trusted confidant of his father, who had accepted his advice on a wide range of issues, including the education and upbringing of his younger brothers. In short, while in Hanover, Frederick had been a person of real consequence in his own right.

In England, however, as he quickly realized, he had no significant role. He was a lieutenant general in a peacetime army and he was Colonel of the Coldstream Guards, which was largely an honorary position. He was not the heir to the throne, and though a son of the king, there were plenty of those at the time. Nor was he even married, with a growing family to occupy his time and energies. During Frederick's childhood George III had set aside some of the revenues from Osnabrück, which by 1786 were enough to buy him an estate of about 4,500 acres at Allerton Mauleverer in Yorkshire, for which Frederick was now responsible.

Situated about five miles from Knaresborough, the estate, owned by the Mauleverer family soon after 1066, passed to several subsequent families and was bought by Frederick from the fourth Viscount Galway. At its centre was a large Georgian mansion, built in the 1740s and remodelled in the 1790s. Frederick took the Prince of Wales with him to stay in the house in October 1787 but clearly George did not think much of it, because shortly afterwards Frederick commissioned Henry Holland (his brother's favoured architect) to rebuild it. The London journal *The World* reported in March 1787 that 'Henry Holland is at present in Yorkshire superintending the improvements now in progress at HRH's house at Allerton in the county', and subsequently it was reported that 'HRH entirely rebuilt the large and substantial residence, erecting commodious stables, and [laying] out the beautiful gardens'. A striking feature of these gardens was (and still is) a 'Temple of Victory' standing on top of a 200-foot hill, and there is a picturesque local tradition that this was indeed the very hill on which the 'Grand Old Duke of York' deployed his 10,000 men – presumably construction workers, toiling ant-like up and down. It is not a plausible story, however, because the temple and hill appear on a map of Yorkshire dated 1771, well before York bought the estate.[14]

When Frederick was appointed Duke of York he was given a parliamentary grant of £12,000 a year and he still received some revenue from Osnabrück.[15] So he had an income, although it was small compared with that of the Prince of Wales. But it would have been enough had he not gambled so much. He was elected to Brooks's Club, where many members of the aristocracy who were far richer than he cheerfully lost thousands in a single game of cards. Some might have made money this way, but not Frederick. During his lifetime he was well known for being not a very smart player, as well as being unlucky.

Inevitably Frederick became drawn into the fascinating circle of his brother, the Prince of Wales: he was a constant guest at Carlton House and soon became part of the petty intrigues, gossip and frolics that made up life there. He could have his pick of the women at court and he was frequently at dinner-parties where vast quantities of wine were consumed. He became less and less in touch with his father and mother, partly because it was George III's avowed policy, like the Hanoverian kings before him, to exclude all his sons, even his heir, from any participation in state affairs or the business of government. The king was still only forty-nine: the future for his elder sons seemed lacking in any real purpose.

A good deal of Frederick's life was centred on Brooks's Club, and in 1828 (a year after his death) a history of the London Clubs was published, 'with anecdotes of their members, sketches of character and conversation'. It contained two passages concerning the youthful Duke of York, though the episodes are not dated and they probably rely heavily on club gossip. The first extract reads:

Several of the Princes, sons to George III, became members of Brooks's Club soon after coming of age. The two eldest sons were of course great favourites with everybody; but this partiality was not so much the consequence of their high rank as of their great good-nature and affability, their convivial habits, and their uniformly genteel deportment. They shared largely, likewise, in the admiration of the fair sex, at whose tea and card tables it was often a matter of serious dispute as to which was the handsomest fellow ... two finer-looking young men than the Prince of Wales and the Duke of York were not to be seen in a day's march.

The second extract is less flattering to York, and sees him in something of a Bullingdon Club mood (founded at Oxford University around 1780):

The Duke of York, Colonel St Leger, Tom Stepney and two others, one morning about three o'clock, came reeling along Pall Mall, highly charged with the juice of the grape, and ripe for a row. They banged on the door of Brooks's so loudly as to wake up all the servants, who let them in, whereupon in the darkness they blundered about, damaging the furniture. One of the waiters produced a blunderbuss and was about to shoot when the housekeeper, who with no other covering than her chemise and flannel-petticoat was fast approaching with a light, which no sooner flashed upon the faces of these midnight disturbers than she exclaimed 'For Heaven's Sake, Tom, don't fire! It is only the Duke of York!'[16]

When the king apparently went mad in the autumn of 1788, a far more sober attitude to life was required from his sons. The king became very agitated and even violent and the queen, afraid for her safety, moved to separate apartments. This made him even worse, and on one occasion he seized the Prince of Wales by the throat and pinned him to a wall. Dr Warren, his physician, shaved the king's head and applied hot blisters to it, but by 5 November he was declared to be totally deranged, raving and gesticulating wildly and howling like a dog. On 8 November York, who had just come out of the king's room, told a courtier that his 'situation is every moment becoming worse. His pulse is weaker and weaker; and the doctors say it is impossible to survive it long, if his situation does not take some extraordinary change in a few hours'.[17] The king subsequently fell into a coma. He did not die but his physicians were completely at a loss to know the cause or correct treatment of his condition, or how long it might last.

Clearly a regent was needed to carry out the king's executive functions. The obvious candidate was the Prince of Wales but this was a disastrous prospect for Pitt and his ministers, who might well be sacked and replaced by Fox and the Whigs if the prince came to power. So Pitt at first advanced the claim of the queen to be regent, thereby causing a major family and political quarrel. In fact, Fox was on holiday in Italy and did not return, utterly exhausted, until 24 November. By then Pitt had accepted that the prince should be regent but only with restricted powers, a notion that infuriated the Whigs. In December Pitt's Regency Bill made its way through Parliament and it is reported that on the 15th the Duke of York spoke very fluently in the House of Lords on behalf of his brother against any restrictions on the powers of the regent:

No claim of right, he said, had been set up by the Prince of Wales; and he was perfectly assured that his brother too well understood the sacred principles which seated the House of Brunswick on the British throne, ever to assume or attempt to exercise any power, let his claim be what it might, that was not derived from the will of the people, as conveyed through the constitutional voice of their legal representatives. This declaration, delivered in a manly and bathetic tone, made a deep impression upon the whole house, which remained silent for some minutes.[18]

Subsequently, York took quite an active part in the proceedings in the Lords, formulating amendments against any attempt to reduce the regent's authority, but he was outvoted and formally disassociated himself from the final proposals. These were that the regent would not be able to create peers or make appointments for life and that the control of the royal household and the person and property of the king should be given to the queen and not to the prince. This undoubtedly caused a breakdown of good relations between the queen and her two eldest sons. Apparently, she and York had a serious row in January 1789 when the duke, in a temper, suggested to her that she was as mad as her husband.[19]

It seemed likely that the Bill would become law before the end of February 1789 and that the glittering prizes of executive power and political office, even if somewhat restricted, would fall into the hands of the Prince of Wales, the Duke of York and the Whig opposition. With only days to go, the king suddenly recovered on 20 February and two days later the prince and York were allowed to see him. We are told that the king 'embraced them both with the greatest tenderness, and shed tears on their faces, and both the Princes were much touched by the scene ... The Queen was present, and walking to and fro in the room with a countenance and manner of great dissatisfaction.'[20]

But the founding editor of *The Times* newspaper, John Walter, chose to describe this tender reconciliation in terms that were certainly libellous, because they were untrue as well as being grossly disparaging to York. Walter's article on the following day said: 'It argues infinite wisdom in certain persons to have prevented the Duke of York from rushing into the king's apartments on Wednesday. The rashness, the Germanic severity and insensibility of this young man might have proved ruinous to the hopes and joys of a whole nation.' York swiftly brought a libel action against Walter, who was given a stiff sentence – a year in Newgate prison, standing once in the pillory at Charing Cross and a fine of fifty pounds. He paid the fine and went to prison but was let off the pillory, perhaps at the suggestion of the duke. However, Walter continued to edit his paper in prison and was in trouble again the following year for libelling the prince and the duke once more and also their brother the Duke of Clarence, for good measure.[21] It is quite possible that Walter received secret service money from the treasury to support the government and undermine the opposition, which of course included the two princes.[22]

The king had been declared deranged for three-and-a-half months and during this time the prince and his brother experienced a number of emotions. At first they were undoubtedly seriously shocked and genuinely upset by their father's unexpected illness, although as time wore on they perhaps became more cynical about it. 'Madness' was not a condition that was sympathetically understood at the time and the princes doubtless felt that their father had been almost dehumanized by his ravings and physical assaults: this was not the father they had known and respected. It was said that after several drinks in Brooks's Club they were both seen imitating their father's wild gesticulations and behaviour, which was not in the best of taste.[23] When it seemed possible that the king would not recover, the important issue became the political one of who should wield his power and to what extent, and here the princes found themselves battling against a majority in Parliament, led by the wily Pitt and his ally, the queen. Given that Frederick was so close to his brother, it would have been personally treacherous and tactically unwise for him to have abandoned the prince's cause and to have supported Pitt. Indeed, in the opinion of Edmund Burke, the influential political philosopher, 'The Duke of York's whole conduct has been such, with regard to spirit, judgement and correctness of honour, as ... every friend of his could wish.'[24]

George III was very popular with the great majority of his subjects and there was heartfelt rejoicing at his recovery. Political opponents of the Whigs portrayed them as a party which had attempted to seize power during the crisis, abetted by the Prince of Wales and Duke of York. The prince, in particular, was lampooned by popular caricaturists as a dissolute wastrel, greedy for power and influence, who had been disloyal and disrespectful to his father and mother, while *The Times* (still under the influence of Walter) went so far as to say that 'Gluttony, drunkenness and gambling were [both brothers'] habitual occupations.' As for the prince and the duke, they largely blamed the queen, who, they felt, had made an unconstitutional bid for power. Only the Irish seemed to be strongly on the prince's side. Early in March (when it was too late), deputies from the Irish Parliament in Dublin came to offer the prince an unrestricted regency in Ireland. Instead the prince and the Duke of York gave them dinner at Carlton House, and the prince entertained them by using his excellent singing voice to render 'a sea-song extremely well'.[25]

On 10 March there were lavish illuminations and displays in the West End of London to celebrate the king's recovery, and so great was the patriotic enthusiasm of the mob that the Whigs had no alternative but to join in or have the windows of their houses smashed. The prince and the duke went to the opera but on the way their coach was held up in a traffic jam and the crowd demanded that they shout 'God Save the King', which they were happy to do and then 'Pitt for Ever', which they refused. When a man threatened to enter the royal coach, the prince was ready to fight but York pulled him back, hit the stranger on the head and told the coachman to drive on. The queen's continued hostility was made apparent in April when the two brothers were told that a concert which the king and queen were putting on at Windsor 'was intended only for those who have supported us through the late business, and therefore you may possibly choose not to be present'. They did attend, all the same, and the king greeted them warmly, though the queen looked 'dowdy and glum'. Finally, there was a five-hour service of thanksgiving at St Paul's Cathedral on 23 April, a magnificent affair attended by enormous crowds, including 6,000 children from the city's charity schools. Critical observers claimed that during the service the prince and the duke chatted to each other and laughed at jokes, and they ate biscuits during the sermon.[26]

There has been much debate about the nature of the king's illness. At the time it was put down to stress caused either by the need to remain faithful to a somewhat unattractive wife, or by the loss of the American colonies, or by the disgraceful behaviour of his eldest son. In the late twentieth century it was suggested by psychiatric experts that the king in fact suffered from a disease called acute intermittent porphyria, which today can be treated relatively simply and successfully. The tragedy is that the king suffered agonies, not only from the disease but even more so from the hardly less than sadistic regime imposed upon him by his physicians, based upon the notion that he might be cured if he were punished for his outbursts by being confined in a straitjacket, among many other indignities.[27]

# Chapter Four

## The Duel, 1789

On 20 May 1789 the Duke of York stunned the nation by fighting a duel with a young officer in his regiment, Lieutenant-Colonel Charles Lennox, the nephew and heir of the third Duke of Richmond. Richmond was Master-General of the Ordnance at the time and he seems to have engineered the appointment of his nephew to a commission in the Coldstream Guards without the knowledge of York, who was very irritated by this, as he was the regiment's commanding officer. Moreover Lennox was a supporter of the king and queen's court party and did not disguise his disapproval of the way in which both the Prince of Wales and York had behaved during the king's illness. According to York himself, at a masked ball he witnessed three masked gentlemen insulting his brother, the Prince of Wales. He intervened and recognizing Lennox to be one of them he told him that he was a coward and a disgrace to his profession. Nothing further came of this incident at the time but Lennox continued to abuse and insult the princes and their friends (in their absence) at the military Daubigny's Club and then on 15 May he approached the duke during regimental exercises, demanding to know whether he had said that he, Lennox, had behaved in a way unfit for a gentleman. The duke said that he had heard someone else say that at Daubigny's Club but that he would not hide behind his rank as a prince and Lennox's commanding officer and that he was ready as a private gentleman to give Lennox satisfaction whenever or wherever he pleased.

Lennox took him at his word and on 26 May the duel went ahead on Wimbledon Common, with Lord Rawdon as second for the duke and the Earl of Winchilsea as second for Lennox. The ground was measured at twelve paces and the combatants were instructed to fire at an agreed signal. Lennox fired first and his shot grazed the duke's head and displaced a few hairs. Frederick refused to fire in return, even though pressed to do so by Lennox but he said that if Lennox was not satisfied, he could fire again. Lennox said he could not possibly fire again if the duke did not intend to fire back and both men left the field. According to the report of the seconds, 'both parties behaved with the most perfect coolness and intrepidity'. The fact was, however, that Frederick had come literally within a hairsbreadth of being shot dead.[1]

York and Lennox both became heroes to their friends and supporters and the popular opinion of York, which had been low during the Regency affair, improved considerably, as many people were impressed by his bravery and determination not to hide behind his rank. Lennox was subsequently snubbed by the Prince of Wales at a ball held in St James's Palace on the king's birthday, 4 June. The king did not attend this, we are told, 'owing to the agitated frame of mind into which he had been thrown by the narrow escape of his son'. However, to everyone's surprise the queen invited Lennox, whom the princes found it impossible to avoid on the dance floor. The Prince of Wales went up to the queen and announced that he was tired, 'not with the dance, but tired of dancing in such company ... I never will countenance insults given to my family, however they may be treated by others'.[2]

After this the queen withdrew, bringing the ball to an end. The Earl of Winchilsea, Lennox's second, was well known to the queen as a member of the royal household and it seems that she was readily prepared to forget and forgive Lennox's duel with her son. Frederick was still the king's favourite son but he had certainly alienated his mother at this stage. When Fox realized the extent to which the queen appeared unconcerned about the danger York had been in, he exclaimed that with such a son as York, there could surely be no mother in the world who would have behaved as coldly as the queen. 'Friend and enemy, except only his father and mother,' he announced, 'agree in praising the Duke of York to the highest degree.'[3] Of course, Fox was no friend of the king or the queen. Meanwhile, Lennox left the Coldstream Guards and joined the 35th regiment of foot in Edinburgh.

As he gradually realized what had transpired during the months of his incapacity, the king became increasingly distressed that his eldest sons had sided with the opposition to his ministers, instead of maintaining a dignified neutrality. He chiefly blamed the Prince of Wales, considering that Frederick had followed him out of a sense of loyalty, which was largely true. The prince saw the need for a degree of reconciliation and wrote a lengthy letter of apology to his father, associating Frederick with the same sentiments. York himself began to mix less with the Whigs and to appreciate the qualities and abilities of Pitt. The prime minister was in many ways a cold and unapproachable figure and this had not commended him to Frederick but it was increasingly clear to him that he was a loyal and very able servant of the Crown.

In August 1789 the prince and Frederick travelled up to York to attend the races there. They had both become keen followers of the turf, which at about this time became perhaps the prince's most consuming passion: he maintained a racing stable which cost him over £30,000 a year. It was he who established Ascot as a fashionable racecourse and who adopted the racing colours used by subsequent sovereigns. Frederick, too, kept a racing stable, though on a more modest scale. The brothers were accommodated in the deanery at York and the prince was presented with the freedom of the city in an elegant gold box. From Frederick's point of view it was his first opportunity to admire this ancient city, whose name he bore, with its vast gothic minster, dozens of medieval churches and guild halls, all enclosed within a medieval wall in a good state of preservation. After the York visit the duke returned home, while the prince continued his 'progress', visiting, among others, Earl Fitzwilliam, one of the richest men in England, in his enormous palace at Wentworth Woodhouse, of which George was probably envious.

Since his return to England, Frederick had resided in a number of London homes. First of all he had an apartment in St James's Palace, but when the king became ill he moved to Windsor Castle to be with him for a few weeks until he was taken to Kew. Then he stayed with his brother at Carlton House. All this was because a mansion was in the course of being prepared for him on Whitehall, very close to the Horse Guards, and he moved into it late in 1789 and renamed it York House. It had been bought from Sir Matthew Featherstone and Henry Holland was commissioned to make changes and additions. The interior was considered to be very fine, although some critics disapproved of the exterior, with its 'heavy and tasteless portico'.[4] Here York was able to run his own establishment with his own friends and he came less under the influence of his elder brother.

York's main problem, like that of all his brothers, sooner or later, was that the allowances he received were inadequate to maintain him in a manner he considered appropriate to his station and he wrote to the king soon after his duel, in May 1789, saying that despite his income and despite the sum that his father had saved for him from the Osnabrück revenues, he had been unable to keep himself out of debt.[5] Marriage to a rich heiress would perhaps be a solution and it seems that he was very fond of two aristocratic British ladies, Lady Tyrconnell and Mary, Duchess of Rutland, a famous beauty. According to one courtier, York had strong feelings for Lady Tyrconnell and 'absolutely turned the Duchess of Gordon out of the supper-room destined for the royal family at the Pantheon, because her Grace was supposed to have said something ill-natured about the object of his affection'. This affair was common knowledge and the subject of an explicit caricature by James Gillray which showed a strapping young prince getting into bed with Lady Tyrconnell while her husband quietly left the room. It was unfortunate that Lady Tyrconnell was married but the Duchess of Rutland, a very rich widow, was not. However, she was romantically entangled with a friend of the Prince of Wales, who persuaded his brother to look elsewhere.[6]

## Marriage, 1791

One way in which Frederick could reduce his expenses might have been to take up employment as a soldier and in October 1790 he was earnestly requesting the king to send him on a military mission. He had been ordered to increase the numbers in his regiment in expectation of a detachment being sent on foreign service and he asked to go with them. But the king replied that only a small force was being considered, certainly not large enough to be commanded by a lieutenant general and a Prince of the Blood. York nevertheless told him that he wished to make clear his 'ardent wishes that the moment may not be far distant that I may have an opportunity of learning my profession in the only way it can be truly taught and of endeavouring to make myself useful to your Majesty and my country'.[7]

While the nation recovered from the shock of the king's illness and gradually returned to the normal pattern of life, events in France during 1789 moved into a drastic political crisis. For many decades the nation's finances had been badly managed and King Louis XVI was bankrupt. Unlike Britain, France was not a constitutional monarchy and the king considered that he governed by 'divine right'. However, with no money he was forced to appeal to the 'Estates General', the nearest thing to a parliament in France, which had not met since early in the previous century. The Estates pronounced themselves a 'National Assembly' and took an oath not to dissolve before they had extracted major constitutional reforms from a reluctant king and they galvanized the 'mob' in Paris, which attacked the royal fortress of the Bastille in July 1789 and later demolished it. A 'Declaration of the Rights of Man' was issued, along the liberal principles advocated by political philosophers such as Rousseau, and in 1790 the king was compelled to accept a constitution, which drastically limited his powers. In the countryside many of the feudal aristocracy were attacked by the local people and their *châteaux* and estates were ransacked, causing a mass exodus of the nobility from France.

In the summer of 1791 Frederick received permission to travel to Berlin to see whether he could persuade the King of Prussia to allow him to take part, on the Prussian side, in hostilities which seemed likely to break out because of disputes between Prussia and Russia over Turkey. Before he left, he again raised with his father the matter of his income, stating baldly that 'I find myself under the utter impossibility of keeping up my present establishment without the assistance of your Majesty,' without which 'I shall find myself under the cruel necessity of making that reform in my ... household, as will in some manner satisfy my creditors.' It is true that he did not receive a very large allowance, but the king must have been aware that some, at least, of his debts had been incurred at the gaming table.[8]

When he reached Berlin a couple of weeks later, the likelihood of war between Prussia and Russia had passed but Frederick wrote to tell his father that he had visited his two brothers, who were still studying at Göttingen. 'They are both grown very handsome lads', he was pleased to relate: 'Ernest is above two inches taller than me and Adolphus is nearly my size.' Ernest was highly thought of by his superior officers, while Adolphus was 'a prodigious fine lad, perfectly natural, [who] seems to have a great deal of sense and a great desire to learn'.[9] In Berlin Frederick was a guest at the military reviews held on 24 and 26 May, and the king gave a grand dinner for him in the Charlottenburg Palace.

With no prospect of joining the Prussian army, Frederick's attention in Potsdam turned once more to the Princess Frederica. He had known and admired her for years and he now came to an important decision and wrote to his father to say:

I think it my duty to inform your Majesty that from the first time I saw the King of Prussia's eldest daughter ... she was not wholly indifferent to me and though I did not think it right at that moment to encourage any hope concerning her, not being acquainted with your Majesty's sentiments, yet the very instant I knew them, she was always my object. Having had an opportunity during my stay here to see her and to enquire very particularly after her, I am perfectly convinced that her person and disposition are such as to make me perfectly happy. Allow me therefore, sir, to entreat you as my father and my King to grant me your consent to marry her, and to obtain her for me of the King her father.[10]

King Frederick II had died in 1786 leaving no children, so his throne passed to his nephew, Frederick William II, considered to be one of the most handsome men in Europe. Frederica was his eldest child and she enjoyed the title of Princess Royal of Prussia. Concerning the marriage, York wrote to his former aide, by now General Grenville:

You knew for many years that the Princess Frederique [sic] has been a flame of mine, and you will not forget that when we left Berlin four years ago I then told you that I should be very glad to marry her if it could be brought about. The different events that have happened during the last four years have hindered me till now from declaring myself but still I can safely say I never lost sight of my object ... I have no doubt of being perfectly happy. The princess is the best girl that ever existed and the more I see of her the more I like her.[11]

'I do not say that she is the handsomest girl that ever was formed,' Frederick admitted to other friends, 'but she is full enough so for me, and in disposition she is an angel. ... Every day I am more attached, and am more convinced that I never could enjoy any happiness without her.'[12]

George III was delighted with this proposed marriage to a highly suitable Protestant princess and he lost no time in giving it his blessing. In almost every respect this seemed to be an advantageous union, with the added bonus that the pair were genuinely fond of each other. Moreover, it was dynastically an extremely prestigious marriage: no British prince of the Hanoverian line had as yet married the daughter of a reigning king. A good many details had to be settled before the marriage could go ahead, one of the most important being a renunciation by York of any claim he might have to the Prussian throne, in the event of the (highly unlikely) failure of heirs male in the Hohenzollern family.

The marriage ceremony took place in the lavishly decorated White Hall of the baroque Charlottenburg Palace in Berlin on the evening of 29 September, in the presence of many royal persons, including the young Hereditary Prince of Orange and his wife. The bridegroom wore his regimental uniform while the bride wore a gown of silver, ornamented with diamonds, and a diamond tiara. They were married according to the rites of the Lutheran Church by the Upper Councillor of the Consistory, after which twelve guns in the garden fired three rounds. Then the royal family played cards for a while before sitting down to a supper served on gold dishes, with the dessert served on a superb set of porcelain made by craftsmen in the Berlin factory.

The new duke and duchess left Berlin on 17 October and arrived at Hanover on the 25th, where they stayed eight days, moving on to Osnabrück for a further four days. In both places they received the congratulations of the local people and both gave and received hospitality. From Osnabrück they travelled to Brussels and then to Lille, where they witnessed the ugly side of the French Revolution at first hand. Travelling in a carriage emblazoned with royal arms, they were detained by the locals, who required the unwelcome signs of royalty to be obliterated before allowing the couple to proceed. At Calais they had to wait five days for a suitable ship to take them across to Dover, where they landed on the beach on Friday, 28 October and were met by the duke's servants and men from his regiment.

On their arrival at York House on Saturday, they were greeted in the Great Hall by the Prince of Wales and the Duke of Clarence but at this point Frederica felt unwell and was ordered to bed by her physician. A round of dazzling receptions and celebrations were held in the following days, including a re-marriage in Buckingham House that were held according to Anglican rites, in order to comply with the provisions of the Royal Marriages Act. In all these appearances the duke and duchess made an excellent impression with their sumptuous attire, the duchess sparkling with diamonds, including ear-rings presented by the queen, while the duke wore a sabre studded with diamonds, a costly wedding gift from the King of Prussia.[13]

Frederica was the child of a disastrous marriage. Her mother, the Crown Princess of Prussia, who was a double first cousin of her husband, became pregnant by a lover in 1767, two years after Frederica's birth. The crown prince divorced his wife and she was placed under house arrest in the castle of Stettin, a social outcast for the next seventy-one years until her death in 1840, aged ninety-three.[14] Frederica was brought up by her grandmother and the crown prince's new wife and by the time of her marriage she was twenty-four years old and not very tall or pretty. She had flaxen hair and china-blue eyes but a pock-marked complexion and poor teeth, although the newspapers enthusiastically printed long columns in praise of her charm, liveliness and agreeable manner. A friend of the Prince of Wales had written to him (partly in French), 'I never saw two people so completely in love as the Duke and Princess are. It is beyond anything I ever saw or heard of. I think your Royal Highness will like your beautiful sister very much: she is very lovable and full of talents: a very good musician, and she sings like an angel.'[15]

Being a small person, Frederica had feet to match and six pairs of tiny shoes were made for her in England, to be worn at her English marriage and its attendant celebrations. This caught the popular imagination and copies of these shoes were made and sold by the hundreds. Later models followed, five-and-a-half inches long and made of purple leather, decorated with diamonds. According to the *Frampton Journal*, it soon 'became the fashion for everyone to squeeze their feet without mercy, in order to be like Her Royal Highness, and as she wore heels to her shoes, so did the rest of the world'. The caricaturist Gillray thought that this rage had become excessive and lampooned it by depicting her very small feet and the duke's big ones as they might be observed when he was lying on top of her in bed.[16] The fact is that York's marriage was the first major royal wedding in Britain since that of George III nearly thirty years before and it caused widespread excitement, winning the enthusiastic approval of high society as well as popular opinion.

On 19 December the Lord Mayor of London, in his state coach, made a formal visit to St James's Palace with his civic entourage, in order to congratulate the new Duke and Duchess of York. The Lord Mayor, in his speech, emphasized the fact that 'we feel a peculiar satisfaction in the present opportunity to testify our sincere joy at your Royal Highness's union with a princess so truly distinguished ...', while the duke, in reply, thanked him for his address, 'so full of sentiments of attachments to the House of Brunswick [i.e. Hanover] and of affection to me'.[17]

Two days later the Duke of Richmond's town house, near the palace, caught fire and was burned to the ground, although a good many of the contents were saved, largely as a result of the speedy action of York, who quickly mobilized three hundred of his Coldstream Guards. They carried out many of the valuable paintings and furniture and also kept back the locals, who were inclined to take advantage of these occasions to make off with any available loot. At one point Richmond's favourite spaniel was seen barking at a closed window on one of the upper floors and his owner offered a reward to anyone who would save it. A waterman from the Thames climbed up by the use of various ladders, smashed the glass and brought the dog down safely, whereupon Richmond gave him ten guineas and York another guinea for good measure. Given that it was Richmond's heir who had nearly killed Frederick in the famous duel, this was generous behaviour.[18]

When opening the parliamentary session in late January 1792 the king drew attention to his son's marriage and hoped that Parliament would assist him in making suitable financial provision for the duke and duchess. After his departure from Westminster, the Commons were told that both the King of Prussia and George III had given Frederica 100,000 crowns and that the duke would provide her with £4,000 a year and the interest on £6,000 a year for daily expenses. In subsequent debates during February the House agreed that the duke should receive £18,000 a year extra from the Consolidated Fund, though at the king's pleasure, to add to his existing £12,000 a year from the Civil List and £7,000 a year from the Irish revenue, making a total of £37,000 a year. Fox argued that he should receive substantially more, and that as York's income was dependent on the king's pleasure, he would not be able to raise loans on the strength of it. However, Pitt was not to be moved and the House voted in favour of the proposed grants. It was not an over-generous settlement, especially as the 100,000 crowns provided by Frederica's father was considered very miserly, given that she was his eldest child.[19]

Because of Frederica's high status within the Prussian royal family, some delicate issues had to be settled about where she stood in the matter of precedence within the British royal family. The matter was left to the College of Arms, which decided that in Britain it was birth and not marriage which granted precedence and so for that reason Frederica had to take her place behind Frederick's sisters. She did not make a fuss about this and indeed she quickly established good relations with all members of the royal family, except for the Prince of Wales. This was because by the summer of 1792 Frederica had offended him by applying the rules of the Prussian Court and refusing to receive Maria Fitzherbert, who as far as she knew was only his mistress. The prince asked his brother to do something about this and when Frederick said he could not, it led to the first serious break in their friendship, which took some time to mend.[20]

At first the duke and duchess were based at York House but Frederick considered that it was too small for his needs as a married man and he negotiated with Lord Melbourne to exchange it for Melbourne's larger house in Piccadilly, for an extra payment of £23,571. This move (to the building subsequently known as The Albany) was eventually made in 1793. It was also essential that the couple should have a suitable retreat in the country, and in 1791 Frederick sold his Yorkshire estate at Allerton Mauleverer for £110,000 to Colonel William Thornton, having the previous year taken a crown lease on the Oatlands estate near Weybridge in Surrey, about eighteen miles from London.

At Allerton there is a 'local tradition' that York lost the estate to Thornton as a result of a wager or gambling debt, and Robert Huish says on the second page of his memoir of the duke, rushed out in the year of his death, that 'this delightful estate was however sacrificed to the high sense of delicacy and honour which always distinguished the character of His Royal Highness in the eager pursuit of play ...', so the local story might well be at least partially true. It does seem strange that having built a new house there, with attractive gardens, York should have disposed of it so soon after completion. Professor Aspinall, the editor of George III's correspondence, thought so too, and took the view that Frederick was forced to sell Allerton 'in order to pay heavy gambling debts'.[21]

The main house of his new estate, Oatlands Park, stood near the site of an enormous Tudor royal palace, not unlike Hampton Court, which was sold and demolished after the execution of Charles I in 1649. Only a former hunting lodge was left standing and it had several owners until it was sold in the mid-eighteenth century to the second Duke of Newcastle. He made additions, including a fascinating grotto in the grounds, built by Italian architects over a period of twenty years. The grotto consisted of four rooms, one of which contained a cold bath, and they were connected by winding passages with walls decorated by millions of pieces of spar, glass and shells. The Duke of York again employed Henry Holland to enlarge and improve his new property and in 1791 he invited the Prince of Wales there to hear a recital by Joseph Haydn, who made a two-day visit in November and was impressed with the house on its slope, commanding magnificent views of the Thames Valley and the North Downs.[22]

The duke resumed command of the Coldstream Guards and in August 1792 found it necessary to write to the king about a 'very shocking and unfortunate affair'. He related how, when he arrived at a parade of the Guards, a prisoner was brought to him who had been 'caught the evening before in a very indecent situation with a gentleman in Hyde Park', said by witnesses to have been a general, no less, who was also a courtier in the queen's household. York interviewed the witnesses himself and came to the conclusion that the general had been involved, whereupon he sent word to him that, if innocent, he should attempt to clear his name, and if guilty, he should flee the country and sell his commission. The general was deeply shocked and decided to abide by the decision of the Bow Street justices, who, however, found against him and committed him to prison.[23]

# Chapter Five

## Revolutionaries and Patriots

While Frederick had been in Berlin from May 1791 onwards, he had been able to watch, with the Prussian Court, as events took an even more dramatic turn in France. In June the French king and queen, in disguise, tried to escape to the Austrian border but their coach was stopped just before they reached it and they were forced to return to Paris. His flight had made it obvious that the king was opposed to the constitutional reforms and the demand for a republic grew stronger. At this point Emperor Leopold of Austria, who was the brother of the French queen, Marie Antoinette, together with King Frederick William of Prussia, signed a Declaration that they would invade France if any harm should come to the royal couple, which served only to strengthen the republican cause.

Between October 1791 and August 1792 France was run as a constitutional monarchy but the government proved ineffective and deeply divided and in August 1792 the royal palace in Paris was stormed by a revolutionary mob and the king and queen were imprisoned. The new government of France declared war on Austria in April, and Prussia shortly afterwards declared war on France in support. Prussian armies invaded France but were defeated at the battle of Valmy on 20 September. On the same day the new government of France, calling itself the Convention, abolished the monarchy and established a republic as well as a new revolutionary calendar. French armies were ordered into Flanders and the Rhineland, where they won a series of minor victories, before defeating the Austrian army at Jemappes on 6 November and annexing most of the Austrian Netherlands, also known as the 'Low Countries' (roughly present-day Belgium).

The Austrian Netherlands, which had previously belonged to Spain, were ceded to Austria in 1714 after the Duke of Marlborough's famous victories over the French had resulted in the defeat of France and Spain in the War of the Spanish Succession. It was mainly Britain and the Dutch who wanted an Austrian presence in Flanders to create a buffer state against France, which had made many attempts to conquer the region. But the Austrians were never very enthusiastic about their new acquisition and were very unpopular with their Flemish subjects. From about 1780 onwards one of the main aims of Austrian foreign policy was to exchange the Austrian Netherlands for Bavaria, as we have already seen. In 1789 the Austrians were driven out of the Netherlands after a successful rebellion and eleven of the provinces declared themselves the 'United States of Belgium'. The following year the Austrians repressed the revolt and recovered control, but this did nothing to add to their popularity and to some extent the arrival of the French invaders was welcomed in Flanders.

On 21 January 1793 Louis XVI's enemies at last got what they wanted and he was guillotined, to the dismay and disbelief of the crowned heads of Europe. The reaction in England was the expulsion of the French ambassador and on 1 February the Convention declared war on England and the Dutch Republic. The following month they declared war on Spain as well. This provided William Pitt with a challenge for which he had little or no preparation. As prime minister during the last nine, peaceful, years, he had been a great success; during his first few years in power he had given priority to the need for more efficiency in government and administration and he had significantly cut costs as well as reducing the number of sinecures. He followed the economic philosophy of Adam Smith and encouraged free trade wherever possible. His India Act of 1784 reduced the authority of the East India Company in favour of a governor-general appointed by the Crown, while his Canada Act of 1791 retained the loyalty of French Canadians by giving them their own province and safeguarding the French language. Pitt was undoubtedly a master of administrative detail and he had a calm and common-sense approach to peacetime problems. But he had never served in the armed forces and had no experience whatever of conducting a war.

Britain had a fine navy with a great reputation, largely because it was considered vital for the defence of an island nation. For that reason there had been no serious objection to the way the navy had traditionally been manned by 'press gangs' who effectively kidnapped young men or got them so drunk they did not know what they were doing when they enrolled. This contrasted strongly with the deep-rooted national hostility to the idea of a standing army, which had been regarded as a potential threat to individual liberty ever since the days when Oliver Cromwell had held the nation in check with a repressive military regime in the 1650s. Conditions in the army were so tough that it was difficult to recruit suitable men on a large scale, though there were part-time militias in all the counties, mainly for self-defence. Since 1715 all three Georges had supplemented their British troops by relying heavily on Hanoverian soldiers for their foreign campaigns as well as mercenaries from other German states, especially Hesse.

So Pitt had a formidable naval force at his disposal, about 600 ships with 100,000 men aboard, but only about 14,000 soldiers in Britain and a further 28,000 in India and the West Indies. These could be augmented by 14,000 men from Hanover and 8,000 from Hesse.[1] Hence Pitt's main strategy was to use diplomacy to support a strong coalition of European powers against France. The new French republic had made this comparatively easy by defiantly declaring war against Britain, Austria, Prussia, Spain, Portugal, Sardinia, the Kingdom of the Two Sicilies and many smaller Italian and German states for good measure. France was in theory bankrupt and divided by civil tensions, her navy was completely outnumbered and she had possibly 270,000 land troops compared with about 350,000 of the allies.

The French government's shortage of money made the banking city of Amsterdam a great attraction and they instructed General Dumouriez to invade the Dutch republic. The Dutch were in a state of complete disarray, partly because their leader, William V, Prince of Orange, was a man of 'almost inhuman dullness, apathy and stupidity', according to one of Britain's greatest military historians, Sir John Fortescue.[2] Professor Simon Schama, in the book that made his name, goes further:

As Willem V pointed out ruefully on many occasions, he was not the man supplied by Providence to restore the fortunes of his dynasty and his Fatherland. Physically, he was singularly unprepossessing, with pop eyes, fat lips and a weak chin, something less than the incarnation of military virility ... He was subject to alternating fits of petulant obstinacy and chronic vacillation and he suffered from the unpleasant malady of spitting bile. No prince of the Ancien Regime can have had a more unanimously damning press and few such an inauspicious upbringing. Bullied by his mother ... and finally hectored by the wife who had been foisted on him ... his was a classic case of inferiority complex.[3]

Between 1568 and 1648 the seven Protestant northern provinces of the Spanish Netherlands had fought a long war to rid themselves of their Catholic Spanish masters. In 1648 they succeeded in having their federated 'Dutch Republic' (often known as Holland after the most important province) internationally recognized at the Treaty of Westphalia, while the southern provinces of Flanders stayed under Spanish control. The success of the Dutch revolt owed a great deal to the Dutch nobleman William, Count of Nassau, the owner of extensive lands in the Netherlands and Germany, who also inherited the title of Prince of Orange – a small semi-independent state, about twelve miles by nine, near Avignon in the south of France. He was appointed

'Stadholder' – a sort of Dutch President – in 1572 and when he died in 1584 it became customary, with a few interruptions, for the head of the Orange-Nassau family to be elected to this post. Faced with a French invasion in 1747 the Dutch Estates-General (Parliament) declared that the Stadholderate, then held by William IV of Orange, would henceforth be hereditary.

William IV married Anne, the eldest daughter of George II of Great Britain, and when he died at the age of only forty in 1751 he was succeeded by his three-year-old son, William V. It is ironic that the hereditary principle had been adopted in Holland just at a time when it was entirely unsuitable. There was a regency, lasting fifteen years, during which all the regents, including William's mother, grandmother and elder sister, were unpopular and incompetent. When he himself was allowed to take control at the age of eighteen in 1766 it was already clear, as we have seen, that he was totally unsuited to a leadership role. In 1767 he married Princess Wilhelmina of Prussia, the aunt of York's Frederica, and their eldest son and heir, William, known as the 'Hereditary Prince of Orange' was born in 1772.

In 1780 the Dutch Republic had drifted into four years of naval warfare with Great Britain, largely because Dutch merchants provided arms and supplies to the American rebels, and the result was defeat and disaster for the Dutch, who lost valuable colonies and trading rights. Continued dissatisfaction with William V's rule led to the formation of a Dutch 'Patriot' party which wanted to be rid of the monarchical and aristocratic trappings of the Orange regime and favoured a democratic republic on the lines of the recently recognized USA. In 1785 William was forced to move his court from the hostile Hague to remote Guelders and eventually Wilhelmina called upon her brother, Frederick William II of Prussia, to send a force to defeat the rebels in 1787. Although cowed for the time being, the Patriots laid low and awaited their next opportunity.

## York Goes to War, February 1793

In 1793 the Patriots' moment arrived when the armies of the new French republic were about to invade, bringing with them the promise of democracy and the overthrow of the House of Orange. Lord Auckland, the British Ambassador in Holland, urged on 15 February that the Duke of York and a few British officers should be sent to Holland to bolster the Dutch troops, which were technically under the control of the very inexperienced Hereditary Prince William, now aged twenty-one. The following day the French invaded the country from Antwerp with a small force of 17,000 men and received a considerable welcome from many of the Dutch population, as well as from the hard core of Patriots.

This development prompted Pitt to act quickly and to the king's delight, as well as that of his second son, he agreed that York should go with all speed with an expeditionary force to assist the Dutch. The constitutional position in Britain at this time regarding the conduct of a war was that the king had the right to conduct foreign policy and declare war and peace and he was the supreme commander of all military and naval forces. However, it was Parliament that paid all the expenses, so it was essential that the king and his ministers should work together harmoniously. Apart from Pitt himself, the two main ministers involved were Lord Grenville, aged thirty-four, the foreign secretary, and Henry Dundas, aged forty, the home secretary, who at first had responsibility for war.

The decision to appoint York to the command of this force resulted from the insistence of the king, despite the doubts of his ministers, who had only known the duke in his more frivolous years since his return to England. Nevertheless, George III was not being foolish in demanding his appointment. Despite York's relative youth and lack of wartime experience, he had been formally educated and trained to be a soldier and commander, he had benefited from the guidance of the Duke of Brunswick, one of the most successful generals of the age, and he knew from first hand how the Prussian and Austrian armies operated and what their strengths and weaknesses were. He was a high-ranking British royal prince and the son-in-law of Britain's ally, the King of Prussia, and as he would be working together with the commanders of coalition troops, high social rank counted for a great deal. Moreover, there were precedents for the appointment of young British princes to military command, notably George II's younger son, the Duke of Cumberland, who had fought against the French at Dettingen and Fontenoy and then crushed the Jacobite rebellion (with alleged brutality) at Culloden in 1745 at the age of twenty-four. Finally, only a small British force would be sent out at first and York's main troops would be Hanoverians, whom he had commanded during his years in Germany.

On 20 February York assembled all seven battalions of the British Guards on Horse Guards and told them that the first battalions of the three regiments would be going on active duty. As these battalions were not up to strength, he called for volunteers and was pleased to find that the entire brigade stepped forward as one man.

Five days later the king and the Prince of Wales rode from Buckingham House to the Horse Guards, where York paraded the chosen three battalions, numbering only about 2,000 men. They were inspected by the king at 7.00

am and marched past in slow time. Then, with York riding at their head, they set off across the river and marched down the Old Kent Road to Greenwich. Along the way they were greeted by enthusiastic crowds who plied some of the soldiers in the rear columns with so much drink that several collapsed and had to be transported in carts.

The king, the queen, the Duke of Clarence and the three eldest princesses all accompanied the brigade down to Greenwich, but not the Duchess of York, who, we are told, 'was so much depressed in her spirits that she could not bear to witness the departure of her consort in the career of peril and glory'.[4] The Guards reached Greenwich by nightfall and transferred to ships, which seem to have been 'too small to carry more than two-thirds of their number in safety, without medicines or medical appliances, without the slightest reserve of ammunition, and of course without transport of any description'.[5] As they boarded the ships, in sight of the royal princesses, some men were heard to say 'Who would not die for them?'[6]

Although York was in overall charge of this expedition and was also expected to take command of about 13,000 Hanoverian troops when they were ready, Major-General Gerard Lake had been given command, under him, of the three Guards regiments. The duke's formal instructions, given by ministers in the name of the king, directed, very vaguely, that he should act 'for the defence of the United Provinces and for acting against the enemy'. He was told not to divide his troops or place them in the frontier garrisons or to take them more than twenty-four hours' march away from the port of Helvoetsluys, which is where they landed. It is very likely that these orders were originated by Henry Dundas, the minister who assumed most of the responsibility for the details of the conduct of the war.

Dundas was a Scot who became MP for Midlothian in 1774 and supported first Lord North, then Pitt, entering the Cabinet in 1791 as secretary of state for the home department. In this capacity he took responsibility for hostilities until his appointment to the new office of secretary of state for war in 1794, a position he held until 1801. He was a close friend and loyal supporter of Pitt but had no personal experience of warfare and most British military historians have blamed the disorganization and bad planning of the 1793 campaign almost entirely on him. From the start, he had no particular confidence in York and tried to make sure, in his orders, that York would be obliged to consult more experienced officers: more often than not this simply resulted in indecisive actions.

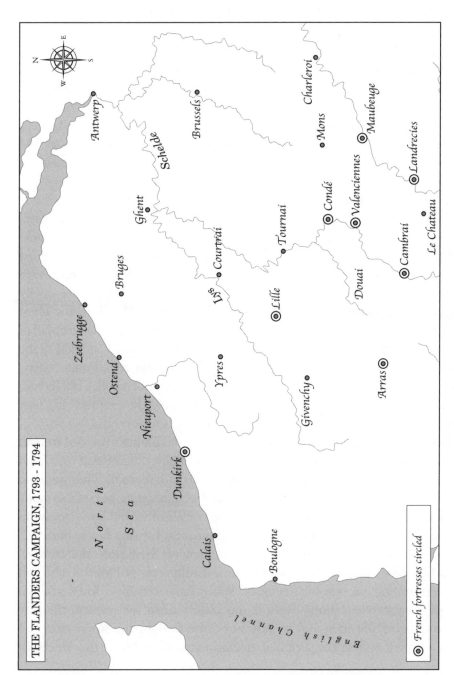

THE FLANDERS CAMPAIGN, 1793 - 1794

The Flanders campaign, 1793–1794.

## Success at Valenciennes, July 1793

Once his small force had landed, York left it under the command of Lake and rode straight to The Hague to discuss the situation with the Stadholder, William V. He found 'everybody here in the greatest consternation at the news which just arrived of the surrender of Breda, through the cowardice of the governor'. After a few days he told his father that he thought the biggest problems in Holland were the irresolution of William V, 'and that no one thing can be done without a written order from him, which from his hurry he very often forgets to sign'. At least York persuaded William to allow his son, the hereditary prince, to accompany him on a tour of the defences of the country, and he decided to move his Guards to a position where they could protect the city of Dort (now Dordrecht).[7]

At this point the Austrians, under the command of an experienced general, Prince Josias of Coburg, made a spectacularly successful strike at the French. Coburg's army of 40,000 men crossed the Meuse at Maastricht and defeated General Dumouriez at Neerwinden on 18 March, moving on to recapture Brussels. Dumouriez abandoned Antwerp and all of Flanders and personally defected to the enemy, urging his troops to do the same. This dramatic act of treachery had drastic repercussions in Paris, where it heralded the downfall of the relatively moderate politicians associated with Dumouriez and led to the rise of the radical politician Robespierre and the Committee of Public Safety. Its members governed France on the ruthless principles of a policy of 'Terror', which they saw as the only effective way of defeating the enemies that now confronted the Revolution at home as well as abroad.

Encouraged by the defeat of Dumouriez, Pitt and Dundas decided to send out reinforcements to York's small British force. These consisted of men from the 14th, 37th and 53rd foot regiments, topped up with recruits. They were not impressive, as the duke was warned by a member of his staff, because so many of them were 'nothing but undisciplined and raw recruits; and how they are to be disposed of until they can be taught their business I am at a loss to imagine'. They were placed under the command of General Sir Ralph Abercromby, aged fifty-nine, a Scottish laird and political supporter of Dundas who had not seen military action for ten years. When they arrived in Antwerp, two out of the three battalions 'were found utterly unfit for service, the new recruits being old men and weakly boys, worse than the worst that had been accepted even at the period of greatest exhaustion during the American War'.[8]

Having been advanced by his father to the rank of full general, York reviewed these troops and took the decision to leave the two weakest regiments behind for further training. He was also sent squadrons of cavalry, which were in better shape, and this brought his British contingent up to a total of 4,200 infantry and 2,300 cavalry. Together with his 13,000 Hanoverians and 8,000 Hessians, he was now in command of a sizeable force, though of varying quality and lacking in cohesion. He was advised by a number of experienced officers, including Abercromby and also his adjutant-general (chief of staff), General Sir James Murray, as well as the foreign coalition generals. York's younger brother Ernest had, meanwhile, been given command of a Hanoverian cavalry regiment. However, towards the end of April York had to deal with a mutiny in the Hanoverian ranks, caused by the fact that they were being paid less than they had been promised. He addressed the Hanoverians through their commander, General de Bussche, and as he reported to his father:

I went out to them and desired General de Bussche to acquaint them from me that I understood they thought themselves injured, but I would give them my word of honour that though I was not acquainted with the treaty, I would take care that whatever was their right should be given them, but that I was ashamed of their conduct as soldiers and that the first man who ventured after this promise to grumble again should be punished in the severest manner. I then told them myself that it was the first time I had ever seen a Hanoverian regiment with disgust and that the disgrace they had brought upon themselves could only be washed away the first time they met the enemy. I cannot express to your Majesty how ashamed and affected the men appear and I have no doubt from what I saw and have heard that this very disagreeable occurrence is totally over.'[9]

General Murray, impressed with the way York had dealt with this potentially tricky situation, wrote back enthusiastically to Dundas, remarking that, by talking to the soldiers 'with firmness, declaring at the same time his intention to do them justice, His Royal Highness succeeded in re-establishing discipline and order ... the Duke seemed to me to act with great judgement in this critical circumstance'.[10]

A conference had been held in Antwerp early in April between the military and diplomatic representatives of the allies, who eventually fell in line with Prince Josias of Coburg's plan to attack the 'barrier fortresses', just over the border from France, which were still in French hands. Built by Louis XIV's great engineer Vauban in the previous century, they were formidable obstacles, but Ypres, Menin, Tournai and Mons had already fallen to the allies. However, ten more fortresses still held out, including Dunkirk, Lille, Condé and Valenciennes. Pitt and Dundas were keen on York capturing Dunkirk, because this would be seen as a tangible victory at home, but they agreed that he should be subordinate to Coburg in his assault on Condé and Valenciennes, after which Coburg promised to lend Austrian support to a British attack on Dunkirk. Aware that Dunkirk was likely to be attacked, the brilliant French engineer and politician Lazare Carnot arrived there in April to supervise the strengthening of the dilapidated fortifications and to make it clear to the inhabitants that anything less than absolute loyalty to the Convention would be savagely punished.

The new French commander, Dampierre, despite being outnumbered by the allies, was under instruction to prevent the fortress of Condé being taken. Accordingly, he attacked the allied line on 1 May and on 8 May the Austrians were driven back near the town and appealed to York for help. As he told his father, 'I immediately told the Coldstream which was nearest the battalion to advance: as they were moving along, I went up to them and said to them, My Lads, I have no doubt of your courage, but be likewise prudent and cool. The whole battalion answered me Never Fear, we will do you Honour, God Save the King. They immediately advanced, formed line, and moved into line, keeping their step and their distance as well as if they had been at exercise.' Unfortunately the Coldstreams suffered about seventy casualties and ultimately blamed York for sending them into a wood bristling with enemy batteries, though the order had actually come from an Austrian commander.

The Austrians were grateful and spoke highly of York and his troops, ascribing eventual success to 'their bravery and to a very quick and able manoeuvre by His Royal Highness'.[11] On 23 May York received orders from Coburg to attack the French camp at Famars, just south of Valenciennes. He had to improvise on the original plan and he was restrained from immediate attack by the Austrians, so that when he did attack, the French army had largely retreated. Nevertheless, the camp was captured and York had won his first victory, details of which he lost no time in conveying to his delighted father.

Military analysts have subsequently argued that Coburg should have ignored the uncaptured fortresses and swept on to take Paris, because the French army was still below strength and there were serious political rifts in the capital as well as a major royalist rebellion in the Vendée. However, Coburg was a veteran of eighteenth-century warfare, which attached great importance to sieges, and he ordered York to besiege the fortress at Valenciennes, partly out of deference to the British success in the campaign so far. The Austrians were so slow and methodical in their preparations for the siege that York objected and was in turn asked to be patient.

By 22 July the Allies had taken Condé and Mainz, and four days later three allied columns attacked Valenciennes from the earthworks they had built on the eastern side. On 28 July the fortress surrendered and Coburg left most of the negotiations to York, who immediately became the object of flattery from the local French, some of whom suggested that he should be proclaimed King of France. The men of the garrison were taken prisoner and made to lay down their weapons but York allowed them to leave with the honours of war. The British were less disliked in France than the Austrians and, although Coburg entered the town ceremoniously with York, it was to the duke that the keys of the town were handed. He seems to have made a good impression there because on their way home the French garrison told their countrymen that 'they loved the Duke of York, who seemed to them worthy of the throne of France'.[12]

The duke wrote constantly to his father during this period, in terms of the greatest courtesy, keeping him abreast of all developments and indeed seeking his permission on a number of counts – for instance in accepting Coburg's offer that he should preside over the siege of Valenciennes. As well as telling him the good news about the capture of Famars and the fall of Valenciennes and commending the bravery of specific officers and men, he also related the bad news. This included an incident involving Hanoverian footsoldiers who had deserted their trenches, encouraged by two of their officers, as well as the more serious problem of Colonel Pennington of the Coldstream Guards, whose unpleasant behaviour to his fellow officers was causing deep unrest. York came to the conclusion that Pennington was 'perfectly mad' and told him so in front of all his officers, in the hope that he would resign. York also had to deal with the awkward question of his brother, the Prince of Wales, who had decided that, not to be outdone by Frederick, he would offer to serve in the Austrian army under Coburg. Not surprisingly, the king forbade him to go.[13]

After the fall of Valenciennes, the allies pressed on southwards to attack the French army in Caesar's Camp, just north of Cambrai. Coburg ordered York with 25,000 men to lead a diversionary attack from the south of the camp, while the Austrians would deliver the main attack from the east. However, the French saw what was happening and retreated during the night of 7 August. The following morning York saw the rearguard of the enemy in the distance and, eager to pursue them, he quickly collected a cavalry force of about 2,000 men and led them to the burning village of Marquion. With only one aide, Count Langeron, he reached a point where he saw two lines of cavalry only twenty yards away. Crying 'There are my Hanoverians', he rode towards them, only to hear Langeron shout at the last minute that they were in fact French cavalry wearing uniforms similar to the Hanoverians'. According to Langeron, he seized the bridle of York's horse and led him back to the safety of the village, and 'but for me he would have been killed or taken – which would have been the same thing for him, for the Convention spared no Englishman'.[14]

In the end it was Prince Ernest, commanding a detachment of Hanoverian cavalry, who managed to have a hand-to-hand skirmish with the French. He told his father, proudly, that he had received a cut on his head. York was very irritated that the French had managed to get away and blamed the caution of the Austrian commanders, with whom he had heated words at the end of the day. This did not prevent him being offered the Grand Cross of the Military Order of Marie Theresa by the emperor, a high honour given only for a battle won or a town taken. However, as York was perfectly aware, acceptance of an award such as this could become an embarrassment if one day the Austrians should become enemies instead of allies.

## Retreat from Dunkirk, September 1793

The allies had achieved considerable success up to this point and the French armies were demoralized and in disarray. Most military historians (sitting in hindsight-blessed armchairs) are agreed that they should now have risked a march on Paris, which is what both Coburg and York were keen to do. However, Pitt and Dundas were adamant that York should take Dunkirk first, partly so that they could demonstrate tangible gains to their political supporters at home and partly to use as a bargaining counter in future negotiations. There was no doubt in York's mind that this was not a wise venture but he had been trained to be a loyal and obedient soldier, so with an additional force of 10,000 Austrians provided by Coburg, as promised, he marched his army of many nationalities north towards Dunkirk. By 17 August they had reached Turcoing. Some Dutch allies attacked the French at nearby Linselles but were driven back, requesting help from York. He immediately sent General Lake with just over a thousand Guardsmen, who, in what has been described as 'one of the most brilliant actions of the war', put the French to flight.[15]

On 14 August Lazare Carnot was appointed to the Committee of Public Safety in Paris and was given responsibility for the formation, training and movements of the French armies. He also worked harmoniously with two other colleagues responsible for arms, ammunition, hospitals and general supply. On 16 August a decree introduced conscription, which was expected to add 450,000 men to the army, and on 29 August a blue uniform was adopted to replace the Bourbon white. With his personal experience of Dunkirk, Carnot perceived that its fall must be prevented, and throughout August he moved as many troops as possible into the vicinity, under the supreme command of General Houchard.

Meanwhile York, despite misgivings, remained true to his orders and continued the march on Dunkirk. He divided his force into two columns, with the Hanoverian Field Marshal Freytag in command of the left column, which consisted of Austrians, Hanoverians and British. They were ordered to protect the siege operations while York with the main column attacked the French and drove them back to the walls of Dunkirk on 24 August. Unfortunately, as York explained, 'the ardour and gallantry of the troops carried them too far and in spite of a peremptory order from me, three times repeated, they pursued the enemy upon the glacis of the *Place* [main square] when we had the misfortune to lose many brave and reliable men by the grapeshot from the town'.[16]

So preparations were made for a siege, but the bad news arrived that an English fleet, convoying transports bringing siege guns, had not landed as expected at Nieuport on 22 August; instead, French gunboats sailed off the coast and fired at York's army from the sea. Then the Dutch, for whom York was rapidly losing all respect, made further blunders, as he told the king: 'Our good friends the Dutch have again behaved with their usual cowardice. On the 28th the enemy attacked their positions at Turcoing, Waterloo and Lannoy, all of which they abandoned without firing a shot and retreated with the utmost precipitation.' They did manage to regroup, but York was told that the Dutch would probably retreat back to Holland, partly because the Hereditary Prince of Orange was annoyed that he himself had not been allowed to lead the offensive on Dunkirk.[17]

The fact that the fleet bringing the siege guns did not arrive for sixteen days after York's army reached Dunkirk turned out to be a decisive factor. Carnot sent commissioners from Paris to emphasize once more that any treachery would be ruthlessly punished and to make sure that the garrison and townsfolk were prepared to withstand a siege. York began firing on the fortress early in September with some cannon captured from a French ship, but Houchard attacked Freytag's Hanoverians on 6 September. They resisted stoutly all day, but were forced to retreat during the night. York's brother, Prince Adolphus, aged nineteen, had recently left his university studies at Göttingen and joined the Hanoverian forces but he was wounded in the shoulder on this day and briefly taken prisoner, until rescued by a detachment of Guards. On 8 September Houchard attacked the Hanoverians again and once more they sustained heavy losses and were forced to retreat. The duke held a council of war that afternoon and decided that, in the absence of the British fleet bringing siege guns and reinforcements, and with French troops massing menacingly in the country round Dunkirk, he had no option but to retreat from the siege in two columns, an operation which was carried out during the night amid considerable confusion, but with no further loss of life. Two days after the retreat, on 11 September, the British fleet arrived.

It is likely that York's army lost about 10,000 men killed, wounded, taken prisoner or dying from disease during the siege of Dunkirk and there was no disguising the fact that it had been a significant defeat. Popular opinion in Britain inevitably held the duke to blame, unaware of the details of the operation. However, it is clear in retrospect that the prompt arrival of the fleet would have made a crucial difference and the reasons for its failure to appear were almost entirely the responsibility of ministers at home, chiefly Dundas. Moreover, most military historians are agreed that the British government's determination to take Dunkirk was a mistake in the first instance. It was also unfortunate timing that Carnot had come to power in the very month of the siege, employing ruthless and efficient administrative measures to great effect. On the credit side, as with the British evacuation of Dunkirk 147 years later, York had successfully pulled his army out of what had become a position of great danger. Carnot recognized this and, far from Houchard receiving praise for his efforts, he was summoned to Paris and guillotined for letting York's army get away.

In a long letter of explanation to his father, which remained private, York blamed above all the failure of the fleet to arrive in time, but also emphasized that superior French numbers had overcome the Hanoverian troops defending his besieging army and complained that, contrary to the Convention signed after the fall of Valenciennes, French prisoners released after the siege had been used again to attack him at Dunkirk.[18] York did not himself go public with any personal defence of his actions, partly so as not to cause dissent among his allies or to antagonize the ministers at home, although it seems clear that in private he blamed the Duke of Richmond, who, as Master-General of the Ordnance, was responsible for the provision of the artillery which had failed to arrive in time. York's case was neatly put in the *Morning Chronicle* two days after the battle by an officer who wrote:

There is but one sentiment through the whole camp. If the gun-boats and floating batteries had been ready, according to the express promise to cooperate with the Duke of York, and if his alacrity had been at all seconded on the part of the officers in England there is no doubt that Dunkirk would have fallen at the first attack. Every man that has since perished ... is to be set down to the score of the ministers ...[19]

York did not waste any time fretting about the failure at Dunkirk and once his force had regrouped he assisted the Austrians in a successful attack on Menin, causing the French to evacuate the town and retreat. He then joined the Austrians in besieging another fortress-town, Mauberge, but a successful offensive by the French not only drove the allies back to Tournai but also recaptured Menin. On 28 October York's troops captured a hundred French prisoners at Lannoy, between Tournai and Menin. According to an eye-witness, 'Every possible assistance was given to the suffering Frenchmen. All the surgeons in the camp were sent to dress their wounds, and His Royal Highness, the commander-in-chief, humanely ordered wine and food to be distributed to them.'[20]

Eighteenth-century armies tended not to fight in the winter and with the arrival of November the allies established themselves in winter quarters between Ghent and Courtrai, with York's headquarters close to the latter town. He asked his father's permission to return home on leave, but it was refused. The king told him that if he went on leave, other officers would expect the same, but that he would summon him home for consultations in due course. Although the king's faith in his son was unshakeable and although he was highly regarded by allied commanders, York had strong critics in the government and also among some of his own officers, especially in the Guards. Many Guards officers came from the highest ranks of society, and several of them wrote to people of influence at home, criticizing the performance of their commander.

The reasons for this may well go back to 1787, when York first became Colonel of the Coldstream Guards. We have seen how, during his six years in Germany, he came strongly under the influence of the Prussian military machine through the Duke of Brunswick and Frederick the Great himself. Two of the main features of that machine were that the men were well cared-for in terms of uniform, equipment and food, but in return they were submitted to a highly punitive system of discipline, which kept them in constant fear of committing any misdemeanour, however trifling. This would result in very harsh punishment, often of a corporal or physical nature. It seems that when York took over responsibility for the Guards he found that there were many instances of slackness and he introduced measures which, by English standards, were considered those of a martinet. Excessive discipline has always been resented in the British army, and after a year or so York realized this and relaxed the rules accordingly.

In addition, many of the Guards officers came from aristocratic Tory families which might have resented York's early political connections with the Whigs, while the duel with Lennox, who had his admirers, doubtless alienated a few young officers. Once the campaign started, York's detractors blamed him for the seventy Guardsmen lost near Condé in May, and a steady number of critical letters trickled back to influential figures in London. Most of them were sent by officers who disliked York on a personal level, probably resenting the fact that he owed his command, at the age of thirty-one, to the personal favour of his father rather than to any outstanding qualities of his own. The failure to take Dunkirk was a golden opportunity for his opponents, most of whom would not have known, or cared, much in detail about the practical difficulties York faced.

Lord Malmesbury, a British diplomat working on delicate negotiations to bring Prussia into the coalition, visited the army in December and found that one British colonel 'spoke most highly of [York] as a man and an able general', while an Austrian minister praised him and his army, and a Dutch minister praised York and criticized the Prince of Orange. Most of the Austrians, indeed, were full of praise for York but were highly critical of their own commander, Coburg. Malmesbury had quite a long conversation with the duke and noted in his diary that 'it confirmed me in the opinion, that the Duke of York has a very good understanding; but he *talks* too much, and is careless to whom. I ventured to tell him so, and took an opportunity of recommending him to ask the superior officers to dinner; and, as he could not prevent their writing home, to try at least to furnish them by his conversation there, with materials which would do no harm. Now they, and particularly the Guards, write nonsense, almost equal to mutiny. To this he attended with great good humour.' On the same subject, the Duke of Portland, writing to Malmesbury from England, referred to 'the licentious, not to say mutinous spirit which prevails amongst the troops and which originated in and is even cultivated in the Guards'.[21]

During the winter York sent one of his staff, Colonel Craufurd, to Vienna, where he had an interview with Baron Thugut, the Austrian minister responsible for the war. He told Craufurd that he and his colleagues had come to the conclusion that the main reasons for the lack of success in 1793 were that the Austrians had been too slow in besieging Valenciennes and had then failed to besiege Maubeuge after its capture. The allies also missed the opportunity for a knock-out blow against the French at Famars, mistakenly abandoned the siege of Maubeuge and engaged in field operations in terrain unsuitable for cavalry, the arm in which the allied armies chiefly excelled. This seems fair comment, and it makes no criticism of York or the forces under his command.[22]

By December York had come to the conclusion that two key individuals needed to be changed before the start of the next year's campaign. One was his own adjutant-general, Sir James Murray, and the other was Murray's Austrian counterpart, Prince Hohenlohe. Although Murray had been loyal to the duke, he was indecisive and unpopular and York persuaded his father to replace him with Colonel Craig, a short, stocky man who had allegedly begun his army career as a private in the Household Cavalry and subsequently fought with distinction in the American War. Craig arrived at York's headquarters early in January 1794 and wrote back to Dundas to say that York treated 'everybody with a degree of good nature and politeness which I know have not had justice done to them in the accounts which have been given of him in London'. He also felt that 'the late Promotion', presumably meaning a considerable clear-out of personnel, 'has in a great degree removed the sources of the misrepresentations which have been made on this subject; at least it is very clear that a certain corps [the Guards] amongst the officers of which it has occasioned the principal removals, has been infinitely more quiet since'.

Still on the matter of the duke's popularity, Craig wrote:

The only circumstance which I have observed in the Duke's treatment of the officers which I could wish changed, is with respect to the invitations to his table; in this it appears to me that insufficient attention is paid to the field officers and those of a higher rank. I am endeavouring as much as lies in my power at present to bring about a little alteration in this respect, which if I can accomplish it I am sure will tend to increase the Duke's popularity in the army. It would not perhaps be unpleasing to you to know that the entertainment that His Royal Highness gave on Her Majesty's birthday – a ball and supper – was perhaps one of the handsomest and best conducted things of the kind that was ever given. There were about 800 people at it. Prince Ernest was here, but Prince Adolphus did not arrive until next day.[23]

This is a strong reminder that we are still dealing here with the practices of eighteenth-century warfare, where royalty and aristocracy held lavish balls and dinners in the vicinity of their military headquarters – admittedly during a suspension of the fighting.

York also wrote to his father urging him to persuade the emperor to replace Hohenlohe with the brilliant tactician General Karl Mack, who was much admired in Austrian military circles. It is not easy to say how influential York's view was but Mack was duly appointed and he and York met in Brussels on 1 February 1794, where Mack showed York his plan for the new campaign. York then left for England to tell the king about this, and invited Mack to come to England himself. Clearly an amicable relationship had developed between the two.

Mack's arrival in England in February came at a good time for York, because Pitt and Dundas, who had never been keen on his appointment as commander, were about to urge the king to appoint Lord Cornwallis in his place. A veteran of the American War, Cornwallis had just returned from a very successful spell as Governor-General of India and most people considered him to be Britain's most able general (despite his disastrous surrender at Yorktown). Mack, however, argued strongly in favour of York retaining his command and as the king never wavered in his support for his son, the ministers gave in and York was present in London when Mack outlined his plan to Pitt, Dundas and Grenville. It envisaged a main advance towards Paris by the Austrians in the centre, with a British army of 40,000 men protecting the right flank by a march on Amiens.

York had about a month's 'leave' in England, during which he was reunited with his wife after a long absence, but he was back at the front on 8 March to make preparations for the beginning of the new campaigning season.

# Chapter Six

## The 1794 Campaign in Flanders

William Hague, in his excellent biography of Pitt, has this to say about the campaign of 1793:

> It is hard to escape the conclusion that the British war effort in 1793 suffered from the lack of a consistent strategic thrust. Furthermore, the mismatch between chosen objectives and the materials available to deliver them was itself a failure of strategy. Pitt ran the war through Dundas, who, as Secretary of State for Home Affairs and the Colonies, had direct responsibility for it, and through Grenville as Foreign Secretary. Their efforts in these early stages suffered from inexperience and a tendency to interfere in operational matters, which combined with Pitt's naturally optimistic nature to produce unrealistic assumptions. On the other hand, Pitt brought to the leadership of the war effort his usual diligence and capacity for controlling government departments. Through his two Secretaries of State he oversaw the whole effort of the British state in a way Lord North in the American War of Independence would never have contemplated. He even deputised for them if they were away ...[1]

Later, Hague states: 'The failure to gain a decisive advantage over France in 1793 was arguably the single most calamitous occurrence in the life of Pitt, for from it so much of the pain and tragedy of later years unfolded.'[2]

For the campaign of 1794 Pitt made a determined effort to raise more troops in England and to secure the support of the Prussians for a new offensive. Accordingly, between November 1793 and March 1794 about 30,000 men were enlisted for the regular army in England, though this was achieved by a corrupt system tolerated by government ministers. Rich young men were effectively bribed with a rank in the army based on the number of soldiers they were able to recruit: the more recruits, the higher the rank. If these officers took to the field, this could mean that very young and inexperienced men were in positions of senior command; if they decided to sell their soldiers on, they could retire for the rest of their lives on the half-pay pension equivalent to the rank they had been granted.[3] Meanwhile, after tortuous negotiations, Pitt was successful in persuading the Prussians in April 1794 to provide 62,000 men in return for a down payment of £300,000 and £50,000 a month. Britain and Holland provided the money, and the Prussians agreed to fight wherever they were asked.

The grand plan was that the allies should advance on Paris and deliver a knock-out blow, and the emperor, Francis II, arrived to command the allied troops in person, although he still relied strongly on the advice of Coburg and Mack, among others. The British government had left York in no doubt that in matters involving the overall strategy of the fighting he was to take his orders from the emperor. Francis held a review on 16 April near Le Cateau, but one Guards officer, at least, felt that he was a poor sight compared with the Duke of York:

> Of diminutive stature, eyes sunk in his head
> Resembling a Mercury moulded in lead,
> With swarthy complexion and pitiful mien
> Judge, beside him, to how much advantage was seen
> With the form of a hero and strength of roast beef,
> Great Frederick! Our noble Commander-in-Chief.[4]

Advancing in five columns, the allies took Le Cateau, Fremont and Vaux and moved on to besiege Landrecies. The French attempt to relieve the fortress was brilliantly countered by York's British cavalry, acting in concert with his Hanoverian troops, and a force of 30,000 French was put to flight, with its commander captured, together with thirty-five cannon. This was a notable victory for York, described by a French historian as showing the French army, 'immobilized in front of a fortress, being outmanoeuvred and turned by an active and enterprising enemy, propelled by the invincible spirit of the offensive'.[5] York's military biographer goes so far as to say, 'If Wellington defeated forty thousand Frenchmen in forty minutes at Salamanca, it can be said with equal exactitude that York defeated thirty thousand Frenchmen in thirty minutes on the plains of Le Cateau.'[6]

Landrecies fell on 29 April and the emperor ordered York to reinforce the Austrian General Clerfait's troops at Tournai, an unpleasant march in heavy rain across muddy terrain. On 10 May the main French army, commanded by General Pichegru, attacked between Courtrai and Tournai, and York achieved another notable success near Willems, causing a larger French force to flee, leaving thirteen guns and over four hundred prisoners. York was so pleased with the performance of his cavalry in this engagement that he presented its commander with his own sword, an unconventional and generous gesture.

At this point York found himself in disagreement with the Austrian high command's insistence on the 'cordon' system of fighting, i.e. stringing out troops thinly over a long line of defence. He much preferred concentrating forces in strategic centres, which would be approved by modern strategists. He wrote to his father, 'I humbly agree with your Majesty that the system of cordons, into which the Austrians have fallen ever since the beginning of this war, is exceedingly pernicious as well as dangerous and has been the real origin of all the misfortune to which they have been subject.'[7]

On 16 May the allies agreed to attack the French positions between Lille, Menin and Courtrai, with the aim of driving them out of Flanders. The troops involved were 4,000 Hanoverians under Bussche, 11,000 British under York, and 52,000 men, mostly Austrian, but including British, Hanoverian, Hessian and Dutch, in separate forces commanded by General Otto, Count Kinsky, the Archduke Charles and General Clerfait. On 17 May York was ordered to advance to Tourcoing, which he considered a dangerously exposed position, with large French armies to his front and rear. He questioned the wisdom of this strategy but his objections were overruled by the Austrians and he pressed on. The following day, with no support in sight from the Austrians, he ordered his army back to a safer position and decided to ride in person to consult with General Otto in the village of Wattrelos. Arriving there, he found that Otto had retreated and the French were everywhere, so under fire from the enemy and an easy target in his elaborate uniform complete with the Garter star and blue sash, he drew his sword and galloped as fast as he could to escape the pursuing French cavalry. When his horse refused to jump a ditch, he had to wade across and find another mount. Eventually he made safe contact with the Austrians.

York blamed Austrian indecisiveness for the very unsatisfactory outcome of this 'battle of Turcoing' and in fact he received a letter of apology from the emperor, expressing his satisfaction with the way York had removed his men from danger. Indeed, one modern military analyst has written that 'as an example of glory snatched from defeat, the battle of Turcoing may perhaps rank with Fontenoy and Dunkirk in British annals'.[8] Yet to York's troops their advance and retreat probably seemed demoralizing, and this is one occasion when some British wag might well have given new words to an old nursery rhyme which can be traced back to the 1620s:

> The King of France went up the hill
> With twenty thousand men

> The king of France came down the hill
> And never went up again.

The jingle that has subsequently gained an extraordinary degree of fame runs, of course,

> The grand old Duke of York
> He had ten thousand men
> He marched them up to the top of the hill
> And he marched them down again.

At Turcoing York had around 10,000 British troops under his command and they were ordered first to advance from the so-called 'heights' (a mild eminence) near Roubaix, and then to return to them, which would not have been popular with the men. So in some ways this scenario seems suitable, although, as we shall see later, it is not likely that the 'Grand Old Duke of York' jingle was ever current during York's lifetime. What is quite clear, however, is that, contrary to oft-repeated myth, York was not in any sense personally responsible for a serious 'defeat' at Turcoing.[9]

The muddled events at Turcoing destroyed York's confidence in the Austrians and he wrote to his father, complaining that the placing of British, Hanoverian and Hessian troops under the command of Austrians was not working well because the Austrian generals tended to give their allies the most dangerous tasks, to save their own troops. Moreover, the Austrians had begun to think that the French armies had become too strong and numerous and were keen to benefit from any partition of the weak state of Poland with Russian and Prussia. Indeed the emperor, with Mack, left the army on 29 May, handing the command to Prince Waldeck.

So far, the Prussian troops which Britain and the Dutch had agreed to finance had taken no part in the action but their arrival was now imminent and Lord Cornwallis was sent, under York's command, to liaise with them. However, Frederick William II, like Francis II, was at this point more interested in the fate of Poland. In 1772 Austria, Russia and Prussia had taken advantage of the serious weakness of the Polish state and agreed a 'partition', each taking large tracts of territory and leaving a much reduced Poland. In 1793 Prussia and Russia annexed further large portions of the country while Austria was engrossed in Flanders and by the middle of 1794 it seemed very likely that Poland would disappear entirely – as in fact happened in 1795, when the rest of the country was divided between Austria, Prussia and Russia. This explains why Britain's Austrian and Prussian allies from the middle of 1794 were increasingly diverted from the war against France, because of the rich gains to be made in the east.

In May 1794 France's National Convention released a document announcing that 'England is capable of every outrage on humanity and of every crime towards the Republic. She attacks the rights of all nations and threatens to annihilate liberty ...' Accordingly, French soldiers were ordered to take no English prisoners: 'When, therefore, the results of battle shall put in your power either English or Hanoverians, strike: not one of them must return to the traitorous land of England, or be brought into France. Let the British slaves perish and Europe be free.' York replied with an instruction to his troops, which he ordered to be read out and explained at three successive roll calls. It said that:

The National Convention of France, pursuing their gradation of crimes and horrors, which has distinguished the periods of its government as the most calamitous of any that has yet occurred in the history of the world, has just passed a decree that their soldiers shall give no quarter to the British or Hanoverian troops. His Royal Highness anticipates the indignation and horror which has naturally arisen in the minds of the brave troops whom he addresses, upon receiving this information. His Royal Highness desires, however, to remind that mercy to the vanquished is the brightest gem in a soldier's character, and exhorts them not to suffer their resentment to lead them to any precipitate act of cruelty on their part, which may sully the reputation they have acquired in the world.[10]

York made sure that this order was made available to the enemy and many French soldiers quietly ignored the instructions of their own government.

By June 1794 it was clear that Carnot's policies had resulted in a significant increase in the number of French troops in the Low Countries, while the morale of the Austrians had declined and half their officers were attempting to resign and follow the emperor and Mack home to Vienna. On 1 June Pichegru besieged Ypres, which fell on 18 June, and General Jourdan, with a second French army, attacked on the other flank and besieged Charleroi. Pichegru marched on from Ypres to Deynse, where he defeated the Austrians under Clerfait on 23 June, driving them back beyond Ghent. Meanwhile Coburg marched to the relief of Charleroi, but arrived on 26 June, the day the city surrendered. Coburg then attacked Jourdan's forces at Fleurus, just north of Charleroi, but in fifteen hours of desperate fighting the French, helped by a reconnaissance balloon which reported the enemy's movements, drove the Austrians back. The French casualties, at around 5,000, were probably higher than those of the allies and Coburg might have regrouped, but he lost his nerve and retreated towards Brussels, thereby conceding a tactical victory which proved decisive. After this the government in Vienna seems to have made the decision to abandon the troublesome Austrian Netherlands and to ensure instead that it would benefit from the next partition of Poland.

On 1 July York rode forty miles at night to meet Coburg for a war council, at which he asked the blunt question 'What are the Austrian intentions regarding the Low Countries?' and received a written reply which read: 'The Archduke Charles and the generals pledge their word of honour that they have no orders from His Majesty [the emperor] to quit the Low Countries, and in consequence, they feel, as honourable men, obliged to defend the country as long as human force will allow them, and to all extremities.'[11] Yet even as this was being written, the fortresses of Tournai, Oudenarde, Ghent and Mons all fell to the French, leaving only Valenciennes, Condé, Landrecies and Quesnoy in the hands of the allies. By 7 July Coburg had retreated eastwards, far away from his ally, and York sent him a pretty straight letter, expressing his feelings: 'I own I am at length driven to the necessity of openly stating to your Serene Highness that the opinion which the British nation must have on a subject cannot be other than that we are betrayed and sold to the enemy, and your Serene Highness knows that in a country such as Great Britain popular opinion is not to be despised.'[12]

Had Pichegru now made a determined attack on the allied troops he might have swept all before him, but the politicians in Paris had decided on an invasion of England and instead ordered him to pull back and secure the ports of Ostend, Nieuport and Walcheren for this enterprise. York received reinforcements in the shape of Lord Moira and 7,000 troops fresh from Britain, and despite the gloomy outlook he maintained a cheerful disposition, for which he was widely admired. Colonel Craig informed ministers in London that it would be impossible for York 'to conduct himself with more temper and resolution than he does in a situation so critical and in which he feels his responsibility to be so great. His Royal Highness is perfectly aware of all the danger, and feels every anxiety incident to it, but is neither cast down nor negligent of the precautions which are necessary. The greatest unanimity prevails among us which in our present situation is of some consequence.' Another eye-witness recorded that 'the Duke of York rises daily in esteem, keeps up no state, has no unnecessary people with him, sometimes hardly a servant, and generally wears a plain coat'.[13]

By the middle of July Pichegru had captured Malines, the Dutch had lost Louvain and the Austrians had retreated still further, so that the British and Austrian armies were entirely separated. In these circumstances, for York to have attacked on his own would have been folly so at the end of July he withdrew northwards to the comparative safety of Holland.

## In Holland, 1794

From August 1794 York was no longer under Coburg's command and the British, Hanoverian, Hessian and Dutch troops looked to him for their leadership. Now that Flanders had fallen to the French, York decided that his main aim should be the defence of Holland itself. The allies were in possession of five Dutch fortresses – Bergen-op-Zoom, Breda, Bois-le-Duc, Grave and Nymegen – so York positioned the Dutch forces close to Bois and stationed his own army near Breda. During August the French were occupied in capturing Nieuport, Ostend and Sluys in preparation for their intended invasion of England, so York was inactive and ten of his generals chipped in with forty pounds each to celebrate his thirty-first birthday in fine style with a dinner for 150 people.

Pitt, Dundas and Grenville had been dismayed by the withdrawal of the Austrians and they sent a deputation to Vienna urging them to re-engage in the war and to dismiss Coburg, whom they blamed for much of the Austrian inactivity and lack of success. Coburg was in fact recalled and replaced with Clerfait but the Austrians, aware of his limitations, suggested to Pitt that if Cornwallis were to be appointed commander of the force currently under York's command and raised to the rank of field marshal, they would be prepared to accept him as supreme commander of all the allied forces, including their own. This was music to the ears of Pitt and Dundas, but there were three obstacles: the views of the king, York and Cornwallis. York made clear that he would be disappointed to have to relinquish his command but that he would do so if ordered, although he would not wish to serve under Cornwallis. Cornwallis's view was that he was reluctant to accept the responsibility and unwilling to command the duke. The king's view was that he would prefer his son to remain at his post and after a good deal of diplomacy and several changes of mind by all parties except the king and the duke, York remained in command.

On 28 August Pichegru began his invasion of Holland and the following day York grouped his forces of about 30,000 men in a secure position by the river Aa, near Bois. Jourdan's army, meanwhile, drove the Austrians even further eastwards towards the Rhine and the fortresses of Valenciennes and Condé surrendered. On 14 September Pichegru attacked one of York's outposts at Boxtel and took prisoner two battalions of Hessians with considerable ease. York sent General Abercromby with a sizeable force to retake Boxtel, but Abercromby decided that he was so heavily outnumbered that it would be foolish to attack. He withdrew, with the loss of about thirty men killed and ninety taken prisoner in an engagement which gave the young Colonel Arthur Wesley (later the Duke of Wellington) his first taste of action under enemy fire. York was informed, inaccurately, that Pichegru probably had about 80,000 troops at this point and he held a council of war to consider his options. Abercromby and Craig were in favour of retreat, as was the civilian William Windham, newly appointed secretary at war, who was present. Although not himself enthusiastic about the retreat, York ordered his troops northwards across the Meuse.

York was sent reinforcements, but we are told that they were 'green troops, inadequately trained, equipped and disciplined and badly officered; some of the new colonels were youths scarcely out of their teens'.[14] Meanwhile, the government looked into the possibility of giving the supreme allied command to the Duke of Brunswick, under whom York would willingly have served, but Brunswick refused. On 10 October the Dutch surrendered Bois and York sent British troops to reinforce Nymegen and renewed his requests that Clerfait should give Austrian support. On 28 October Clerfait sent a force of 7,000 Austrians under General Werneck towards Nymegen but at this point the Hanoverians under Walmoden got cold feet and urged York to abandon Nymegen. Werneck, acting on his own, constructed a bridge across the Rhine at Wesel in order to attack the French from the east, but his forces were easily repelled and the bridge was dismantled.

For most of the campaign York's opinion of his Dutch allies as a fighting force had been very low and his relations with their young commander, the Hereditary Prince William of Orange, had been strained. Increasingly he had also become disillusioned with the Austrians, whose appetite for the war in Flanders had steadily diminished. The Hanoverians had generally been very reliable, but now their commander, Walmoden, seemed to have lost the will to fight. As for York's British troops, the more recent recruits were untrained and ill-disciplined and there were many incidents of looting and criminal behaviour, some of them punished by courts martial, but not all. Moreover, the outlook for the campaign looked far from good. The Austrians were gradually pulling out; the Prussians, despite promises and payments, had never appeared on the field of battle and the Dutch, as ever, were weak and indecisive. The French, on the other hand, were growing stronger with every month and they had already taken control of Flanders and were poised to capture Holland. Letters describing the seriousness of the situation reached Cornwallis in England and he passed them on to ministers, who had already decided that a change of command was necessary, if only to appease political critics.

On 23 November Pitt wrote a long letter to the king regretfully insisting that York should be recalled to London, highlighting the indecision among his commanders and the indiscipline of some of his troops. Pitt's main argument, however, was that, as a subordinate to Coburg, York had acquitted himself well, but that he had encountered more difficulties when left to his own devices:

It seems generally felt [he wrote] that, when the Duke of York was originally appointed to the command, it was under circumstances in which he would naturally act in conjunction with officers of the first military reputation, with whom the chief direction of operations would naturally rest. But by the course of events he is now placed in a situation where the chief burden rests upon himself and where his conduct alone may decide on the fate of Holland, and perhaps on the success of the war. Such a risk appears to be too great to remain committed to talents, however distinguished, which have not the benefit of long experience, and which cannot therefore be expected at such time to command general confidence.[15]

This time the king acquiesced and Dundas wrote to York, recalling him to London, on 27 November 1794. It was not a letter of dismissal and York was instructed to hand over temporary command of the British forces to General William Harcourt, and of the Hanoverians to General Walmoden. Once in England, he went first to Oatlands to see his wife, and then to Windsor, where he was warmly greeted by his father. There then followed a period of about ten weeks when he was technically still in command, though not responsible for the fate of his army, which was left in the hands of ministers and the generals in the field.

He did not find Oatlands the same as he had left it, because earlier that year, on 6 June, while he was away with his army, a fire broke out in a wing of the house which contained the laundry and grand armoury. It blazed away furiously for one and a half hours, destroying two thousand pounds worth of weapons. Frederica was in her bedroom in the main house, which would probably have been destroyed as well but for the help of local people who demolished a gateway linking the burning wing with the main house, thereby bringing the blaze under control. The king went to Oatlands on the following day to view the damage and immediately gave orders for the destroyed wing to be rebuilt at his expense.[16]

Meanwhile, in Holland the French showed no sign of taking up winter quarters and this imposed further strains on the British forces, which were ill-equipped for a winter campaign. Many of the infantry had no greatcoats and they were often housed in barns and other inadequate accommodation.

Typhus fever and exposure to the cold caused major casualties and it has been estimated that in November 1794 nearly half of the 21,000 soldiers in British pay were sick.[17] By the middle of December the weather was so exceptionally cold that the rivers of the Rhine delta, the natural defences of Holland, froze over, allowing the French to cross and threaten the British and Dutch positions. Marching across the ice on the Meuse, Pichegru attacked the allied line near Arnhem on 14 January 1795 and, although the French were beaten back, both Walmoden and Harcourt came to the conclusion that they could not fight on for long.

On 20 January 1795 the French captured Amsterdam and a few days later the icebound Dutch fleet surrendered to a force of French cavalry. The rebel Dutch 'Patriots', who had opposed the House of Orange since the beginning of the French Revolution, supported the French in the establishment of the 'Batavian Republic', a client state of France comprising both Flanders and Holland, and William V of Orange and his sons fled into exile in England. Fortescue calls the period that followed these events 'amongst the most tragical in the history of the Army'.[18] The Hanoverians made their way back to the electorate, but Harcourt had to lead his increasingly indisciplined and bedraggled men through Germany to Bremen, on the north German coast, from where they were eventually transported home in the middle of April 1795.

In many ways it was fortunate for the Duke of York that he had been recalled to London in November the previous year, before the fall of Holland and the subsequent repatriation of the demoralized British army. In February 1795 he was appointed to the administrative post of commander-in-chief of the army and raised by his father to the rank of field marshal. Certainly George III felt that, faced with an exceptionally difficult mission, his son had acquitted himself honourably and had not lost heart or shown weakness of character despite having to deal with unsupportive ministers, vacillating and temperamental allies and, above all, a determined and resilient enemy.

In 1973 Professor Richard Glover, one of the leading military historians of this period, surveyed the evidence and made this judgement on York's performance as a field commander:

> At the siege of Dunkirk everything that York could do was done brilliantly; but he was atrociously let down by his own government (whose failings he most magnanimously covered up) and he was ill-supported by his Hanoverian subordinate Field Marshal Freytag. In the five-pronged attack which his Austrian allies directed against the French at Turcoing in 1794, York carried out his orders to the letter. But only one other commander did so. As a result the British received the punishment that comes all

too naturally to detachments thrust unsupported into exposed positions; and but for the Duke's skilful leadership they would have been still worse handled. His attempted defence of Holland in the autumn of 1794 was frustrated by the incredible ineptness of his Dutch ally. These failures, little as he deserves blame for them, have eclipsed his remarkable successes in lesser actions where he was in full command . . .[19]

# Chapter Seven

## Commander-in-Chief, 1795–1799

I n 1660 King Charles II created the post of 'General-in-Chief-Command' for the professional head of the army and it was subsequently filled by many famous British soldiers, notably the Duke of Marlborough, as well as by George II's soldier son, the Duke of Cumberland. During the Seven Years War, however, the post remained vacant, largely because the elder William Pitt was determined to take charge of all aspects of the war effort himself. The Marquess of Granby, a successful general who was very popular with his men (hence all the public houses named after him) held the post from 1766 to 1769 but it was vacant again until the appointment of Lord Amherst in 1778. He had been mainly responsible for the conquest of Canada during the Seven Years War and was thought to be a suitable person to advise the government during its contest with the American colonies. He was a member of the cabinet, but very uncomfortable and monosyllabic in the presence of politicians, so that the war was mainly run by Lord George Germain, the secretary for the colonies.

Amherst was succeeded in 1782 by Field Marshal Henry Conway, but he retired the following year and the office remained vacant until Amherst was reappointed in 1793 after the outbreak of hostilities against France. He was then aged seventy-seven and a spent force, incapable of reforming the corrupt and decadent administrative structure of the army, which had so much hampered York and other generals in the field. His replacement by York in 1795 was widely welcomed because, as Pitt told the king, tactfully, 'the feelings of personal regard and esteem which everyone bears towards Lord Amherst cannot prevent a very general sense that his age and perhaps his natural temper are little suited to the activity and energy which the present moment seems to call for'.[1] Dundas put it more frankly when he told Grenville that because of Amherst's idleness and incompetence, 'The mischief he did in a few years will not be repaired but by the unremitting attention of many.'[2]

Up to July 1794 Henry Dundas bore the main responsibility for the war in his capacity as secretary of state for home affairs and the colonies, but Pitt wished to give this post to a new political ally, the Duke of Portland, although he did not want him to have control over the war. So he appointed Dundas to the new position of secretary of state for war, with a seat in the cabinet, and an overall responsibility for strategy. His chief assistant was William Windham, in the new post (confusingly named) of secretary at war, whose main responsibility was the control of finance and expenditure. Hence, when York was appointed commander-in-chief, these two civilians were between them responsible for the overall management of the army, as well as for the appointment and promotion of officers. York's office was in the room above the archway leading into Horse Guards from Whitehall, and his deputy was the adjutant-general, Sir William Fawcett, whose responsibility lay mainly in the area of discipline.

As someone who had suffered at first hand from gross inadequacies in the organization of the army, York was in many ways the ideal person to introduce reforms. He was young and energetic, he had the complete confidence of the king, he was a field marshal and second in line to the throne, and he had commanded an army in the field for two years. Moreover, as his letters show, he had a fluent and straightforward way of expressing himself and a capacity for conducting business efficiently. He was the sort of man who would have been popular with soldiers: the novelist Thackeray wrote of him that he was 'big, burly, loud, jolly, cursing, courageous; he had a most affectionate and lovable disposition, was noble and generous to a fault and was never known to break a promise'.[3]

He soon established a steady routine, arriving at his office around 9.00 am and often staying until 7.00 pm and dealing with a huge correspondence, amounting to 300 letters a day, mostly from officers and concerning the issues of promotion. He appointed a military secretary to whom officers could write – instead of to the secretary at war – and he gave the adjutant-general responsibility for the drill and general efficiency of the troops. Gradually he managed to wrest from William Windham many of the financial powers previously exercised by the secretary at war.

One of the main weaknesses of the army was the time-honoured system of purchasing commissions. This could result in able young men being promoted rapidly but more often than not it resulted in the promotion of men who were not devoted to their profession and lacked experience, competence and discipline. So deeply embedded was this system that York could not abolish it but he put a stop to the more obvious abuses, such as teenage boys being made colonels. He also greatly increased the number of promotions made on merit rather than for payment and specified that a captain had to have at least two years' service and a field officer at least six years'. A system of annual confidential reports on officers was also instituted and York kept a very personal eye on the qualifications of individuals recommended for promotion. Generally speaking, he was a good judge of men and their abilities.

York had observed at first hand the desperate conditions under which many soldiers were forced to serve and he eventually raised the pay of privates by 80 per cent, increased their rations and improved the standard of barracks. Military uniforms were modernized by the abolition of the long skirt and the unpopular pigtail, and greatcoats were provided for all soldiers. York had seen how poor were the medical services provided in Holland and one of his main priorities was to establish military hospitals with trained staff and to insist on vaccination for all troops.

The duke also lost no time in making rapid and wide-ranging tours of inspection of regiments in their various headquarters. He was not impressed with the general standard of drill and training and considered that the 'Rules and Regulations for the Formations, Field Exercises and Movements of H.M. Forces', compiled by General Sir David Dundas and issued by direct command of the king in 1792, had been widely ignored. In May 1795 he ordered that these instructions should be strictly followed without any deviation and he set out a training plan specifying particular exercises on certain days of the week. Thursday was to be a day of rest, except for any troops considered to be negligent or backward in their training.[4]

One of the instructions in the 'Rules' was that regiments of infantry should be drawn up three deep in line of battle but York discovered that this was widely ignored. In September 1795, for instance, after a tour of inspections in the area between Newcastle and Whitby, he wrote to his father complaining that all but one of the regiments he had inspected had been drawn up two-deep. Over time and with due persistence, York was able to overcome what Richard Glover calls this 'disparity, inefficiency and negligence of British troops in so vital a matter as the actual battle drill to be used in the face of the enemy'. In Glover's view, thanks to York, 'British officers did all learn one common method of handling their troops in action. It is likely that no one reform [between 1795 and 1809] did more to make the British Army an effective force than this steadily applied system of training.'[5]

York was also aware that the British army lacked 'light troops', which could rapidly form advanced and rear guards, gather intelligence, occupy outposts, maintain communications and use vigilance and rapid movement to cover a front.[6] As early as 1798 a scheme for the creation of a 'light division' was sent with his blessing to the war office, which took no action. So instead he created two light companies from regiments of the line and eleven more from regiments of the militia, with two troops of light horse and a brigade of horse artillery, and gave them to the American War veteran Sir William Howe to be trained in Essex. Although interrupted by the campaigns of 1799 and 1800, this was the beginning of a significant change in the structure of the army.

When York took over at Horse Guards in February 1795 the war against France was still the highest priority. In addition to York's own campaign in the Low Countries, the government had also sent 12,000 troops to Toulon in the summer of 1793 to support a royalist rebellion against the French Republic, but this promising development was ruined by the outstanding tactics of a young French officer called Napoleon Bonaparte, who successfully attacked the port's defences and defeated the rebels, forcing the British to withdraw. In November 1793 a British naval expedition was sent to the Caribbean, where by the following summer it had captured the French islands of Tobago, Martinique, Guadeloupe and St Lucia. In May 1794 Admiral Hood captured Corsica and then on 1 June came a great naval victory when Admiral Howe defeated a large French fleet in the Atlantic and captured six ships of the line. Late in July Robespierre's enemies at last brought him to the guillotine, the 'Terror' calmed down and from the summer of 1795 France was governed by a more moderate – but no less determined – 'Directorate' of five ministers.

An invasion of England was still high on the French agenda and it was York's responsibility as commander-in-chief to prepare for such an event. He had about 60,000 troops stationed at home, mostly militia and Fencibles, who were regulars enlisted only for home defence. The militia came under the control of the home secretary, and it took the duke a considerable time to establish his own authority over this vital defensive force and to mould it into a more coherent organization. Two battalions per regiment were maintained on a territorial basis and York also increased the numbers of light dragoons.

General Harcourt and York's former army of about 23,000 men arrived back in Britain during the spring of 1795 and were variously deployed in home defence and on new initiatives. These included support for a force of French royalists who were landed on the coast of Brittany and a naval expedition which eventually captured Ceylon and Cape Colony from the Dutch – former allies, who, in defeat, were now under the thumb of France. In September a large naval force with an army of 32,000 men under General Abercromby set sail for the West Indies, where he eventually added St Vincent, Grenada and some small Dutch islands to Britain's conquests.

The need to recruit more men for use at home and abroad was a pressing necessity and in 1795 York set up fifteen recruiting districts in England, four in Scotland and five in Ireland, with an inspecting field officer in charge of each and an inspector general of recruiting responsible for the whole structure. Recruiting was not an easy matter because the pay of a soldier from 1797 was only about seven shillings a week, whereas a civilian artisan could earn eighteen shillings. Moreover, conditions for the foot soldier were notoriously harsh, with wives suffering such poverty that soldiers were officially advised not to marry. Most recruiting operations involved spinning yarns of dashing military success and glory in public houses, thereby attracting recruits, who were also enticed by an initial 'bounty' of around five guineas, which enabled them to buy their uniforms and other requirements and still have a little left over.

Once a soldier, a man could run foul of a system of harsh discipline, where a thousand lashes or more was not an unheard-of punishment. York had this reduced to a maximum of 300 lashes and instructed that, in any case, corporal punishment should be a last resort. Officers and NCOs were forbidden to strike their men and York held regular 'levees' at which he personally heard complaints from those who alleged unduly harsh treatment. Moreover York instructed his officers in no uncertain terms that:

> The timely interference of the officer, his personal intercourse and acquaintance with his men (which are sure to be repaid by the soldier's confidence and attachment), and, above all, his personal example, are the only efficacious means of preventing military offences . . .[7]

Another serious abuse that York had to deal with was the frequent absence of lazy and irresponsible officers from their posts. He tackled this by sending letters to regiments, demanding to know which officers were absent and giving a date by which they were required to present themselves or face the possible loss of their commissions. All this did not make him popular with some officers, who were usually men of birth, wealth and influence, used to doing things at their own pace. However, the fact that York was a royal prince who was known to have the king's ear gave his orders a force that had to be reckoned with.

York also turned his attention to the state of military hospitals and issued detailed orders concerning the way they were to be run. Commissioned medical officers were to visit hospitals at least twice every twenty-four hours and all the wards were to be 'purified' each day with a specified fumigation process. Hospital bedding and the clothes of the sick were to be 'baked in an oven' or steeped in running water for at least forty-eight hours, special wards were to be set aside for smallpox patients and medicines were to be carefully stored and regularly checked. Impressed by Dr Jenner's research into a smallpox vaccine, York gave permission for the 83rd regiment in Colchester to be vaccinated, which proved entirely successful. After this, York used his influence to ensure that vaccination was available to British soldiers all over the world.[8]

The duke was an active patron of a large number of charities, especially the 'Philanthropic Society' in St George's Fields, London, which admitted juvenile criminals and the children of convicts in the hope of educating them to a better standard of life. He also supported organizations which gave refuge to people discharged from prisons and to destitute women. His wife assisted him in much of this and became patroness, for instance, of the 'Lying-In Charity for the Wives of Foot-Soldiers belonging to the regiments of Foot Guards'. The duke also made sure that military chaplains were provided for the troops, although liberty of conscience was respected: presence at the Church of England services was compulsory but no questions were asked about individual beliefs.[9]

## Mutiny and Rebellion, 1797–1798

In 1795 the Prince of Wales reluctantly agreed to an official marriage between himself and Princess Caroline of Brunswick, whom York had admired as a young girl during his years in Germany. The prince, as we have seen, was already secretly married, although his relationship with Maria Fitzherbert had by now cooled as a result of his interest in a succession of mistresses. His current favourite was Lady Jersey. He only agreed to get married in return for the payment of colossal debts of around £600,000 that he had incurred over the years. He had never met Princess Caroline, who was essentially the choice of his father, and he did not much like her when they did meet, just before the wedding, finding her something of a show-off and an indiscreet chatterbox, as well as being on the plump side. She, on her part, was not impressed by the fact that she was met on her arrival in Britain not by the prince, but by his mistress, Lady Jersey, who made disparaging remarks about her appearance. Nevertheless, the wedding went ahead on 8 April 1795 and on 6 January the following year Caroline gave birth to a daughter, Charlotte. This affected York in so far as up to this date he had been second in line to the throne after the prince, but now he moved down to third.

York's own marriage to Frederica remained happy and they continued to live in the London house in Piccadilly and at Oatlands in the country. However, after four years of marriage there was no sign of children and indeed medical opinion had come to the conclusion that Frederica was not likely to have any, a blow that inevitably imposes a strain on any marriage, particularly one that had taken place in order to provide an heir to the British throne. Many people who knew him well described York as a very likeable personality in a domestic setting and he would probably have made an excellent father. Frederica had no ambitions to be a leader of fashionable society or the centre of a brilliant social circle or even an active member of the royal family: instead she preferred a quiet life at Oatlands, surrounded by a growing number of pet dogs. She and the duke worshipped on many Sundays in Weybridge parish church and she devoted a good deal of her energies to local charities and the welfare of the poor, for which she was much admired and respected. She was also a gifted needlework artist.

One of her local friends was Horace Walpole, the son of George II's prime minister, an elderly lifelong bachelor, man of letters and aesthete whose main legacy has been his vast correspondence and his remarkable house at Strawberry Hill, near Twickenham. In 1747 he bought this as a 'cottage' in five acres and developed it over many years into a mock castle that had a considerable degree of influence on the Gothic revival in Victorian times. Until his death in 1797, Frederica enjoyed visiting him and being shown round the house:

> The same ritual was always observed. Walpole would lay down a piece of carpet from his front door to the gate, and would be waiting to help the Duchess out of her carriage. Inside the house there would be some little surprise for her: on one occasion it was a little couplet written by Mr Walpole, extolling the military fame of the Duke of York, hanging round the frame of a brass eagle he had in the hall. Then he would show her the house, and afterwards there would be chocolate. She always tried to make him sit, but he never would. He explained that as a child his father had taken him to see George I and there was something about that terrible old gentleman that made him think it impossible to sit in the presence of his descendants.[10]

During 1796 the French discovered that they had a military genius at their service when the youthful General Bonaparte swept the Austrians out of Italy in a brilliant campaign. In August Spain became an ally of France, a move which posed a great threat to Britain because the fleets of France and Spain combined were a numerical match for the Royal Navy. Pitt spent most of this year raising new taxes to pay for more troops and ships, while the threat of a French invasion remained very real. In fact, a French fleet sailed from Brest to Ireland in December 1796 with 15,000 men and forty-three vessels, including seventeen ships of the line. Luckily for the British, they were battered by a gale and reached Bantry Bay with eight ships missing, and were then blown out to sea by another gale and were back in Brest by the middle of January 1797, with the loss of one ship of the line.

The following month twenty-seven Spanish ships of the line with 2,300 guns and including the largest ship in the world, the *Santissima Trinidad*, set sail from Cartagena. Their destination was Cadiz but they were blown into the

Atlantic by an unfavourable wind and on their way back they were caught in fog in the vicinity of Cape St Vincent by the British Mediterranean fleet under Admiral Jervis with only fifteen ships. In the ensuing battle on 14 February the Spanish fleet was badly damaged and four prizes were taken. The remaining Spanish ships made their way back to Cadiz but were blockaded by the Royal Navy for the next three years, much reducing the threat of a successful Franco-Spanish invasion of England.

This victory raised morale in Britain and honours were showered on Jervis as well as on Horatio Nelson, one of his captains, who stunned the navy during this battle by capturing one Spanish ship and audaciously using it to capture another. Unfortunately, in an attack on the Canary Island port of Santa Cruz in Tenerife in July Nelson made some serious tactical errors and, while stepping ashore from the leading longboat to direct operations, he was hit in his right shoulder by a shot from the Spanish defenders and had to be taken back to his flagship to have his arm amputated. He took an almost self-destructive risk on this occasion and was lucky not to have been killed. This rare defeat of the famous Nelson is still celebrated with gusto in Santa Cruz each year on its anniversary, 25 July.

On land, however, Bonaparte continued his successful campaign against the Austrians in Italy with further victories at Arcole and Rivoli, eventually taking his army to within a hundred miles of Vienna. The Austrians were obliged to make peace in April 1797 and the great 'First Coalition', which Pitt had done so much to keep together since 1793, now collapsed. The Austrians made a humiliating peace with France, involving the surrender of the Netherlands. Pitt, too, began to put out feelers for a peace settlement but the French demands were impossibly high. With all her allies knocked out of the war, Britain now faced France alone.

The Royal Navy was Britain's only effective defence, the backbone of the nation. And yet on 16 April 1797 the Channel Fleet based at Spithead in Hampshire refused orders to put to sea. The chief grievance was that whereas the army and militia, thanks to the Duke of York, had recently received increases in pay, sailors had been paid the same amount for over a hundred years. Moreover, as the sailors were well aware, it was the navy and not the army which had achieved the main successes in the war so far. Negotiations were carried out at first in a civilized manner and Pitt promised that navy pay would be increased. But he had to get this measure through Parliament and that took time and by May the pay had not arrived. On 7 May the men of the Channel Fleet forced their officers to go ashore and sailed to St Helen's, off the Isle of Wight. Sympathy mutinies then broke out on ships in Plymouth, Weymouth, Yarmouth and at the Nore, a major anchorage in the Thames estuary.

The sailors' favourite admiral, Lord Howe, managed to defuse the situation everywhere except at the Nore, where the mutineers were led by Richard Parker, a determined and aggressive troublemaker who had political and even revolutionary motives. Pitt decided that the time had come to break off negotiations, stop supplies to the Nore Fleet, train the shore guns upon them and remove the navigational buoys from the Thames. By June most of the mutineers had returned to duty, except for Parker, who attempted to surrender his ship to the French. This was too much for his men, who turned him over to the naval authorities and he was hanged with twenty-three other mutineers.[11]

During this dire emergency, the fact that the government could rely upon the loyalty of the army was a crucial factor. John Watkins, writing about the mutinies some twenty years later, attributed the loyalty of the army during this period to the high regard in which York was held by officers and men as the result of his humanitarian reforms and his concern for the soldiers' welfare:

Under these appalling circumstances, the military in every part of the kingdom maintained a dignified firmness: and while the seamen of the grand fleet were dictating their own terms, obviously with the expectation of seeing their example generally followed by the kindred service, not a single defection occurred in the army at home or abroad. This conduct had the happiest effects, for it strengthened the state, revived the spirits of the people and ultimately reduced the revolters themselves to moderation and their duty. Had it not been for the timely and spontaneous measures of prudence adopted by the Duke of York as Commander-in-Chief, in all probability a great proportion of the British army would have imitated the example of the seamen; the consequences of which must have been humiliating and destructive to the government and the nation.[12]

Within a few months of their mutiny, the sailors of the Nore ships, led by Admiral Duncan, confronted the Dutch fleet at Camperdown, off the coast of Holland, on 11 October. The fleets were evenly matched and it was a fierce struggle but the Dutch were defeated and Duncan sailed back to the Nore with seven captured vessels.

Even so, the French were still hoping to get an invasion fleet to Ireland, where disaffection against the British was very strong among a wide spectrum of Irishmen, including Roman Catholics as well as patriots with revolutionary ideas inspired by France. In May 1798 the Irish authorities arrested Lord Edward Fitzgerald, who was killed in the ensuing struggle. He was found in possession of detailed plans for a widespread rebellion throughout Ireland, with the assistance of the French.

A youthful Prince Frederick in Germany, aged about eighteen, by A. Ganz.

King George III, after Johann Zoffany. *(Taylor Library)*

'A scene on Tuesday the 26 of May between a prince and a poltron.' Caricature of the duel between the Duke of York and Lieutenant Colonel Charles Lennox on Wimbledon Common, by James Gillray, May 1789. *(National Portrait Gallery)*

The Duke of York, aged twenty-four, after Sir Joshua Reynolds. (*National Portrait Gallery*)

'The Soldier's Return.' Caricature by James Gillray showing Prince Frederick with his new bride, Princess Frederica of Prussia, November 1791. (*National Portrait Gallery*)

The Duke of York (left) and his brother the Prince of Wales, from a wax relief by Thomas Poole. (*National Portrait Gallery*)

King George III (centre) with his sons the Prince of Wales (left) and the Duke of York, after C. Tomkins. (*National Portrait Gallery*)

The Duke of Wellington at the battle of Waterloo, June 1815. (*Taylor Library*)

The Duke of York in Flanders, aged thirty-one, after John Hoppner, 1794.

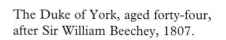

The Duke of York, aged forty-four, after Sir William Beechey, 1807.

Mary Anne Clarke, a watercolour
miniature after Adam Buck, 1803.
(*National Portrait Gallery*)

Mary Anne Clarke, after Thomas
Rowlandson, 1809. (*National Portrait Gallery*)

Frederica, Duchess of York, after Sir
William Beechey, 1802. (*National Portrait Gallery*)

Monument to the Duchess of York by Sir
Francis Chantrey, currently in the bell
tower of St James's Church, Weybridge.
(*Photo by the author; reproduced by courtesy of the Rector and
Churchwardens*)

Nineteenth century engraving of the Duke of York's memorial column and statue in Waterloo Place. (*Taylor Library*)

The Duke of York in 1822, after Sir Thomas Lawrence.

The newly cleaned Duke of York monument, photographed in 2015. (*Author*)

Sir Richard Westmacott's statue of the Duke of York on top of his memorial column before the 2014 cleaning. *(Taylor Library)*

Statue of the Duke of York on the Esplanade, Edinburgh Castle, by Thomas Campbell. *(Andrew Murray)*

Statue of the Duke of York
on the main staircase of
the Institute of Directors
(formerly the United
Service Club), by Thomas
Campbell.
*(Reproduced by kind permission of the
Institute)*

A commemorative
medallion struck in
1827 to mark the
death of the Duke
of York, mourned as
'The Soldier's Friend'.
*(Author's collection: photo by
Morrison, Isle of Man)*

On the news of Fitzgerald's arrest, there were revolts in Wicklow and Wexford but his death and the arrest of other ringleaders crippled the effectiveness of the rebels, even though tens of thousands of Irish peasants, mainly led by priests, flocked to the cause. The government sent across several thousand regular troops and militia, with Lord Cornwallis as both lord lieutenant and commander-in-chief in Ireland: he arrived in time to confront a small French invasion force of 1,100 men that landed in August at Killala and was quickly surrounded. Naturally, the Duke of York was closely involved with all these events and it was ultimately his responsibility to select the relevant troops and to make sure that they were properly provisioned and provided for in their despatch to Ireland. He may well have been considered for the post given to Cornwallis but it would not have been tactful to have a Prince of the Blood involved in the complex issues of rebellious Ireland.

John Watkins argued strongly that without the wise and benevolent policies of York as commander-in-chief it would not have been safe to use British troops in Ireland in this way because so many soldiers in British regiments were Irish – attracted to the army because of the dire poverty that afflicted them at home. He maintained that the causes of the loyalty of the Irish troops were:

> not in the strictness of discipline or the severity of the executive power, but in that wisdom and benevolence which had provided the most effective security for the nation in the establishment of a general system of well-organized economy through every department of the military service ... and the personal comfort of the humblest individuals employed in this complicated body of moral machinery.

He also recorded that:

> Considering, therefore, the extraordinary and seasonable benefit rendered to the public by the judicious regulations which the Duke of York introduced for the management of the army, the University of Oxford, in a solemn convocation held on the 16 June 1799, presented to his royal highness the degree of Doctor of Civil Law, by diploma.[13]

While Pitt was persuading the House of Commons to pass the necessary legislation to deal with the Irish emergency, he chose to accuse an opposition MP, George Tierney, in the House of Commons of 'obstructing the defence of the country' by his objections and delaying tactics. When Pitt refused to withdraw this unparliamentary language, Tierney challenged him to a duel, which took place on Putney Heath on 27 May. Both duellists missed with their first shot and, as York had done, Pitt then fired his second shot into the air and the seconds declared that honour had been satisfied. Whether York and Pitt later compared notes on their respective experiences has not been recorded.

Certainly Pitt had become a politician hardened in the fire. During the peacetime years he had been liberal and tolerant but since 1789 there had always been the danger that revolution might eventually raise its head in Britain. The king and queen were much respected by the average citizen but the antics of the Prince of Wales and his circle, and indeed the extravagant behaviour of many aristocrats, were much criticised. The 'London Corresponding Society' and the 'Society for Constitutional Information' were set up by radicals with ideas inspired by the reformers in Paris and as times became more difficult during the war, with higher taxes and shortages of bread, the government became increasingly intolerant of dissent. In August 1795 dissatisfaction at the high price of bread had led to riots in many cities, including London, where Pitt's windows in Downing Street were smashed. During 1796 Pitt introduced his so-called 'Gagging Acts', which banned any meeting of more than fifty people without the consent of magistrates and he was also prepared to take the drastic step of suspending the Act of Habeas Corpus, which effectively prevented arbitrary arrests. None of this would have been possible without the loyal support of the commander-in-chief at the Horse Guards.

In May 1798 Napoleon Bonaparte set out with a fleet carrying a large French army to Egypt. He had defeated the enemies of France on land, the government (known as the Directors) regarded him as too much of a rival to remain in Paris and he himself conceived the grandiose plan of conquering Egypt in order to strike at British commerce in India and the East. Admiral Nelson, by now in charge of the British Mediterranean fleet, knew that Napoleon had set sail but not where he was going, so it was several weeks before, more by luck than judgement, he found thirteen French ships of the line moored in Aboukir Bay, close to the mouth of the Nile. As a result of the battle that took place there on 1 August 1798, the French fleet was totally destroyed and Napoleon's army was marooned in Egypt.

It took three months for the news of this triumph to reach England and in the same month as the battle, York was carrying out routine inspections of his troops on the home front, in case Bonaparte should suddenly appear off the British coast. In August he wrote to the king:

The Hampshire Fencible Cavalry are a very pretty corps, exceedingly well mounted, particularly the bay troop, and rode very well except that their stirrups are too long. The Royals are in the highest order possible: they ride perfectly well and have strictly kept their stirrups to your Majesty's orders with regard to the length of stirrups. The only error I found in them was that they rode too much by the snaffle. The troop of the Horse Artillery and the park are in a very high order and exercise perfectly well.[14]

Aboukir Bay was a massive setback for the French. Their navy was shattered and demoralized, Bonaparte's army was confined to unproductive campaigns against the Turks and he himself suffered a serious loss of credibility. Everywhere, France's enemies took fresh heart and Pitt set to work to create another Coalition, inventing a new, but temporary, British tax on income to pay his allies. Britain could afford it because the new factories of the 'industrial revolution' were producing goods of all kinds, many of them needed by the armies of Europe in the shape of uniforms and weapons.

In February 1799 Britain signed a treaty of alliance with Russia, by which Britain would pay over £1 million a year for 45,000 troops and in March Austria abandoned her peace treaty with France and declared war. By June 1799 the French had been driven out of southern Italy by local forces and revolts against the French Republic were imminent in Flanders as well as in parts of France itself, such as the Vendée and Brittany. In March one Austrian army crossed the Rhine and another defeated the French in Northern Italy. Meanwhile the Russian General Suvorov captured Milan, Turin and Mantua, and by August all the Italian lands conquered by Bonaparte had been regained.

There was a real possibility that the French might crack under this pressure, and Pitt was fairly confident that he could persuade the reluctant Prussians to join the coalition for the right price. The cabinet, by now full of warlike enthusiasm again, foresaw a successful invasion of France along its eastern and southern frontiers by Austrian, Russian and Prussian armies and decided to make a British contribution to the war by sending a military force to invade Holland.

# Chapter Eight

## The Helder Campaign, 1799

As we have seen, after the French success in the Low Countries campaigns of 1793–1795, France established a client 'Batavian Republic', consisting roughly of the present Holland and Belgium. It was occupied by a French army of 15,000 men under General Brune, but by November 1798 Brune was under pressure because of a growing mood of rebellion throughout the country. In the same month York wrote to the king:

> I have the honour to report to your Majesty that I met Mr Pitt this morning by appointment at Mr Dundas's, where he mentioned to me that account had been received from Holland which could be relied upon that the French troops have been for the most part removed out of Holland into Brabant on account of the insurrection and that the Dutch are so exceedingly discontented with the French that if a body of troops could be sent there, it could be easy to seize upon Flushing.[1]

This idea, thus floated, solidified into a firm policy in the following months and Pitt offered large subsidies to both Prussia and Russia if they would assist in an invasion of Holland. Prussia ultimately refused, but Russia agreed to send a force of 18,000 men.

The cabinet authorized the raising of a British army of 30,000 men, some of whom were drawn from the militias; thanks to York's work in the preceding four years, they were troops of good quality and well equipped. The cabinet moreover decided that York should be the commander-in-chief of this force, without any pressure from the king, and Dundas wrote to Pitt: 'This is certainly a command fit for a king's son and I cannot help thinking that with a view to future connection, it is desirable that a Prince of the Blood should have a chief part in the deliverance of Holland and the re-establishment of the House of Orange.'[2] The Tsar of Russia was also keen that the supreme commander of the coalition troops should be a royal prince. The fact that Pitt, Dundas and Grenville all warmly recommended the appointment of York makes it clear they had accepted that the problems he encountered in the 1793–1795 campaign were not essentially of his making and that his achievements as commander-in-chief since then had been impressive. However, the government also gave important roles to General Sir Ralph Abercromby, the experienced and popular veteran (although he was now aged sixty-six and very shortsighted), as well as to General David Dundas, and it was understood by all parties that York would benefit from their advice.

The plan was that, as an opening move, Abercromby should sail in Admiral Mitchell's fleet to either the Zuider Zee or the naval port of the Helder, where his instructions were to land, capture what was left of the Batavian fleet after Camperdown and eject the French from Holland. He set sail on 13 August, waved off by Pitt himself, and decided to land a few miles south of the Helder, the Batavian naval base on the tip of the peninsula separating the Zuider Zee from the North Sea. On the western shore there was a strip of sand dunes about one and a half miles wide, and the rest of the territory was very flat, much of it below sea level. As with many parts of Holland, the sea was kept out by a system of dykes consisting of large earthen banks with roads running along the top.

Bad weather delayed the landing until 27 August, so the Franco-Batavian army had plenty of warning of an impending invasion, although they did not know exactly where. The Batavians had about 20,000 men and the French 10,000 but they were thinly deployed all along the coast. Abercromby's landing near Callantsoog was a great success and the Batavians fell back to the south. Unfortunately, Abercromby failed to pursue them or to capture the garrison of the Helder itself, which escaped. However, on 30 August Admiral Mitchell received the surrender of the Batavian fleet, consisting of eight ships of the line, three frigates and a corvette – amounting to 632 guns and 3,690 men – without firing a shot, largely because many of the Dutch sailors mutinied against the Batavian Republic on sighting the Orangist flag among the invaders.[3] Now that one of the main aims of the expedition had been accomplished, this should have been the time for Abercromby to press his advantage, but instead he waited for the arrival of York with reinforcements. He was attacked by the French on 10 September but beat this off with heavy losses and again failed to pursue the rapidly retreating enemy, or to join with Admiral Mitchell in a new offensive.

In fact, he was waiting for York to take the ultimate responsibility, which he did on his arrival on 13 September, at the same time as a Russian division which he reviewed before riding to his headquarters. As York well knew, one of his most important roles as commander was to maintain good relations with his Russian allies, under General Herrmann, and with his much less numerous 'Orangist' Dutch allies, led by the Hereditary Prince William of Orange, with

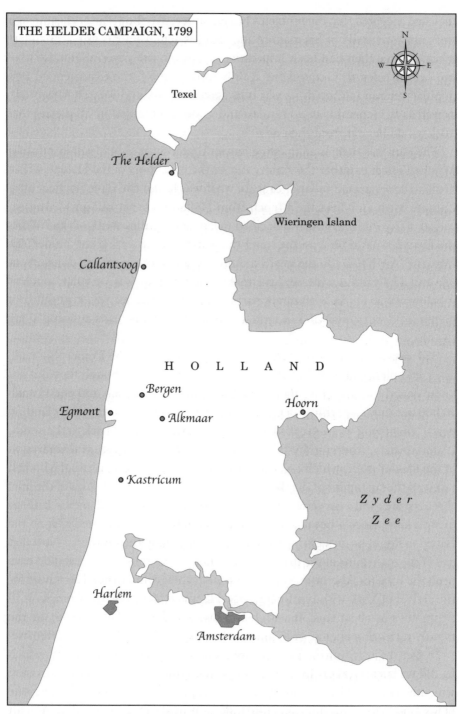

**THE HELDER CAMPAIGN, 1799**

Texel

The Helder

Wieringen Island

Callantsoog

H O L L A N D

Bergen

Hoorn

Egmont

Alkmaar

Kastricum

Z y d e r
Z e e

Harlem

Amsterdam

The Helder campaign, 1799.

whom he had served in 1793–1794. After due reconnaissance of the terrain and the positions of the combatant armies, York produced a bold plan of attack. It began early in the morning on 19 September with a Russian advance on the right flank of the town of Bergen. This was at first successful, although marred by extensive pillaging and the burning down of the church, which was still in ruins 150 years later. Despite this setback, the French regrouped and counter-attacked the Russians with vigour: the Russian line gave way and 2,000 men were killed, 800 wounded and 1,500 taken prisoner, including General Herrmann himself.[4]

However, on the left flank General Pulteney drove the Batavians back towards Alkmaar and their retreat became a rout. At this moment Abercromby should have attacked. The previous night, as planned, he had marched to the town of Hoorn, which surrendered, and his orders were to join in the battle the following day wherever seemed most advantageous to him. But Hoorn had not surrendered until about 4.00 am and Abercromby's men were tired, many of them lying down in the roadside to catch some sleep. On the day of the battle all he did was send messengers to discover how the fighting was progressing. He later claimed that 'the state of the roads, the fatigue of the troops, the broken nature of the ground, above all, the uncertainty of events on the right made [an advance] impossible'.[5]

By the mid-afternoon, with the Russians out of the contest and Abercromby immobile at Hoorn, York and his staff decided that the battle was lost and both Abercromby and Pulteney were ordered to return to the British lines, even though Pulteney's attack had been successful. So ended the battle of Bergen, in a defeat of the allies by a numerically inferior force. An anonymous poem published a few months later runs:

> Ten thousand troops to scatter wild dismay,
> Were marched to Hoorne, wisely detached by night,
> To stop the hostile army in its flight;
> That when they shrunk from Russia's conquering spear,
> This corps might charge them on the flank and rear,
> But when, alas, the fatal mine was sprung
> And the sad news confirmed by every tongue ...
> They beat to arms, pursued their former track,
> Rejoined the prince – and to a man came back.[6]

Here is another possible scenario for the 'Grand Old Duke of York' and his ten thousand men. There is certainly an advance and a retreat by the requisite number of troops (although not up and down a hill) and the incident was lampooned in a contemporary verse. Even Alfred Burne, York's most enthusiastic defender, had to admit that the order to recall the troops was a serious mistake, judging that 'the duke, or his staff, or both, temporarily lost their heads'. He goes on to say:

> Bergen should, in fact, go down in history as one of those battles in which the commanders, not the troops, were defeated. There may have been extenuating circumstances of which we know nothing. We are reduced to judging by results. The result of the recall order was that the battle was lost and the Duke, as Commander-in-Chief, must take the blame for it. One cannot picture a Wellington or a Lee issuing such an order. But then, they were not saddled with war councils and Abercrombys.[7]

There was no denying that the Russians had performed badly at Bergen and the Tsar was disposed to punish them, despite the fact that York wrote to him saying that he had 'been a witness of the order and bravery with which all these corps fought against the enemy'. Captain Bunbury, on Abercromby's staff, described them as 'angry, sullen and scarcely to be counted as allies', and according to one report, when issued with grease for their vehicles, they spread it on their bread and ate it. Anxious not to cause dissent among his Russian allies, York, on his own authority, ordered that they should be paid on the same basis as the British troops.[8]

The British fleet, initially so successful in capturing the Helder and the Batavian fleet, did very little for the next three weeks. An obvious target was Amsterdam and a French official there feared that 'a few bombs directed against so populous and so rich a town would cause it to capitulate. This would be the coup de grace of the [Batavian] government; it would have no more money or resources to pay its forces.' York saw the possibilities here, and proposed to his generals that the land forces should combine with the fleet against Amsterdam. He explained in a despatch: 'I thought it my duty to ask the opinion of Sir Ralph Abercromby and General Dundas upon these plans but they deemed it infinitely too dangerous to be adopted.' Admiral Mitchell, in a despatch to the Admiralty, adopted a distinctly pessimistic tone, saying that after the defeat at Bergen he had 'doubts of success' and could not understand why Abercromby had done so little. French historians of this campaign have come to the conclusion that, having captured the Batavian fleet, the British navy should have easily been able to attack Amsterdam and the Hague, thereby cutting off the retreat of the French forces in North Holland and leaving them at the mercy of the allies. York probably felt the same because soon afterwards Mitchell was recalled and replaced by Admiral Dixon.[9]

Bad weather swept in after Bergen; rain lashed down, wind whipped up the sand on the dunes and the next attack was held up until 2 October. Abercromby was ordered to march along the seashore and his troops fought a stiff engagement with the French one mile north of Egmont. Abercromby himself displayed great personal bravery, having two horses shot under him, and the French fell back to the south of the town. To the east, the Russians and General Dundas made less progress on the dunes and the Russians refused to advance south of Schoorl, the Russian commander, General Essen, merely informing the duke 'We do not move from here'. York wrote to the Tsar asking for his replacement the next day. However, enough had been done to ensure a French withdrawal, and York was able to write in modest terms to his father about the bravery of his troops, saying, 'It is to their steadiness and gallantry alone that through Divine Providence the victory was gained.'[10]

On 6 October York ordered his forces to advance south of Alkmaar and Egmont but they clashed with the enemy, who were making an unexpected counter-attack, near the village of Kastrikum. Both sides suffered heavy casualties, but the French retreated and 500 of their troops were taken prisoner. At this point the British had 28,000 men and the Russians 14,000, compared with 14,000 French and 10,000 Batavians, so the enemy were heavily outnumbered, though the allies were probably not fully aware of this.

After the battle was over that evening, York called his generals together and asked them for their opinion of what should be the next move. He eventually received a written reply, probably composed by Abercromby, which was pessimistic in the extreme, emphasizing:

hardships due to the wet weather, difficulty of supplying troops owing to bad roads, paucity of horses and barges, heavy losses in the recent battle without any balancing advantage, sickness owing to exposure, absence of good billets, the difficulty of the terrain in their front, the strength of the French position at Haarlem, the fact that the farther they advanced the greater would become their difficulties, whereas the French were being reinforced by 6,000 fresh troops; finally the great fatigue of the troops who had been out in the rain for several days.

The conclusion of the generals' report was:

From what we see and what we feel we are humbly of opinion that however we might have given efficacy to a revolution in Holland, we are not at this moment equal to the conquest of the country or of remaining (even if it was an eligible one) in our present situation and that any further advance affords no prospect of decided advantage but on the contrary is fraught with much difficulty and dangers should we fail; that therefore we should return to the position ... which we quitted and then await a more favourable change of circumstances.[11]

The following morning Abercromby and David Dundas saw the duke and repeated their opinion that he should retreat. Given that York had received overall command on the understanding that he would take careful notice of the opinion of Abercromby, he decided that, as he explained to Henry Dundas, 'I found myself under the necessity of complying.' He gave orders for the retreat that day and the allies were back behind their original line on 9 October. Abercromby and David Dundas then saw York on 12 October and said that they did not think the Helder naval base could be retained over the winter and advised a full evacuation of the allies back to Britain. York's engineers produced reports which foresaw great difficulties in defending the Helder and fortifying the army's lines and the naval authorities warned that it would be very difficult to enter the Helder after the middle of November.

Faced with this, the duke agreed to an evacuation and began negotiations with the French, who demanded that in return for a ceasefire the Batavian fleet must be handed back and 15,000 prisoners of war in England must be returned. York refused the first item outright but eventually agreed to the release of 8,000 prisoners. On this basis, the Convention of Alkmaar was duly signed, hostilities ceased on 29 October and the British and Russian evacuation was carried out speedily and without incident. York took all these decisions without express permission from London and his main worry was that the terms of the ceasefire might be censured by the government and his father. In fact, they were very supportive. Pitt wrote to him that 'every part of the transaction is marked with dignity, firmness and wisdom, and as far as Y.R.H. is personally concerned must entitle you to the confidence and gratitude of the country in at least as great a degree as the most splendid and prosperous issue which would ever have attended our enterprise'. The king's view was:

The situation [into which] the army under the command of my dearly beloved son the Duke of York was placed by the supreme strength of the country and the difficulty of getting off the troops without the loss of the rearguard fully exculpates him for the steps he has taken of negotiating and concluding a suspension of hostilities without previous directions from hence, and on these grounds I fully give my sanction and approbation for that measure.[12]

Pitt and Dundas had hoped that the Helder campaign would result in the capture of the Batavian fleet, the encouragement of a revolt by pro-Orangist Dutch against the French and the expulsion of French soldiers from the Low Countries. Moreover, it had been conceived as part of an attack on France on a number of fronts by the Prussians, Austrians and Russians. The Prussians had refused to take part and the Austrian and Russian campaign to strike at France through Switzerland came to nothing. York's army had been unable to fight its way south of Amsterdam and it faced the serious danger of being trapped on a peninsula too small to provision it throughout the harsh winter months. Pitt and Dundas were probably over-optimistic about what might have been achieved and they were prepared to accept the verdict of an experienced campaigner such as Abercromby that, with the Batavian fleet captured and its ships destined to be valuable additions to the Royal Navy, evacuation was the best option. This was the only seasoned land force that Britain possessed and it might have been lost altogether. Its safe return to Britain provided the government with the option of using it for other projects, such as an attack on the French fleet in Brest. This is why ministers, on the whole, were grateful to York for bringing his army home under honourable conditions.

Yet no one could pretend that it was a glorious result and many felt that the duke had failed to make the best use of a great opportunity. Henry Bunbury, who, as the duke's 21-year-old ADC, had carried many messages to and fro between York and Abercromby, wrote in his *Narrative of the Campaign in Holland*, published fifty years later, that, as he perceived it, York had faults as a commander:

> Much as I loved the Duke personally, much as I felt many good and amiable qualities in his character, much as I owe to him in gratitude for long kindness to myself, I cannot but acknowledge that he was not qualified to be even the ostensible head of a great army on arduous service. ... He was of cool courage: he would have stood all day to be shot at: but he had no active bravery. With a very fair understanding he had little quickness of apprehension, still less of sagacity in penetrating designs or forming large views: painstaking, yet devoid of resources, and easily disheartened by difficulties. (He could not bring himself to say no.) To these defects must be added habits of indulgence, and a looseness of talking about individuals after dinner which made him enemies, and which, in the unfortunate campaign, probably excited the rancour of the Russian generals.[13]

It should be said, however, that a young ADC is not necessarily the best person to understand the complexities of a commander-in-chief's position and too much notice has possibly been taken of this judgement, written fifty years after the event. Pitt's elder brother, Lord Chatham, who accompanied the army, told his brother that the disappointments of the campaign could 'fairly be attributed to the misconduct of the Russian general and the Russian troops'.[14] French historians later conceded that York's plan for the battle of Bergen was 'a bold, but also a just, extensive and skilful application of the principles and rules of the art of war', and Professor Glover has emphasized that: 'In the event, the duke's plan for Bergen was to be wrecked by the insubordination and the rout of his Russian allies.' In his view the duke's hands were tied by orders to do nothing without the approval of a council of war, and York might have achieved more if he had been 'left free to follow his own good judgement'.[15]

York in public blamed the Russians and perhaps in private blamed Abercromby, who in turn blamed York. A Scottish laird and a lawyer, philosopher and MP as well as a soldier, Abercromby was a long-standing friend of Dundas and a man with intellectual and enlightened tastes not always found in the military. After his part in the 1793–1795 campaign in the Netherlands, his West Indies expedition had met with reasonable success and in 1797 he had been appointed to command the troops in Ireland, where he resigned after differences of opinion with the lord lieutenant.

After this, Abercromby was placed in charge of the garrisons in Scotland, before being transferred to the Helder campaign. Some might say his performance in Holland was sensible, prudent and wise; others might argue that his attitude was timid and defeatist. He was not himself particularly proud of his achievement, as he indicated by refusing the offer of a peerage on his return. However, he went out in a blaze of glory, because the following year he was appointed to command British troops in the Mediterranean and after a successful attack on the French near Aboukir in 1801 he died from his wounds in almost Nelsonic style. His widow was created a peeress and monuments were raised to him in St Paul's Cathedral and St Giles's in Edinburgh.

# Chapter Nine

## An Eventful Day

In the early summer after his return from the Helder, York put the Grenadier Guards through a series of manoeuvres in Hyde Park, which were attended by the king. Suddenly, a musket-ball was fired from the centre of the ranks and hit a junior clerk in the navy office, called Ongley, who was standing only six or seven yards from the monarch. It went right through one of his thighs and lodged in the other, near the groin. Surprisingly, despite vigorous investigations, no culprit was identified and the matter was declared to be an accident. Ongley recovered and the authorities made sure that in due course he received a suitable commission in the navy.

That night the king and queen, the Duke and Duchess of York and other members of the royal family attended a first performance of Mozart's *The Marriage of Figaro* at Drury Lane. As the king entered the royal box, a contemporary recounted,

> ... the whole house was thrown into confusion by the discharge of a pistol from the front row of the pit; but though the bullet struck the pilaster just over the head of the King, it providentially did no mischief, owing to the sudden jerk to the hand of the assassin at the moment he was taking his aim. Immediately the perpetrator of this atrocious deed was seized and dragged over the rails of the orchestra into the music room, where Mr Sheridan and the Duke of York soon entered, to attend the examination. On seeing His Royal Highness, the man recognized him instantly and enthusiastically exclaimed, 'God bless you! I know you: you are the Duke of York under whom I served on the continent.' Then, turning to the people about him, he went on and said: 'Ah, he is a good soul: he is the soldier's friend and love.'[1]

York remembered the man, whose name was James Hatfield (or Hadfield), because he had been one of the dragoons who formed his personal guard at Famars, back in 1794. Formerly a silversmith, he had fought bravely, but was badly wounded in the head at Lincelles, so that he had to be discharged on a pension. For his attempted assassination of the king he was tried for high treason the following month, before Lord Kenyon in the Court of King's Bench in Westminster Hall. York was called as a witness. Upon seeing him, Hatfield, who had sat listlessly throughout the trial so far, exclaimed brightly, 'Ah, God bless His Highness! He is a good soul!' York explained that his personal guard had been chosen from men of the best character and the court heard several witnesses testify that Hatfield had become deranged as a result of his wounds. Lord Kenyon stopped the trial and committed the prisoner to the Bethlehem Hospital (nicknamed 'Bedlam'). On one occasion he escaped from there, but was recaptured on the coast of Kent. York made sure that his wife and family received some support, and, it would appear, sometimes called at the hospital to see him.[2]

George III was a very popular king and this was one of only two attempts to assassinate him in a very long reign. Both would-be assassins were deranged. The first, in 1786, was a woman called Margaret Nicholson, who tried to stab him while he was getting off his horse at St James's Palace. In the ensuing panic the king remained 'the only calm and moderate person then present', according to Fanny Burney. After the Drury Lane incident, the singer Michael Kelly, who was on stage in the role of Don Basilio, wrote later in his memoirs, 'Never shall I forget His Majesty's coolness. The whole audience was in an uproar.' It seems that the king merely got out his opera glass and looked steadily round the theatre. Meanwhile, Richard Sheridan quickly penned another verse for the National Anthem, which was sung from the stage that very night. It ran:

> From every latent foe,
> From the assassin's blow,
> God Save the King!
> O'er him thine arm extend,
> For Britain's sake defend
> Our Father, Prince and Friend,
> God Save the King![3]

## The Royal Military College

Resuming his duties as commander-in-chief with the benefit of even more practical experience, York strongly favoured the establishment of a college for the training of army officers. King George II had founded the Royal Military Academy at Woolwich in 1741, where about fifty young men, rising to ninety by 1793, lived under a regime similar to that of the public schools except that instead of being taught Latin and Greek, they studied the practical sciences that would equip them for a commission in the Ordnance (the Royal Corps of Artillery and Engineers). The education and training at Woolwich were excellent, probably providing the best grounding in the sciences on offer in Britain at the time, but it was limited to a minority destined for a career in the Ordnance.

When York became commander-in-chief in 1795 it was clear to him that a similar college was needed to train young officers entering the army at large. Hitherto, new officers received very little formal training or education for their profession save what they could pick up from the drill-sergeants in the regiments they joined. Soon after his appointment, York issued instructions that 'Commanding officers of regiments are equally responsible for the instruction and improvement of the officers under their command as they are for the drill of the men.'[4] But any practical training of this sort fell far short of the study of military theory or tactics, for instance, about which there was little available information. Indeed, this was the very reason why Frederick himself had been sent to Prussia as a young man, to study the art of war from experts such as Brunswick and Frederick the Great and to observe the impressive exercises and manoeuvres carried out by the Prussian and Austrian armies. By contrast, the best that the British army could do was to arrange modest 'field days' for the Guards in London's Hyde Park or Phoenix Park in Dublin. This was largely because, despite the dangers of the war, there was still a strong public and political prejudice against the massing of military forces within the UK.

In 1798 the duke received an offer from an exiled Frenchman, General Francis Jarry, to set up a military school in England. Although he was French, Jarry had served throughout the Seven Years War on the personal staff of Frederick the Great and had been head of the Prussian Military School from 1763 to 1786. After this he went back to France and held a high command under Dumouriez at the victory of Jemappes, although he was subsequently targeted by political extremists in France and eventually moved, in exile, to a large house in High Wycombe. He suggested to York that pupils should be sent to him there and the first thirty young officers, approved by the duke, arrived in May 1799. Unfortunately Jarry spoke only French, so his lectures were not readily understood and his pupils made fun of him. Translators and administrative staff had to be called in, as a result of which the establishment needed a subsidy of £1,000 in its first year.[5]

In January 1799 Colonel John LeMarchant, who had recently designed a new sword for the British army and was a respected instructor in its use, put to the duke an ambitious plan for the setting up of a new army college. York felt that this would probably founder in the face of public and political hostility to the 'militarization' of the UK, so he sent LeMarchant to work with Jarry at High Wycombe in the first instance. From there LeMarchant used his considerable gifts of charm and persuasion, as well as a wide range of military contacts, to win support for his college scheme among the influential colonels of yeomanry regiments across the country. York also arranged for LeMarchant to have access to the cabinet, and eventually Pitt was persuaded to set up a committee to review his scheme, chaired by York and including Sir William Fawcett and Henry Calvert, as well as General David Dundas, all of whom were supporters of officer training.

LeMarchant actually proposed a three-tier structure consisting of a staff college for serving officers, a junior college for training future officers and a school which would provide free education to the sons of NCOs and serving soldiers. A Royal Warrant in June 1801 set up 'The Royal Military College', with a board of governors and based at High Wycombe, while another Royal Warrant, in December of the same year, laid down details of the training and curriculum. This was to be essentially a 'staff college' and an entrant had to be at least nineteen years old with at least two years of regimental service. The subjects taught included French and German, mathematics and drawing, with practical courses in reconnaissance and the movement of troops.[6]

A third Royal Warrant early in 1802 founded the junior department of the Royal Military College, based a few miles away at Great Marlow. There were to be a hundred cadets, aged between thirteen and fifteen at entry, thirty of whom would be freely educated as the sons of officers who had died or been maimed on active service. Of the paying cadets, twenty would be the sons of serving officers, thirty the sons of noblemen and twenty the sons of those in the East India Company's service. The pupils at both colleges behaved badly to begin with and the duke found it necessary to demand enquiries into several quite serious misdemeanours, which were suitably punished. Gradually the new institutions settled down and in 1813 the junior department moved into fine new buildings at Sandhurst, designed by James Wyatt and John Sanders. The senior department of the RMA moved to Sandhurst from High Wycombe a few years later and it has played a highly important part in the training of army officers ever since.[7]

LeMarchant's suggested school, although it was not incorporated within the Royal Military College, was nevertheless taken up by York, who in 1801 laid the foundation stone of 'The Royal Military Asylum for Children of Soldiers of the Regular Army', which had been set up by Royal Warrant that year as a direct result of his personal initiative. It was housed in another new and impressive classical structure, also designed by John Sanders, standing close to the Royal Hospital in Chelsea, and it was ready to admit the first pupils in

1803. Based on the same principles as the 'Royal Hibernian Military School', founded in Dublin in 1769, it was at first intended for the education of children of soldiers killed in the war against France. The first pupils were transferred to Chelsea in August 1803 from a military orphanage in the Isle of Wight and thereafter the school flourished under the watchful eye of the duke and a board of governors drawn from some of his most senior officers at the Horse Guards.

Despite its fine buildings in Chelsea, the asylum was not intended to be a grand school for the privileged but rather a place where the orphaned and destitute children of rank and file soldiers could be educated instead of being sent to the workhouse or relying on other forms of charity. As such, its historians claim, it 'provided the country with the first large-scale system of education for working-class children'.[8] Moreover, it opened its doors to girls as well as boys and by about 1810 it housed 1,500 military orphans, of which 1,000 were boys and 500 were girls. The duke was impressed with the monitorial system of instruction, first introduced by Joseph Lancaster and modified by Dr Andrew Bell, by which older children of thirteen and fourteen would, after initial tuition themselves, give instruction to younger pupils, and this was employed as the general method of basic education. Up to 1815 many of the boys leaving the school were destined for the army but in peacetime they were provided with indentured apprenticeships in a variety of trades. The Asylum was a ground-breaking and enlightened educational development which brought great benefits to its pupils and the nation at large and it would not have seen the light of day without the enthusiastic support of the Duke of York.

## A Short-lived Peace, 1802–1803

As a result of the Fitzgerald rebellion in 1798, Pitt came round firmly to the view that a full political union with Ireland was necessary. After lavish distribution of bribes to the affected parties an Act of Union, passed by both the British and Irish Parliaments in 1800, established the 'United Kingdom of Great Britain and Ireland', which came into effect on 1 January 1801. The Irish Parliament in Dublin ceased to meet and a hundred MPs representing Irish constituencies joined the 558 already sitting at Westminster. Far more controversially, Pitt also advocated the granting of concessions to Roman Catholics, who were in the majority in Ireland, yet suffered under serious restrictions concerning religious practice and civil rights. Here Pitt came up against the opposition of George III, who considered that any concessions to Roman Catholics would be a violation of his coronation oath to protect the Church of England. Because of this conflict, Pitt felt obliged to announce his resignation as prime minister in

February 1801, but before he could leave office the king suffered another bout of insanity. Pitt had to stay on and begin negotiations with the Prince of Wales about a regency but then the king suddenly recovered in March, blaming his relapse on the strains of the Catholic Emancipation issue. Pitt left office on 14 March and was succeeded by his political ally Henry Addington, the Speaker of the House of Commons. Pitt's supporters were dismayed: 'Pitt is to Addington as London is to Paddington,' they joked.

Addington dropped the contentious issue of Catholic Emancipation (which York, following his father, also strongly opposed) and began to look for an end to hostilities with France. While York had been at the Helder, dramatic events had occurred in Paris. General Bonaparte had been marooned in Egypt as a result of Nelson's destruction of his fleet in Aboukir Bay in August but after a number of successes against the Turks he abandoned his army and reached Paris in October 1799, aware that the rule of the Directory was unpopular. After a coup in November, he established himself as 'First Consul' of France, with a plebiscite which voted overwhelmingly in his favour. He then took an army into Italy and defeated the Austrians at Marengo in June, while General Moreau won another victory at Hohenlinden in December. After these defeats, Austria made peace at Lunéville in February 1801, granting France extensive gains including recognition of the Batavian Republic.

In April 1801 a British fleet under Admirals Parker and Nelson defeated the Danes at Copenhagen and destroyed the 'League of Armed Neutrality' that had hampered the British war effort. News then filtered through of the defeat of the remains of Bonaparte's Egyptian army by Abercromby's force. To Addington (and also Pitt, who continued to advise him), it seemed sensible to make peace with France under terms which were embodied in the Treaty of Amiens of March 1802. The French agreed to give up Egypt, Naples and the states surrounding Rome, but kept extensive territories on the left bank of the Rhine and remained dominant in the Netherlands and Northern Italy. Britain retained Trinidad and Ceylon but returned all other gains, including Martinique, Minorca, the Cape of Good Hope and Malta, as well as some Dutch settlements in the East and West Indies. Critics thought that Addington had given away too much but in general the peace was well received. Addington grew in confidence and the king showed his pleasure by giving him White Lodge in Richmond Park to use as an official residence.[9]

In fact, the peace lasted less than fourteen months because on 18 May 1803 Britain again declared war on France, where Napoleon Bonaparte had become First Consul for life. Britain complained that France had abused a generous Treaty at Amiens by occupying the Netherlands and Switzerland, while France countered that Britain had not given up Malta. The reality was that, after Amiens, Napoleon, instead of demobilizing his troops, continued to increase both his army and naval forces to an extent that could only be a serious threat to Britain's interests and Addington, unlike Chamberlain in 1938, was not an appeaser.

The decision to resume war against France had disastrous consequences for the Electorate of Hanover and the Bishopric of Osnabrück. In March 1803 the Imperial Diet, under pressure from Napoleon, granted the bishopric to the electorate, and in July the electorate was forced to surrender to Napoleon's army. It was then abolished and occupied by French troops until 1807, when Napoleon incorporated it into a new Kingdom of Westphalia. This meant that from 1803 the Duke of York ceased to be Prince Bishop of Osnabrück and to enjoy its revenues, while his father lost control over Hanover. George III did not recognize the electorate's dissolution and a body of Hanoverian exiles maintained a theoretical government in London. More effectively, a large body of Hanoverian officers and men came to England after the dissolution of the Hanoverian army and formed the 'King's German Legion'. This eventually numbered about 14,000 men and was one of the best-disciplined forces in the British army, fighting with distinction in many campaigns, including the Peninsular War and at Waterloo. Given his knowledge and experience of Hanover, there was a close tie between these men and their new commander-in-chief, the Duke of York.

No doubt intoxicated by the general enthusiasm for the renewed conflict, the Prince of Wales asked Addington for an army appointment suitable to his rank and dignity. Receiving evasive replies, he appealed directly to the king, who as directly refused permission for him to do anything other than act in the largely ceremonial role of Colonel of the 10th Light Dragoons, an appointment he had received in 1793. Given that all his brothers except one were serving in the armed forces, the prince felt he had a strong case, but from the point of view of the king, he was the heir apparent to the throne and – even more significantly – had had little military training nor shown much interest in it. The prince then turned to his brother Frederick, who as commander-in-chief was, of course, responsible for all military appointments.

In a series of letters which went to and fro between the brothers from 5 to 14 October George became more and more exasperated at York's explanation that he could not give him a command without the king's permission, and he ended: 'Feeling how useless, as well as ungracious, controversy is upon every occasion, and knowing how fatally it operates on human friendship, I must entreat that our correspondence on this subject shall cease here, for nothing could be more distressing to me than to prolong a topic, on which it is now clear to me, my dear brother, that you and I can never agree.' Relations between the two cooled for a while, but George got over it.[10]

When Pitt resigned as prime minister, Henry Dundas resigned with him and Addington replaced him as war minister with Lord Hobart, a man almost forgotten now except for having given his name to the capital of Tasmania. Yet he was an able and conscientious minister, who first undertook a moderate demobilization of troops after the Treaty of Amiens and also continued the work of incorporating the Irish Army and Ordnance within the British army, as a result of the Act of Union in 1801. This meant, from the Duke of York's point of view, that after 1801 he was effectively commander-in-chief of all Irish troops as well as British. Addington can take the credit for not demobilizing too quickly, because when hostilities began again, there were still 50,000 men in the navy, while the army had 132,000 men, three times its normal peacetime strength. Moreover, thanks to York's reforms, the army was better trained and organized than ever.[11]

The threat of a French invasion was very real and all the ports from Brest to the Texel were full of French troops, waiting to be shipped over to Britain, though as York wrote early in July 1803, 'The extent of army which an enemy may land depends not upon his numbers at home, but upon his means of transporting them to this country.'[12] Not content with the forces that already existed, Addington's ministry determined to raise a huge force of militia and in July 1803 passed an Act empowering the government to 'train every able-bodied man whether he liked it or not', following the example of the French *levée en masse*. Ultimately 380,000 'volunteers' were raised in Britain and a further 70,000 in Ireland, creating a demand for firearms which the Ordnance was at first unable to supply. As commander-in-chief, York saw to it that inspecting field officers were appointed to monitor the volunteer militias every month and report back to the Horse Guards.

While Pitt was still a serving MP, very few at Westminster believed that Addington could face the demands of war as well as he could and gradually Addington's support slipped away and he resigned on 9 May 1804. Pitt returned as prime minister and Henry Dundas, by now Lord Melville, joined the cabinet; Hobart was replaced as war minister by Lord Camden until July 1805, when the post went to the brilliant Lord Castlereagh. That month Castlereagh wrote to York that Britain 'should be prepared to ... menace or attack the enemy on their maritime frontier, and, by compelling them to continue in force on the coast and in Holland, [to] weaken their efforts proportionately in other areas', a sensible policy that York dutifully pursued by establishing a fully equipped fleet of transports capable of carrying 10,000 men near Cork, Portsmouth and Dover.[13]

To deal with the very real threat of a French invasion of the south coast, the Duke of York initiated a number of far-reaching measures. In 1794 an army camp had been established on land in Shorncliffe, Kent, which lay only twenty miles from the French coast and in 1803 York made the brilliant appointment of General John Moore (knighted in 1804) to command an army brigade there. Moore was a Scot who had fought with distinction in many theatres of war from American Independence onwards and he was a leader noted for wise and humane treatment of the troops.

It has sometimes been said that Moore initiated the training which led to the emergence of Britain's first light infantry regiment during his time at Shorncliffe but, according to Richard Glover, 'the idea that Moore originated any system of light infantry training is ... a mistake. The system he taught, like the plan of training whole regiments as light cavalry, was but one thing more provided by the foresight of the commander-in-chief and his staff.'[14] As early as 1798 York authorized Baron de Rottenburg, an Austrian in the British service, to circulate his up-to-date manual on the exercise of riflemen and light infantry, in which he provided instruction in weapon-handling, marksmanship and drill, and it was this which Moore used as the basis of his training scheme, together with another manual in the same vein, written by Francis Jarry of the Royal Military College.[15]

About 1800 York founded the Royal Staff Corps, led by Lieutenant Colonel John Brown, and it was they who built the 28-mile-long Royal Military Canal from Shorncliffe westwards to Rye, effectively making the Dungeness peninsula and the Pett levels into islands. Brown met Pitt and the Duke of York in September 1804 and outlined his plans for the canal, which would defend the Romney marshes from invasion. They both approved the scheme enthusiastically and it was complete by 1809. In February 1794 two British warships had unsuccessfully attacked a defensive tower at Mortella Point in Corsica and it was only captured after a hard-fought land attack led by John Moore. When York appointed Moore to take charge of the defence of the coast from Dover to Dungeness, he urged the building of similar defences, consisting of round 'Martello' towers with thick walls, about 40 feet high and housing between fifteen and twenty-five men, with a piece of heavy artillery on the roof. Eventually about 140 of these towers were built in England and Ireland, as well as larger redoubts at Harwich, Dymchurch and Eastbourne.

The immediate threat of a French invasion was drastically reduced when, on 21 October 1805, Admiral Nelson, with twenty-seven ships of the line, engaged the combined French and Spanish fleets of thirty-three ships off Cape Trafalgar and inflicted one of the most crushing blows in naval history, capturing twenty-two enemy vessels and losing none. This success was diminished partly by the death of Nelson himself and also by an exceptionally vicious storm which blew up immediately after the battle, scattering the British fleet and wrecking many of the captured vessels – which had the lamentable effect of greatly reducing the prize money due to British sailors. However, the short-term result of the battle was that a French invasion of Britain was rendered impossible until Napoleon had built another fleet, although he began to make plans for this without delay.

Trafalgar did nothing to prevent French success on land, however. Napoleon, who had become 'Emperor of the French' in December 1804, forced the surrender of one Austrian army at Ulm on 19 October 1805 and then on 2 December, in the 'Battle of the Three Emperors' at Austerlitz, he soundly defeated an Austro-Russian force, commanded by Francis II and Alexander I in person, with a masterly display of tactical strategy. By the resulting Treaty of Pressburg, Austria recognized French gains in Italy and in 1806 Napoleon created the Confederation of the Rhine, composed of many German states which had formerly been part of the Holy Roman Empire. This outdated anachronism was now dissolved and Francis henceforth ruled as Emperor of Austria and King of Hungary.

It was claimed at the time that the shock of Austerlitz, which destroyed the Third Coalition and Pitt's entire foreign policy, was a direct cause of his death. Certainly he died less than two months later, at the age of forty-six, worn down with worry and stress after a lifetime of heavy drinking, often in solitude, and probably suffering from peptic ulceration of his stomach or duodenum.[16] His former political ally, Lord Grenville, succeeded him as head of a short-lived 'Ministry of All the Talents', as the wits called it. The most disastrous aspect of this administration was the appointment of William Windham as war minister. Although charming, well-meaning and a fine speaker, his policies regarding army recruitment were muddled and wrong-headed. He abolished the ballot for the militia, which reduced recruitment drastically and introduced a Training Act which conscripted 200,000 men a year but gave them only twenty-four days of training. He did raise pay by 50 per cent to one shilling and sixpence and introduced pensions for old soldiers, but these measures had no practical effect on recruitment.

Moreover, the Duke of York gave Windham his strong professional advice that he should not abolish the Volunteers, which Windham had criticised in the past for being expensive and ineffective 'painted cherries which none but simple birds would take for real fruit'. Faced with York's objections, Windham compromised by retaining the Volunteers but abolishing the inspecting field officers, which York had introduced, and reducing the Volunteers' days of training and rates of pay. As a result, according to one analyst, 'he did not save the country the whole expense of maintaining these "painted cherries", but he did abolish everything calculated to preserve the real usefulness for which the commander-in-chief valued them . . . This alone is surely enough to justify our calling Windham a national disaster, quite apart from the effect of his policies on the regular army, the fatuity of his Training Act, and his failure to aid his allies.'[17]

Under the Grenville administration, a 'Fourth Coalition' was formed against Napoleon, consisting of England, Sweden, Prussia and Russia. French armies crushed the Prussians at Jena and Auerstadt on 14 October 1806, causing King Frederick William III to flee into Russia. Napoleon entered Berlin and from there inaugurated the 'Continental System', by which all European governments were required to wage economic war against Britain through ceasing to trade with her. In February 1807 Napoleon forced the Russians to withdraw after a battle at Eylau and followed this with a decisive victory over them at Friedland in June, after which the Tsar made peace at the Treaty of Tilsit the following month. At this point in his career Napoleon was triumphant everywhere and there was little that Britain could do but look on.

Fortunately for the British war effort, Grenville's ministry fell in March 1807 because the king refused to consider its plans for Catholic Emancipation. Thanks to the work of Pitt's friend William Wilberforce, however, it did manage to pass one worthwhile measure: the abolition of the slave trade. The king now turned to the elderly and infirm Duke of Portland to form his second ministry, in which Castlereagh returned to the war office, where he was able to concentrate his exceptional ability and energy on restoring the strength and effectiveness of the army, no doubt to the relief of the Duke of York, who had been very unhappy with Windham's unsatisfactory 'reforms'. Castlereagh began by encouraging men from the militia to volunteer for the regular army once more and thereby gained nearly all of the 28,000 reinforcements for which he had hoped, while subsequent losses to the militia were filled by a revival of the ballot system.

## Spain and Portugal

Throughout the eighteenth century both Spain and Portugal were absolute monarchies, ruled respectively by the royal houses of Bourbon and Braganza. When the French Revolution broke out in 1789, Spain was ruled by King Charles IV and Portugal by Queen Maria I, although in 1792 she was declared insane and her son John ruled as prince regent. Spain and Portugal were both horrified by the progress of the Revolution and after the guillotining of Louis XVI they joined Britain in the First Coalition against France. Spanish and

Portuguese armies invaded the French Pyrenees in that year but were driven back by 1795, after which France occupied part of north-east Spain.

After this reverse Spain changed sides and allied with France but, because of the long-standing friendship between Portugal and Britain, cemented by mutually advantageous trading treaties, Portugal declared neutrality. In 1801 France persuaded Spain to take part in a successful invasion of Portugal, which was forced to cede territory to both Spain and France. After this, Prince John's Spanish wife, egged on by Paris and Madrid, attempted a coup in 1805 to take power herself, although it was not successful. John subsequently refused to join Napoleon's Continental System and maintained close diplomatic relations with Britain, which secretly pledged to evacuate him to Brazil if the French should invade again.

In November 1807 Napoleon sent Marshal Junot into Portugal with a large army that soon threatened Lisbon. Helped by the British, Prince John decided to abandon his country to the French and embarked in a fleet of ships bound for Brazil, with several thousand Portuguese nobles, civil servants and military personnel. Despite storms, cramped conditions and disease, most of the ships arrived safely and John set up a new capital at Rio de Janeiro. He instructed those remaining in Portugal to cooperate with the French and avoid the destruction of the country.

Meanwhile, in Spain there was conflict between Charles IV and his heir, Prince Ferdinand, who staged an unsuccessful coup against his father in 1807, backed by 'liberals'. In March 1808 a popular revolt forced Charles to abdicate in favour of his son, who became king as Ferdinand VII, but Charles appealed to Napoleon, who summoned both of them to Bayonne in April 1808 and announced that the Bourbon dynasty in Spain had come to an end. He had appointed his elder brother Joseph Bonaparte King of Naples and Sicily in 1806 and he now declared him to be King of Spain, supported by 100,000 French troops. Although Joseph was able, liberal and well-intentioned, this French upstart, the puppet of his younger brother, had no chance of winning the support of the vast majority of the Spanish people.

On 2 May 1808 Spanish rioters killed 150 French soldiers in Madrid and the following day the French shot hundreds of citizens in retaliation, an event immortalized in Goya's iconic painting *The Third of May*. Sporadic rebellions occurred throughout Spain, which were given the name *guerillas*, or 'little wars'. By the end of the month nearly all the Spanish provincial governments had repudiated French rule and Joseph was faced with a national revolt. Many of the rebel local governments sent delegations to London requesting assistance and Castlereagh despatched three army officers to Gijon in June to assess the situation. Then, in July, Spanish rebel forces inflicted a significant defeat on the

French at Bailen and Castlereagh sent out General Sir James Leith to consider how the north of Spain might be reinforced. In August a British army under Sir Arthur Wellesley landed in Portugal, assured of local support.

## The Wellesley Factor

Born in 1769, Wellesley was the third of the five sons of Garret Wesley, Earl of Mornington, an Irish peer living on his estates at Dangan, in County Meath. When Lord Mornington died in 1781, his eldest son Richard inherited the earldom and after a brilliant career at Eton and Cambridge, he seemed destined for greatness. Meanwhile Arthur did not enjoy Eton, left prematurely and attended the French Royal Academy of Equitation at Angers, where he learnt good horsemanship and became fluent in French. Through Richard's influence he was able to buy a commission in an infantry regiment and was appointed ADC to the Lord Lieutenant of Ireland. Then he became a member of the Irish Parliament for the local constituency of Trim. In September 1793, with money borrowed from his brother, he was able, at the age of twenty-four, to purchase the rank of Lieutenant Colonel of the 33rd Regiment of Foot and in June 1794 he sailed with his men to Flanders to reinforce the Duke of York's army, which was facing a major French counter-offensive.

As we have seen, the army that York was given was badly provisioned and equipped and had been raised hastily, often from the dregs of society, while many of its officers were young men with little training or experience who had bought their commissions, just as Wesley (as he then was) had done. On 14 September 1794 Wesley saw his first action when his regiment helped to check a French attack at Boxtel and he was later complimented by York for his calm and effective conduct. Wesley expected, as many officers did, that he would be returning home for the winter but the French attacks continued and he remained with his men on the Waal for several months in freezing temperatures. During this time (when York had been recalled home) he was only once visited by a general and when he himself went to headquarters, he was surprised to find it 'a scene of jollification'. In later life he criticized the allied high command, although not York specifically, for being out of touch in this campaign and put it on record that 'the reason why I succeeded in my own campaigns is because I was always on the spot – I saw everything and did everything for myself'.[18]

In 1796 Wesley, by now a full colonel, was sent with his regiment to India, where in 1798 his brother Richard was appointed governor-general, after changing the family name to Wellesley. Arthur was part of General Harris's force that defeated Tipu Sultan at Seringapatam and he was then appointed

Governor of Mysore in 1801 and promoted major-general in 1802. In 1803 he won his first battle as an army commander, against the Marathas at Assaye, a decisive victory during which he remained in the thick of the action. He followed this with two further victories, leading to the ultimate defeat of the enemy. He was knighted in 1804 and returned with his brother (who had been created Marquess Wellesley) to England in 1805. During Richard's period of office the influence of France had been destroyed in India, and the often haphazard rule of the East India Company had been transformed into the makings of a new British empire. Inevitably, Richard had promoted his brother over the heads of more senior officers and this caused a good deal of ill-feeling in some quarters. He was a leading Whig and the Tories sought to discredit him by demanding an enquiry into his Indian administration, which subsequently found no fault.

Arthur Wellesley, meanwhile, became MP for Rye in 1806 and was soon appointed chief secretary for Ireland and a privy councillor. However, he relinquished these appointments in order to command an infantry brigade on an attack on Copenhagen in 1807, which captured the Danish fleet and prevented it from falling into the hands of Napoleon. It was after this success that he was promoted lieutenant-general and received orders to command a modest force which would be sent to oppose the French in Portugal.

Arriving there in August, he won a tentative victory at Rolica, immediately after which reinforcements from England arrived off the coast, commanded by Sir Harry Burrard, a more senior general with orders to supersede Wellesley. Before the new troops could fully disembark the French attacked Wellesley, who beat them off with great success at Vimeiro on 21 August. Wellesley then urged Burrard to take the offensive, but he refused. The following day Sir Hew Dalrymple arrived from Britain to take overall command and he also refused to sanction Wellesley's plan for an offensive, which inevitably caused friction between them.

At this point, and unexpectedly, Junot concluded that his position was untenable and he asked for an armistice, under which his army could be safely evacuated from Portugal. Discussing the details between themselves, the three British generals formulated the Convention of Cintra, which allowed the French army, along with 'their arms and baggage, with their personal property of every kind', to be transported in ships of the Royal Navy to the French port of Rochefort. All three generals signed the Convention, which caused public outrage at home when its details became known. Wellesley was very unhappy with it, especially when he saw how much loot the French were taking with them and he resigned his command, allegedly to resume office as chief secretary in Ireland. Soon afterwards, Dalrymple and Burrard were recalled to England, when the government, under pressure from the opposition, announced an official enquiry in November.[19]

Inevitably, the Duke of York was closely involved with many of these important events and decisions. He was aware of Wellesley as a young officer because he had noted his steady conduct at Boxtel, but he formed an unfavourable impression of him subsequently, probably because he had acquired rapid promotion through the influence of his Irish aristocratic family, especially his elder brother, and the system of purchasing commissions, which York had tried so hard to dismantle. York made clear his disapproval of the fact that in India General Harris had given Wellesley the Mysore command in preference to more senior officers and he was very suspicious about the fact that Wellesley had political as well as military ambitions. At this point he considered him less than trustworthy and together with the king he opposed Wellesley's initial appointment to command the expeditionary force to Portugal on the grounds that he was too junior in the service, and he was very influential in the decision to send out Burrard and Dalrymple to supersede him.[20]

York and his duchess were no strangers to the Wellesley family because one of Richard and Arthur's sisters, Lady Anne, was first lady of the bedchamber to Frederica. They had clearly known each other well for several years because the daughter of Anne's first marriage had been christened Georgiana Frederica. After the death of her first husband Anne married the 24-year-old Charles Culling-Smith in 1799 and York appointed him a personal equerry and favoured the couple by becoming godfather to their son, who was named Frederick after him. Seemingly the Culling-Smiths were close friends of the duke and duchess, but an entry in the journal of the politician and diarist Lord Glenbervie, dated 12 February 1804, runs: 'According to gossip the Duke of York returned to Oatlands unexpectedly one day and actually surprised the Duchess and Mr Smith in the very fact. Violent fury. The king said "I am very sorry for it, Frederick. It is an infamous business, but it must be hushed up."'[21]

This episode seems out of character for Frederica, but if Glenbervie was not just passing on malicious rumour, all parties concerned followed the king's instructions because nothing more came of it and the duke, no doubt reflecting that he was by no means an innocent himself in such matters, evidently decided to forgive and forget. In 1805 Charles Culling-Smith and his wife built a fashionable gothic-style house in Virginia Water, Surrey, which they called Wentworths, and Charles served briefly as under-secretary of state for foreign affairs as well as remaining an equerry to the duke until Frederick's death in 1827. Wentworths, together with 200 surrounding acres, was bought in 1920 by George Tarrant, who made it into the famous golf course.

Whether the Culling–Smith episode had any bearing on York's opinion of Arthur Wellesley or not, it was widely thought at the time that he would have liked the supreme command in Portugal for himself. Many in opposition to the government were strongly against this, partly because of York's mixed fortunes as a commander in the past and partly because he was becoming, as we shall see, the centre of a major scandal. A popular caricature of September 1808 depicted the duke on Horse Guards, surrounded by his wife Frederica, a woman called 'Eliza', George Canning (the foreign secretary), and a group of Guards officers. The duchess is saying: 'I will return and bury my cat. If he go or stay, I will have his presence equally. He always turns a dead side to me. Oatlands for me.' Meanwhile the duke says to 'Eliza' (presumably his mistress, Mary Anne Clarke), 'Eliza adieu ... I am yours, but my country calls. Canning is an insolent upstart. Holland and Dunkirk indeed! Popular clamour! Lost confidence! ... Not go? When Sir Hew expects me?' Canning meanwhile is saying: 'He shall not go ... I will resign first ... No, No, ... death to his hopes or my countrymen.' Finally, the group of officers say: 'Aye, turn him out – go out yourself – go, go, go. We could do without you.'[22]

As was often the case, this caricature was politically motivated. It was common knowledge that the duke had kept several mistresses, while Canning's hostility stemmed from rivalry between himself as foreign secretary and the war minister Castlereagh, who was an ally of York. The suggested attitude of the officers is less credible, unless they represented men disappointed of promotion or appointments. In fact, the Portuguese command went to Sir John Moore, who had worked closely with the Duke of York on the defence of the south coast and whose abilities he valued highly. Meanwhile, it was York's responsibility to appoint seven senior generals, chaired by Sir David Dundas, as the board of inquiry into the Convention of Cintra and they met in the great hall of Chelsea Hospital in November. Dalrymple, Burrard and Wellesley all presented their own points of view and the board eventually absolved them of blame, deciding that although an unconditional surrender of the French would have been preferable, the Convention had served a useful purpose.

Taking up his command in Portugal in September 1808, Sir John Moore left 10,000 men in Lisbon and marched another 20,000 as far as Salamanca, hoping to unite with further British reinforcements under Generals Hope and Baird, as well as a large Spanish army. But Napoleon himself had invaded Spain with 160,000 men, driving back the Spanish and entering Madrid on 4 December. Moore and Baird together attacked a French army under Soult with some success but were pursued by Napoleon with his main army. Moore was forced to retreat 200 miles over the mountains in a harsh winter to Corunna, with despondency and lack of discipline ever-present in his ranks. The disorganized force reached Corunna on 11 January 1809 and began evacuating in British ships two days later. On the 16th Soult attacked and was beaten back, but Moore was hit by a cannon ball that mangled his left shoulder and arm. He died that evening, while the rest of his army was evacuated under the cover of darkness. Nine days later some 28,000 men, including about 6,000 sick and wounded, arrived in a very bedraggled state in Portsmouth harbour. Moore's valiant death and the successful evacuation of most of his army tempered what was really a tactical disaster, with the British expelled from the Peninsula, and the French once more in control.

On 1 February 1809 the Duke of York issued a general order praising Moore. 'During the seasons of repose', it ran, 'his time was devoted to the care and instruction of the officers and soldiers. In war he courted service in every quarter of the globe ... his virtues live in the recollections of his associates, and his fame remains the strongest incentive to great and glorious action.'[23] Yet by 18 March, as a result of a scandal which had riveted the attention of the nation for the past two months, York himself felt obliged to inform the king of his decision to resign as commander-in-chief.

# Chapter Ten

## Mary Anne Clarke

As we have seen, the Duke of York was very fond of his wife, and she of him, and part of his domestic world consisted of their home at Oatlands, where he would be from time to time when not involved in his military duties, or at their London house. It was known, however, that the duchess was not able to bear children, so the duke was deprived of the pleasures and responsibilities of bringing up a family and there was nothing in this regard to bind them closer together. Frederica was not socially ambitious, having no desire to cut a figure on the London scene or to be influential in politics. She was content, in the main, to live quietly at Oatlands, surrounded by an alarming number of pet dogs, to dispense charity in the locality, and to attend Weybridge church on Sundays with her husband.

In the world in which the duke had been brought up, it was no great crime for a prominent member of society to keep a mistress, as long as this was done with some discretion. All Frederick's brothers had mistresses, as did many members of the aristocracy: indeed, one of the few exceptions to this general state of affairs was the king himself. Frederick had a strong sexual drive and experienced little difficulty in finding women to suit his tastes. In 1803 he was introduced to Mrs Mary Anne Clarke and fell seriously in love. She was about twenty-seven, undoubtedly pretty and vivacious but also very clever, witty, ambitious and manipulative. The daughter of a journeyman printer, she received a respectable education for two years and then became involved with Joseph Clarke, a stonemason, with whom she had two children, George and Ellen. They were married, but soon separated, although without a divorce. Claiming to be a widow, she became an actress and 'courtesan', rising gradually through the social ranks with her clients until she hit the jackpot with the Duke of York.

By 1804 Frederick had provided for her use a house in Gloucester Place, off Portman Square, and he granted her £1,000 a year so that she could live there in considerable style, give parties and entertainments and keep her bed ready for him. Not content with the two carriages, eight horses, butler, postilion, coachman, groom, chef, gardener and two footmen she enjoyed there, she also persuaded Frederick to rent her a house near Weybridge so that they could even be together when he was supposed to be at Oatlands over the weekend. One day she made the tactical error of attending church when the duke and duchess were also at the service. The duchess said nothing, but wrote to Pitt (prime minister at the time) saying that he must have a word with her husband and make sure such a thing did not happen again.[1]

In fact, York's infatuation with Mary Anne lasted for only about two and a half years. He began to suspect, rightly enough, that she was abusing his trust and he was alarmed by her reckless extravagance and constant demands for more money. In 1805 a tradesman threatened to sue Mary Anne for debt and call the duke as a witness, so that he was forced to bail her out. Worse still, in the autumn of 1806 Mary Anne's husband, Joseph Clarke, emerged from the shadows and threatened to sue the duke, claiming damages from him on the grounds of adultery. As Mary Anne had said that she was a widow, this came as a considerable shock and embarrassment.

York's loyal secretary William Adam was influential in persuading the duke that Mary Anne was a danger and with some reluctance he authorized Adam to tell her that their relationship was at an end. Moreover, Frederick's interest by then had begun to shift to Mrs Carey, who lived in Fulham. This was widely known, because the caricaturist Charles Williams produced a drawing which he called 'The Rival Queans [sic] – or a scene in the Beggar's Opera', which shows Mary Anne and Mrs Carey jealously ranting at each other, separated only by Frederick, who is saying, with his hands over his ears, 'Zounds, the thunder of Valenciennes was music to this!'[2]

In May 1806 Mary Anne was informed by William Adam that her relationship with the duke was over, that she was required to leave her houses and that she would be paid £400 a year. In shock, she maintained that this was nothing like enough to meet the debts she had run up and she felt wronged and aggrieved, to put it mildly. A less skilful and manipulative woman might have melted into obscurity but Mary Anne plotted revenge. She became the lover of William Dowler, an official in the commissariat, and in June 1808, when the duke discontinued payments on the grounds that she was being insufficiently discreet, she blackmailed him by threatening to publish their love letters if she did not receive a far more generous 'pension'.

This increasingly public animosity between the duke and his former mistress was steadily developed by a small but determined group of men into a plot to discredit him, and through him, the government. In 1806 Henry Dundas, Viscount Melville, had been impeached in the House of Lords for alleged financial misdemeanours when he held the office of treasurer of the admiralty between 1782 and 1800. Although he was acquitted, his reputation was seriously discredited. His case showed that it was possible to bring down one of the most powerful politicians in Britain, despite his close friendship with William Pitt. The Duke of York might be a royal prince, but he held a public office and he was not beyond the reach of the law.

One of the 'plotters' was Captain Dodd, secretary to Frederick's brother, the Duke of Kent. Kent was also a professional soldier, but an unsatisfactory one because of his excessive attention to matters of discipline, which tended to cause unrest wherever he held command. In 1803 he was recalled by York from his post as Governor of Gibraltar, where he almost caused a mutiny. York had never been keen to advance the professional career of his brother because he was aware of his weaknesses, and Kent resented this. However, Kent was a field marshal and it seemed to Dodd (who was clearly daydreaming) that if the Duke of York could be toppled, his master would have a good chance of becoming commander-in-chief himself.

Two more malcontents were Pierre McCallum, who had unsuccessfully appealed to York against what he considered unjust treatment from General Picton when he was serving in Santo Domingo, and Captain Glennie, who had a grudge against the entire military establishment as a consequence of being dismissed (although not by York) from the Royal Artillery. These three men knew each other and, over time, hatched their plot. They needed someone with political influence and recruited Colonel Gwyllym Lloyd Wardle, a retired militia officer from Mold in North Wales, who had a rich wife and who had become MP for Okehampton in 1807. He was a member of the radical opposition, led by Sir Francis Burdett and Samuel Whitbread, who had instigated the impeachment of Melville. Despite being a recently elected backbencher, Wardle had already gained some prominence by alleging corruption in the granting of army clothing contracts, which were part of the Duke of York's responsibilities. His general motive was political: if the commander-in-chief were to be disgraced, the government which supported him might well fall also.[3]

These four men proposed to Mary Anne Clarke that she should help them bring down the duke by making public the fact that, while she was his mistress, she took money from officers who wanted military promotion. There is no doubt that she did this and that the amounts were considerable. Naturally, she intimated to the men concerned that her influence with the duke was so great that any wish of hers would be granted. In return for admitting these activities, the conspirators promised that she would receive £100 as a down payment, and be moved to a house in Westbourne Place until a new house was furnished for her. Then the four men took Mary Anne on what was ostensibly a four-day inspection of the south coast Martello tower defences, during which time she told them as much incriminating detail as she could remember.

On 20 January 1809 Colonel Wardle announced in the Commons that he intended to propose a motion about the conduct of the Duke of York and on the 27th he formally called for a committee of investigation into a number of detailed charges against him. At this point Spencer Perceval, the chancellor of the exchequer and leader of the House of Commons, made a disastrous decision. He was so convinced that the charges against the duke would quickly be considered ludicrous that he decided they would be heard not in private by a board of inquiry, but in the most public way possible, by a Committee of the Whole House. Under this procedure the House of Commons switched from being a legislative body to its other function as a high court of law. The rules of an ordinary law court did not apply: the accused was neither present nor represented, and evidence was not taken on oath.

The detailed charges that Wardle put before the House were that a Captain Tonyn had paid Mrs Clarke to be promoted major, that she had taken money 'to hasten the exchange of lieutenant-colonels Brooke and Knight', that a Major Shaw had paid to be made barrack-master at the Cape of Good Hope, and that as he only paid half the fee she asked, he was placed on half-pay. Furthermore she obtained for a Colonel French the right to raise a levy of troops in Ireland and secured rapid promotion to the rank of captain for one Malling, who had been merely a clerk in the office of an army agent. Mrs Clarke also, allegedly, acquired a commission for her footman, Samuel Carter. The duke must have known about all these matters, argued Wardle, so he was guilty of corruption.[4]

On 27 January Sir Arthur Wellesley told the House of Commons that in his experience the records of army promotions were meticulously kept in the commander-in-chief's office, 'so that all these transactions may be completely traced through their history'. As to the case of the barrack-master, he said, 'such removals are circumstances of common occurrence'. Addressing the Speaker, he concluded:

There is still, Sir, one topic upon which I would feel myself much to blame if I did not now say a few words. I allude, Sir, to the state of the army which I had the honour to have under my command last summer. I am bound to declare, Sir, that never was there an army in a better state, so far as its condition depended upon the care and exertion of the Commander-in-Chief. Nay, Sir, I must go further because I must say that, if the army had not performed the service for which it was destined, the blame would not have rested with the Commander-in-Chief but with myself; and whatever enthusiasm they felt in the execution of that service was the result of the example set, and the discipline established, by the illustrious personage at the head of the army.[5]

The House began to listen to the evidence in this case on 1 February and the hearings lasted for seven weeks, with members often sitting well into the early hours, sometimes all night. Moreover, the evidence and arguments for and against were widely circulated in newspapers and pamphlets so that the case escalated to the status of a national scandal, obsessing not only the literate and influential classes but also the wider public. Too many mistakes, it was widely felt, had recently been made by the authorities. Back in 1806 the trial of Melville had dealt with alleged corruption in the administration of the navy; in January 1808 General Whitelocke had been court-martialled and cashiered for surrendering his British force after a failed attempt to capture Buenos Aires; the Convention of Cintra had seemed to indicate incompetence and inefficiency in the military high command; and now the commander-in-chief himself was accused of selling commissions. And all this at a time when the war was going extremely badly, General Moore had been killed at Corunna, and British forces had been driven from the Peninsula.

For the first three weeks the House laboriously sifted through the evidence, calling many witnesses, including Mary Anne, who appeared twelve times. With her blue gown, striking looks and coquettish manner, she became a star attraction. Alfred Burne describes her as 'undoubtedly one of the cleverest courtesans of her century and among the most remarkable women of her generation', noting that she had 'gained an astonishing hold on members by her air of assurance, her flashing wit, her ready retort, and her pert and saucy manner'. Indeed, the contemporary *Annual Register* considered that she 'carried her ease, gaiety and pleasantry to a degree of pertness which was very reprehensible'. However, many members were gradually impressed by what she had to say, while to the mob outside she became a heroine.[6]

At first it seemed clear that, as far as Wardle's initial charges were concerned, they could be explained legitimately and there was no evidence in these instances that Mary Anne had taken money from any of the men concerned. However, as the case proceeded, a certain Captain Sandon produced forty-one letters from Mary Anne in which she mentioned a number of men who were looking for promotion and gave the impression that she could influence the duke in their favour. Only one letter actually incriminated the duke because it seemed to be written by him to Mary Anne, concerning Captain Tonyn; it read: 'I have just received your note, and Tonyn's business shall remain as it is – God bless you.' Hearing of this letter, the duke went immediately, even though it was late at night, to the house of his military secretary Colonel Gordon, and said to him indignantly 'This is most extraordinary: it must be a forgery,' and that remained his consistent view about the note, repeatedly stated. However, popular opinion was not disposed to believe him.[7]

Then Miss Taylor, a friend of Mary Anne, claimed that she had been present at dinner when Mary Anne and the duke discussed a Colonel French, while a letter from the duke to Mary Anne stated:

> [General] Clavering is mistaken in thinking that any new regiments are to be raised; it is not intended; only second battalions to the existing corps; you had better therefore tell him so and that you were sure there would be no use in applying for him.[8]

Mary Anne's butler later gave his opinion that Miss Taylor had never dined with her and the duke, while the Clavering letter was no proof of corruption, only that the duke did discuss military personnel with his mistress, as well as some of his military activities – although there was no harm in that. He told her in the same letter, for instance, written from Sandgate in August 1804, early on in their affair, that:

> Nothing could be more satisfactory than the tour I have made, and the state in which I have found everything. The whole of the day before yesterday was employed in visiting the works at Dover; reviewing the troops there, and examining the coast as far as this place. From Folkestone I had a very good view of those of the French camp. Yesterday I reviewed the camp here, and afterwards the 14th Light Dragoons, who are certainly in very fine order; and from thence proceeded to Brabourne Lees to see four regiments of militia, which altogether took me up near thirteen hours. I am now setting off immediately to ride along the coast to Hastings, reviewing the different corps as I pass, which will take me at least as long. Adieu, therefore, my sweetest, Dearest Love, till the day after to-morrow, and be assured that to my last hour I shall ever remain, Yours and Yours alone.

Unfortunately, other parts of this letter contained enthusiastically amorous passages that seemed laughable and embarrassing when read aloud to the House of Commons, as intimate communications between lovers are bound to do:

> How can I sufficiently express to my Darling Love my thanks for her dear, dear, letter or the delight which the assurances of her love give me? Oh, My Angel! Do me justice and be convinced that there never was a woman so

adored as you are. Every day, every hour, convinces me more and more that my whole happiness depends upon you alone. What a time it appears to be since we parted, and with what impatience do I look forward to the day after tomorrow: there are still, however, two whole nights before I shall clasp my darling in my arms! . . .[9]

Another letter, written a year later, was equally full of amorous declarations:

How can I sufficiently express to my Sweetheart, my Darling Love, the delight which her dear, her pretty letter gave me, or how much I feel all the kind things she says to me in it? Millions and millions of thanks for it, My Angel, and be assured that my heart is fully sensible of your affection, and that upon it alone its whole happiness depends . . . What a time it appears to me already, My Darling, since we parted. How impatiently I look forward to next Wednesday night![10]

These letters did not make a good impression and public hostility to the duke grew stronger. Many MPs, at first quite sure of his innocence, began to wonder. Sir Arthur Wellesley, who witnessed the trial from his seat as an MP and (as chief secretary for Ireland) a member of the government, was questioned at the end of this period of the trial and loyally defended the duke. He told the House:

I know that since His Royal Highness has had command of the army, the regulations framed by him for managing the promotion of the army have been strictly adhered to, and that the mode in which the promotion is conducted has given general satisfaction . . . the officers are improved in knowledge; that the staff of the army is much better than it was . . . that the system of subordination among the officers in the army is better than it was . . . and everything that relates to the military discipline of the soldiers and the military efficiency of the army has been greatly improved since His Royal Highness was appointed Commander-in-Chief. . . . The improvements to which I have adverted, have been owing to the regulations of His Royal Highness and to his personal superintendence and his personal exertions over the general officers and others who were to see those regulations carried into execution.[11]

Wellesley had been 'positively certain' that the duke was innocent of any corruption when the trial began and felt common cause with him when Mary Anne even hinted that Sir Arthur himself was involved in improper conduct (he certainly had a mistress at the time). As effigies of York were burnt by mobs in Suffolk and Yorkshire, Wellesley told the Duke of Richmond that this was because country people were shocked about the revelations concerning his private life. Gradually, however, he came to the conclusion that York would have to go or he would pull the government down with him. It was unlikely, he thought, that York did not at least suspect what was going on, and he wondered whether 'a Prince of the Blood, who has manifested so much weakness as he has, and has led such a life (for that is material in these days), is a proper person to be entrusted with the duties of a responsible office'. There was more than a touch of hypocrisy here: Wellesley, like York, had a wife and many mistresses, and his Kitty was neglected far more than York's Frederica.[12]

Aware that the tide was running against him, York wrote a formal letter the day after the completion of the taking of evidence on 22 February to Spencer Perceval, the Speaker of the House, in which he said:

> With respect to any alleged offences connected with the discharge of my official duties, I do, in the most solemn manner, on my honour as a Prince, distinctly assert my innocence, not only by denying all corrupt participation in any of the infamous transactions which have appeared in evidence at the bar of the House of Commons, or any connivance at their existence, but also the slightest knowledge or suspicion that they existed at all.[13]

After this, the House turned its attention to the war once more, only to return on 8 March to debate the evidence in the Clarke case, one of the longest debates ever known in the Commons. Spencer Perceval opened with a powerful speech in defence of the duke, which he adjourned at 3.30 am and completed the next day. The second defence came from Francis Burton, a blind judge noted for his brilliant grasp of details and exposition, who damned Mary Clarke's evidence as a tissue of lies, citing at least twenty-eight falsehoods. Finally there came an outstandingly forensic speech by the Irish lawyer and MP John Wilson Croker, who showed convincingly that, despite Mary Anne's claims that she had secured the appointment of many a suitor, the evidence did not bear this out. Opposing speeches, mostly falling back on 'sweeping assertions and general abuse', came from Samuel Whitbread (the leader of the opposition), William Wilberforce, Lord Folkestone and the well-known radical, Sir Francis Burdett.

The debate that began on Thursday, 16 March dragged on until 6.30 am the following morning before at last a division was taken on Wardle's motion, which stated that a number of specified abuses could not have existed 'without the knowledge of the Commander-in-Chief', and that 'the Duke of York ought to be deprived of the command of the army'. The motion was lost by 241 votes, 123 for and 364 against. As the wording of this motion did not mention the duke's possible corruption through knowledge of Mary Anne's activities, another motion was proposed that afternoon which declared 'that there were grounds from the evidence at the bar to charge HRH with a knowledge of these practices, with connivance at them, and consequently with corruption'. This was defeated by 334 votes to 135, a reduced majority of 199. Spencer Perceval then proposed a third motion, that there were no grounds on which to charge the duke with personal corruption or connivance, but this was passed by 278 to 196, a majority of only 82. Perceval managed to postpone a further motion, calling upon the duke to resign, from that Friday to the following Monday, and the next day, Saturday, 18 March, the duke resigned of his own accord.

In very few nations at this time would a favourite son of the king, third in line to the throne, who had proved himself without question a very able military administrator, have been forced into this position as the result of a parliamentary trial in which the evidence had been far from conclusive. It would have been unthinkable, for instance, in Russia, Prussia, Austria and even in post-revolutionary Napoleonic France, by now more or less a dictatorship. In that sense, the Clarke affair is a fine testimony to the extent to which Great Britain was truly a constitutional monarchy and not far from being a democracy. Addressing the question of why so many voted against the duke, Alfred Burne came to this conclusion:

United in the same lobby were members of many different factions. There were Jacobins and Republicans, who saw in this case a grand opportunity to aim a blow at the throne. There were the less extreme partisans of the Opposition, who, when they saw the Government ranged on one side, instinctively favoured the other. There were persons of the strong Puritan strain who felt they were striking a blow for morality. There were those whose legal faculties were not strongly developed and who were swayed by sentiment and the strong effect of a mass of apparently incriminating evidence, in the absence of the duke's own testimony. Finally, there were those who were frankly swayed by the popular clamour outside, and either by fear or by favour of the mob voted in the way that they hoped would render them popular with that mob – as it did.[14]

With the resignation of the duke, who was replaced by General Sir David Dundas, Colonel Wardle became a national hero, the object of florid expressions of thanks and adulation from municipal authorities and social organizations across the entire country. On 19 June he made a three-hour speech in the Commons demanding reforms in the military administration, which the government felt obliged to accept. The City of London voted him its freedom, presented in a silver box worth a hundred guineas, noting that 'Colonel Wardle is deserving the thanks of the country for his manly and independent conduct in having boldly dared single-handed to attack the Hydra of corruption, and to assail her even in her very den.' A book about his achievements was soon published, claiming that he had been 'instrumental in obtaining a new era in British politics'. Mary Anne, meanwhile, became the toast of London.[15] She soon announced that her memoirs were about to be published, and because of their damaging nature, she was able to procure a settlement by which in return for her rights to the memoirs and any letters concerning the Duke of York in her possession, she would receive a cash payment of £7,000, as well as the restoration of her £400 annuity. She duly handed over all the letters (so she claimed) and 18,000 copies of her memoirs were burned.[16]

However, this bizarre story had an even more remarkable end. His main aim having been achieved, Wardle made the serious error of sidelining Mary Anne and conveniently forgot his promise to pay for the furnishings of her new house. An upholsterer named Francis Wright sued him for payment and Mary Anne appeared as a witness when the case was tried before the lord chief justice, Lord Ellenborough, on 3 July 1809. The prosecutor was the attorney-general, which signified the government's determination to strike back at Wardle, and he lost the case and had to pay £1,300 in damages. Worse still, for him, was the fact that during the trial Mary Anne got her own back by telling the whole story of how Wardle and his associates had bribed her to incriminate the Duke of York, whom she now cast in a more favourable light.

The day after this trial Wardle wrote a piece entitled 'To the people of the United Kingdom', which claimed that he had lost the case because of lies told by the witnesses and he made arrangements to sue Mary Anne, Francis Wright and others for 'conspiracy'. Lord Ellenborough heard this case in December 1809 but the jury found against Wardle after Ellenborough stated that he had undoubtedly used bribery. These two cases produced a new sensation, which provoked articles and pamphlets from the supporters of both sides. In 1810 Mary Anne herself, who could write in a talented journalistic style, produced a thoroughly libellous work entitled *The Rival Princes*, in which she suggested that the plot had originated in the jealous mind of Frederick's brother the Duke of Kent, abetted by Wardle. She also stated, very frankly, that she would not have put herself through the huge strain of the Westminster trial and public exposure merely for the sake of what she described as 'a pure patriotic zeal to serve the public'. She did it for the promised financial benefits, she wrote, and she had been swindled out of these.

Wardle's reputation and his finances were both ruined by the two verdicts against him. He was not re-elected as an MP in 1812 and to avoid his creditors he left for the continent and lived in Florence, where he died in 1833. Mary Anne continued to write libellous pamphlets and articles but she came seriously unstuck in the summer of 1813 when she was successfully sued for libel by the youthful and ambitious William Fitzgerald, a lord of the treasury and chancellor of the Irish exchequer. In an open letter she had written: 'I am anxious in the first place to caution the Irish nation in particular against the intrigues of one of the most vicious and profligate of men, who at present most mysteriously presides over the finances of that nation . . .' The letter continued in this manner for many pages, accusing Fitzgerald of various improprieties, such as seducing the wife of a friend. These were falsehoods inspired by Mary Anne's desire for revenge against the Fitzgeralds, who had destroyed a letter from the Duke of York, which, she alleged, had promised a commission for her son George.

When Fitzgerald sued for libel, she could only plead guilty and engaged the services of the able lawyer Henry Brougham to try to secure a light sentence. In fact, she was sentenced to nine months in the Marshalsea Prison for London debtors, where, according to a complaint she sent to Samuel Whitbread, she was badly treated. She claimed that she was put in a cell nine feet square with a small barricaded window and that she was denied fresh air and exercise, becoming seriously ill as a result. However, while she was in prison her son George reached his sixteenth birthday and on 17 March 1814 he received a commission 'without purchase' as a cornet in the 17th Lancers. This could not have happened without the express permission of the Duke of York, by then restored as commander-in-chief.[17]

Mary Anne was released in November 1814 and she left the country in disgrace to live in Paris with her daughter Ellen. She was thirty-eight years old and lived many years longer, dying in Boulogne in 1852. During her Paris years she was visited by a few loyal English friends, one of whom, Lord Queensbury, found that her manners were remarkable, that she still retained traces of her past beauty in old age, was still lively, sprightly and full of fun and still telling scandalous stories about the royal family.[18] Her son George enjoyed a respectable career in the army, while her daughter Ellen, no great beauty, in due course married a minor French nobleman and somewhat eccentric inventor called du Maurier. Their son was George du Maurier (1834–1896), a famous cartoonist and illustrator for *Punch* and the author of a popular novel, *Trilby*, which gave its name to the hat and became one of the first 'best-sellers'. His son was Sir Gerald du Maurier (1873–1934), a famous actor and theatre manager in his day, and his daughters were Angela (1904–2002) and Dame Daphne du

Maurier (1907–1989), both well-known novelists. The latter was fascinated by Mary Anne and set out to discover whether there was any foundation in the du Maurier rumour that Ellen was in fact the daughter of the Duke of York, and that royal blood flowed in the du Maurier veins. She wrote an account of her family's history in 1934 and a book entitled *Mary Anne* in 1954, both of which were essentially historical novels. However, neither in real life nor in fiction did she ever claim descent from the Duke of York.

# Chapter Eleven

## Out of a Job, 1809–1811

The Duke of York's reaction to his disgrace and resignation was to retire quietly to Oatlands and his wife. The trial at Westminster had involved the reading out of love letters sent by York to Mary Anne, which must have been mortifying for Frederica. According to Roger Fulford:

> Six hundred men had sat rocking with laughter while his love letters to Mrs Clarke were read: they had been distributed by the newspapers to every corner of the country. Mrs Clarke's drunken butlers and abandoned friends had come forward to say how they had seen the Duke and Mrs Clarke together and how it had been 'Darling this' and 'Darling that' between them. [The duke] could hear the children in the street, as they tossed up those heavy Georgian pennies, crying out 'Duke or Darling', instead of 'Heads or Tails'. The figure of Britannia on the obverse side was made to do service for Mrs Clarke.[1]

No doubt Frederica needed some winning round, but most of the royal family, especially the king, were sympathetic, while York's sister Princess Augusta wrote to a friend of hers, 'I have seen many military men and live chiefly in intimacy with men of that profession. All agree that the army owes everything to the duke. ... I am also miserable to think that the Methodists are doing all the harm to him they can and there are many of them in this country, they are vile canters, cheating the devil, paying with their mouths but denying with their hearts; and they think it will command popularity to condemn and abuse the Duke of York for what I daresay they do themselves.'[2]

The Prince of Wales, however, was worried by the Clarke scandal, partly because it showed what might happen to him should his own illegal marriage and illicit relationships come to light. Being far from popular with the public himself, he was concerned that his brother's disgrace would weaken his own position. He tried to distance himself from the whole matter and announced, 'I have been no party to my brother's irregularities. I have never been connected with the women with whom my brother has been connected. Indeed, I dislike such society.'[3]

Meanwhile, there was still a war on. After the evacuation of the British army from Corunna, the *Junta*, or council, of patriots in Spain signed a treaty with the UK in January 1809 as Napoleon himself left Spain and handed over the French armies to Marshal Soult, who invaded Portugal and captured Porto. In April Wellesley was appointed as supreme commander of a new British army bound for Portugal, and as the Duke of York was no longer commander-in-chief, the fact that he was still a junior general was overlooked. Moreover, the king had no doubt been informed of Wellesley's loyal evidence in the House in favour of the duke. He arrived in Lisbon late in April and in May drove the French out of Porto. He then joined forces with the Spanish and won the battle of Talavera in July, receiving a peerage as Viscount Wellington in August.

At this point, it might have been sensible to reinforce Wellington's army but instead Castlereagh, the war minister, went ahead with yet another ill-starred expedition to the Netherlands. A force of 40,000 men, with artillery and siege trains, sailed across to Walcheren Island in July 1809, intending to destroy the French fleet in Flushing harbour and take the pressure off Britain's Austrian allies. However, by the time the expedition had arrived, the Austrians had already been defeated at Wagram, and although Flushing was captured, the French fleet had by then moved to Antwerp. Worse still, some 8,000 men caught malaria fever, and British medical supplies were inadequate to deal with this epidemic. In September the expedition was abandoned, with heavy casualties. It was a far more ignominious affair than York's Helder campaign had ever been. York, of course, was not involved in the planning of the Walcheren campaign, because of his resignation, and in the view of military historian Roger Knight, writing in 2013, 'the duke's judgement and authority were sorely missed when he resigned'.[4]

Walcheren was Castlereagh's scheme, conceived against the strong advice of George Canning, the foreign secretary, who felt that it was a pointless diversion and that the troops should be sent to Wellington in the Peninsula. Relations between the two men became so bad that Castlereagh, said to be a very fine shot, challenged Canning, who was very inexperienced in this regard, to a duel, which took place on 21 September on Putney Heath. Canning missed, but Castlereagh wounded him in the thigh, much to the disgust of the general public. When the Duke of Portland resigned as prime minister because of ill-health the following month, the king considered neither Castlereagh nor Canning for the post, despite the fact that they were the two most brilliant ministers in the cabinet, and instead appointed Spencer Perceval. A small, slight man, he was the younger son of an Irish earl, and, in the mould of his hero

Pitt, he was modest in his tastes, incorruptible and hard-working. He gave the post of war minister to the Earl of Liverpool, while Richard Wellesley became foreign secretary.

From November 1809 onwards Wellington, impressed by the Martello towers in the UK, began the construction of complex lines of forts known as the 'Lines of Torres Vedras', stretching from that town south to Lisbon, with a branch out to Cintra. A large French army under Masséna was checked by Wellington at Busaco, after which his Anglo-Portuguese force retreated behind the lines, forcing Masséna's increasingly starving and diseased soldiers to return to France for provisions and reinforcements. Masséna returned in 1811 but was checked by Wellington at Fuentes de Onoro and by Beresford at Albuera, but at the end of the year the French remained in possession of the strategically vital towns of Ciudad Rodrigo and Badajoz.

At home, there had also been dramatic events. On 25 October 1810 the nation celebrated the fiftieth anniversary of George III's accession to the throne, but on that very day the king slipped once more into a state of mental turmoil, generally thought at the time to have been caused by the long illness and impending death from consumption of his favourite daughter, the young Princess Amelia. He remained confused for the next few months and agreed with Spencer Perceval, who had been prime minister for the last year, that it was time to unload many of his responsibilities. Accordingly an Act of Parliament appointed the Prince of Wales as prince regent from 6 February 1811 and in May he reappointed his brother commander-in-chief after Sir David Dundas obligingly retired.

This move greatly pleased the king, and the queen wrote to the prince regent on 23 May that, 'He desired me to return you his thanks for having employed me to convey such agreeable news, and to assure you that he never could forget your conduct upon this occasion.' Unfortunately the king's illness worsened in July and he became so violent that restraint was necessary. By 1812 he had lost touch with the real world and was excessively talkative, although otherwise calm. By 1814 his doctors did not expect a recovery and he remained at Windsor, in the official care of the queen and visited daily by his doctors, all of whom charged high fees for pronouncing on a regular basis that he was no better.

In June 1811 the prince regent inaugurated what would become nine years of 'Regency' England with a fabulous dinner and ball for 2,000 guests, held at Carlton House, ostensibly in honour of the exiled Bourbon claimant to the throne of France (later Louis XVIII). On this occasion the prince wore the elaborate, gold-bedecked uniform of a field marshal, a rank he had lost no time in bestowing upon himself. Soon afterwards, another lavish ball was given by the Duke and Duchess of Devonshire, where again women dressed in the height of fashion and men wore brilliant uniforms spangled with gold. The prince, having waited impatiently for the reality of power, was determined to enjoy it.

There was very little public opposition to the reappointment of the Duke of York as commander-in-chief, though the government faced a motion of censure from die-hard radicals in the Commons for permitting it. The MPs were the same as in 1809, but several rose to say that they regretted their former vote cast against the duke, and when a member remarked that 'the Duke of York had been victim of a foul conspiracy', Hansard recorded that the speaker 'was interrupted by a general cry of "Hear, Hear" from all parts of the House'. Colonel Wardle was present and voted for the motion, which was defeated by 297 to 47 votes.[5]

## Last Stages of the War, 1811–1815

When the Duke of York resigned as commander-in-chief in March 1809 there was no significant change of direction in military policy at the Horse Guards. This was largely because he was succeeded by Sir David Dundas, aged seventy-four, who had been for some time his deputy there. Dundas had been a divisional commander under York at the Helder, he was a personal friend and he had himself written several important manuals on training, most notably his *Principles of Military Movements* of 1788, which York had used as the basis for his own reforms. Moreover, Dundas, who was appointed directly by the king without ministerial consultation, understood perfectly well that his role was to mount a holding operation at Horse Guards until it was time for the duke to return.

One of the results of the Clarke affair was that rapid promotion within the army began to be looked upon with grave suspicion. Immediately on taking over as commander-in-chief, Dundas had to deal with a case of alleged favouritism regarding promotions in the army, which was the subject of a debate and division in the Commons, which the government lost. After this, Dundas was very cautious, much to the annoyance of Wellington, who frequently recommended the promotion of his favoured officers, without success. In January 1811 Wellington complained in frustration that 'I am the commander of the British army without any of the patronage or power that an officer in this situation has always had. I have remonstrated against this system in vain.' York, when restored to the Horse Guards in 1811, did not feel able to change the system of promotion by rotation and seniority, but he did at least assure Wellington of his 'cordial support in the dismissal of any officer, from the senior general to the lowest ensign'. Even so, Wellington considered, as late as March 1814, that 'the utter incapacity of some officers at the head of regiments ... and the apathy and unwillingness of others' was caused by 'the promotion of officers in regiments by regular rotation, thus holding forth no reward to merit or exertion'.[6]

The prince regent had initially been given limited powers, in case his father should recover, but in February 1812 the limitations came to an end and the Whig party, which the prince had favoured throughout his life, hoped that he would dismiss Spencer Perceval's Tory administration in favour of a Whig ministry led by Lords Grenville and Grey. However, as often happens, the overall scene usually looks different when one is sitting in the top job and the regent realized that this was not the time to cause major disruption in the domestic political world, when everyone needed to concentrate on the war. So he wrote a letter to York 'expressing the gratification I should feel if some of those persons with whom the early habits of my life were formed, would strengthen my hand and constitute a part of my Government'. In other words, he was suggesting a coalition, and he entrusted York with the task of conveying this to Grenville and Grey. York showed them the regent's letter, but they said that they disagreed too much with the Tories over Ireland and Catholic Emancipation to join the government. York then seems to have suggested that, in that case, the regent would probably allow them to form their own government. This was, of course, not the case and York was made to look somewhat foolish when the regent was obliged to make this clear. According to the diarist Thomas Creevey, the regent, in his mock-jocular way, when introducing his brother to him on an earlier occasion, said, 'He's a damned bad politician, Creevey, but I'll introduce you to him.'[7]

A few weeks after this, in the late afternoon of 11 May 1812, Spencer Perceval walked into the lobby of the House of Commons on his way to a routine meeting and was shot in the chest with a pistol at point-blank range. He died a few minutes later. He was aged fifty-nine and he left a widow and twelve children. His assassin was John Bellingham, a merchant, who made no attempt to escape. He had decided to kill Perceval because he had been, in his view, unjustly imprisoned in Russia for debt and the British government had failed to secure his release or provide compensation. At his trial he was found to be sane, and was duly hanged. Perceval's place as prime minister was taken by the Tory Robert Jenkinson, Earl of Liverpool, aged forty-one, whose post as war minister went to Henry, Earl Bathurst, aged forty-nine. Both men remained in these offices for the next fifteen years and both were a 'safe pair of hands' with whom the Duke of York maintained very good relations.

In the Peninsula, during the course of 1812 Wellington captured Ciudad Rodrigo and Badajoz and then routed the French at Salamanca in July. But an attempt to push northwards into France was prevented by his failure to capture Burgos and he was forced to retreat behind his lines in Portugal. By June 1813 he had emerged to destroy Joseph Bonaparte's army at Vitoria, after which he crossed the frontier into France. Soult successfully resisted him at Toulouse but then agreed to a ceasefire after hearing of the defeat of Napoleon by the combined armies of Russia, Prussia, Austria and Sweden at Leipzig in October. By March 1814 the coalition armies had captured Paris and in April Napoleon was deposed and exiled to the island of Elba.

This apparent end to the conflict with France allowed Britain to concentrate more fully on a war with the United States, which had broken out in June 1812 when Congress declared war on Britain. The main reason given was a series of trade restrictions imposed by Britain on all countries trading with France, as well as resentment at the Royal Navy's interference with American ships on the high seas, the impressments of American sailors and British support for Indian tribes. The early stages of the war were mainly defensive but, after Napoleon's abdication, experienced regiments from Europe were sent out to the USA and it was even mooted that Wellington himself should take command. The British General Prevost was defeated at Plattsburg, but another British force landed at Chesapeake Bay, captured Washington and set the White House ablaze.

In December 1814 negotiators meeting in Ghent signed a treaty which restored relations and boundaries to what they had been before the war began. But before news of the treaty reached America, a British invasion of Louisiana in January 1815 led to the defeat at New Orleans of Wellington's brother-in-law General 'Ned' Pakenham, who was beaten back with heavy losses by General Andrew Jackson. This gave the USA a boost in morale, although in truth they gained little from the war and their hopes of taking over territory in Canada were dashed.

The defeat and abdication of Napoleon soon led to the collapse of his Kingdom of Westphalia and the return of the former Hanoverian electorate to the British crown. In 1814 the Congress of Vienna created an enlarged Kingdom of Hanover, which included the former Prince-Bishopric of Osnabrück, so that George III, secluded in Windsor, now became the wearer of four crowns. As commander-in-chief, York was given due credit for his part in the defeat of Napoleon. When the restored King Louis XVIII visited London in April 1814, he invested both the prince regent and York with the French insignia of the Holy Spirit, in thanks for 'the restoration of myself and family to our beloved country, and to the throne of our ancestors'.[8] Inevitably, the real hero was Wellington, now the recipient of a dukedom and a parliamentary grant of nearly half a million pounds. After taking his seat in the Lords, he asked if he could thank the Commons in person, and was granted permission to do so. He also made a point of referring to the role of the Duke of York over the years. According to John Watkins,

> on the first of July the noble warrior made his appearance in the body of the house, all the members rising uncovered at his entrance. After a short pause, he addressed the Speaker in a plain and modest speech, expressive of his obligations to the parliament for its liberality, and to the government for its energy, during the arduous services in which he had been engaged. The noble duke, on this occasion, took the opportunity of paying a tribute of respect to the commander-in-chief, which was the more impressive for being couched in a few simple words.[9]

The House also passed a vote of thanks to York for his part in the victory and he wrote to the Speaker that: 'It is with particular pride I learn that the favour of the House of Commons has induced them to ascribe to any effort of mine the smallest share in securing these splendid successes.'[10]

Tsar Alexander of Russia and King Frederick William of Prussia came to London at the beginning of June and were treated to a round of festivities, with York prominent among the hosts. He accompanied them on a visit to Oxford, where they received honorary degrees, at a civic banquet at the Guildhall and at a naval review at Portsmouth. At one point the Tsar asked Frederick where the English kept their poor, as he had seen none so far on his visit. The next day Frederick took him to see St Martin's workhouse in London, but the Tsar still asked where the really impoverished people were kept. He was told that every parish had a similar workhouse, where the poor were cared for under the law, and the Tsar exclaimed: 'It is no wonder that England is mistress of the world.' Also that summer York laid the foundation stone of the Westminster National School for the education of a thousand children and early the next year the prince regent appointed him Grand Master of the Order of the Bath, now reorganized so that more military honours could be distributed to veterans of the war.[11]

Celebration of the defeat of Napoleon proved to be premature, however, because he escaped from Elba late in February 1815 and made a successful appeal to the French people and army to turn out the Bourbons once more and follow him. The allies, who had been planning post-Napoleonic Europe at the Congress of Vienna, decided, despite the reluctance of some nations, to resort to force yet again. There was an Austrian army in Italy, another one on the upper Rhine and a Prussian army on the lower Rhine.

After a good deal of argument and discussion among the allies, and even in the UK Parliament, Wellington was given overall command of a combined British, Hanoverian, Brunswick and Netherlands force totalling about 92,000 men, with 120 guns. The largest element in this force came from the new 'Kingdom of the Netherlands', founded as recently as March 1815. This new state, incorporating both 'Holland' and 'Belgium', had been set up with the blessing of the Congress of Vienna, and its king was the former hereditary crown prince who had campaigned with the Duke of York. His son, the Prince of Orange, nicknamed 'Slender Billy' because of his very thin neck, was in command of many of the Dutch–Belgian forces, despite being only twenty-two years old. His inexperience, and the fact that many of his 40,000 troops came from French-speaking parts of Belgium, gave Wellington cause to be anxious about the reliability of these allies. Another 16,000 troops came directly from Hanover and Brunswick but they, too, were relatively inexperienced.

The Duke of York and his Horse Guards administrators were faced with assembling as strong a British force as possible, given that many seasoned troops were still in the United States, that many other veterans had already been released from the service and that a good many opposition MPs even opposed the renewal of warfare. The army that York eventually provided for Wellington consisted of about 30,000 British troops (including Irish) in twenty-two battalions, as well as 6,000 men of the highly dependable King's German Legion. Fifteen of the British battalions had served with Wellington in the Peninsula campaign, although veteran soldiers mingled in the ranks with recent recruits and militia. However, as a result of York's military reforms and capable administration, this was a very efficient force, well trained, highly disciplined and well equipped. About 20,000 of the men were infantry, in whom Wellington had the greatest confidence.

Despite Wellington's eminent military reputation, York's instructions to him on taking up this command left no doubt that his authority had limits. He wrote:

On all subjects relating to your Grace's command you will be pleased to correspond with me or with my Military Secretary for my information, and your Grace will regularly communicate to me all vacancies that may occur in the troops under your command, and as the power of appointing to commissions is not vested in you, you will be pleased to recommend to me such officers as may appear to you most deserving of promotion, stating the special reasons where such recommendations are not in the usual channel of seniority.

The Waterloo historian David Hamilton-Williams regards this instruction as unduly officious, but York was surely right, faced with a campaign that could well change the course of European history, to make it clear exactly where each man's responsibilities lay. Moreover, York's military secretary at this time, Major-General Sir Henry Torrens, was, as Hamilton-Williams admits, 'devoted to the Peninsula hero and assisted him to the limit of his authority', something he would not have done without York's express approval.[12]

By the summer Wellington and the impressive Prussian army of his ally Marshal Blücher, about 120,000 strong with 350 cannon, were in the countryside south of Brussels, waiting for Napoleon, with his army of 125,000 men and 350 cannon, to make a move. On 15 June Wellington and many of his officers attended a ball given in Brussels by the Duchess of Richmond, whose husband, as young Charles Lennox, had nearly killed the Duke of York in the famous duel years before. The following day the French drove the Prussians back in a battle at Ligny, but they were checked at Quatre Bras by Wellington's coalition forces. On the 17th Napoleon probably made a serious mistake by remaining relatively inactive, which allowed Wellington to position his army along a ridge near the small town of Waterloo, placing defenders in the strategically vital walled farms of Hougoumont and La Haye Sainte. There he prepared to give battle, assured by Blücher, who had regrouped about fourteen miles away, of his support. After a night of torrential rain which brought misery to all combatants, the French attacked the defenders of Hougoumont at around 11.30 am on Sunday, 18 June, although both it and La Haye Sainte successfully held out. French cavalry regiments then made repeated attacks on Wellington's infantry squares, alternating with artillery fire that caused massive damage inside the allied ranks. By 6.30 pm the French had at last captured La Haye Sainte and Wellington's position began to look perilous because the Prussians had been held up by boggy terrain and French attacks.

Fortunately, a frontal assault on Wellington by the infantry of Napoleon's allegedly undefeatable Imperial Guard was beaten back by musket fire at close range and this, combined with the arrival of the Prussians in full force, led to a French retreat which soon became a rout. The two victorious commanders embraced on horseback at the former French stronghold of La Belle Alliance at about 9.00 pm, assured of a momentous victory. Wellington wrote to his brother Richard:

> It was the most desperate business I was ever in. I never took so much trouble about any battle, and was never so near being beat. Our loss is immense, particularly in the best of all Instruments, British Infantry. I never saw the Infantry behave so well.

He is reported to have said, subsequently, 'I hope to God I have fought my last battle ... I am wretched even at the moment of victory, and next to a battle lost, the greatest misery is a battle gained.'[13]

Fickle Paris turned against Napoleon once more and he abdicated on 22 June. After surrendering to the British, he was imprisoned on the remote island of St Helena, where he died in 1821. Louis XVIII again reigned in Paris and the French, who had been Britain's natural enemies for many centuries, now became allies. Powered by her industrial revolution and protected by her navy, Britain was poised to become a world power with a global empire. The outstanding generalship of Wellington had over many years played a critical role in the eventual defeat of Napoleon, but he could hardly have been successful in the Peninsula and at Waterloo without a well-trained and well-equipped British army and an efficient system of transportation and provision. For this, it can certainly be argued, the Duke of York must be given a great deal of the credit. This was also Wellington's publicly stated view, and the House of Commons responded again with a fulsome tribute to the Duke of York, voting:

> That the thanks of this House be given to His Royal Highness the Duke of York, Captain-General and Commander-in-Chief of the British forces, for his continual, effectual and unremitting attention to the duties of his office, for a period of more than twenty years, during which time the army has improved in discipline and in science to an extent unknown before; and, under Providence, risen to the height of military glory.[14]

## Keeping the Peace, 1815–1820

Britain's war against Revolutionary and Napoleonic France lasted, with only a short break, for over twenty years and it has been calculated that about a million men and boys from the British Isles fought in the army or the navy out of a population of about 14 million in 1800. Of those who fought, about 315,000 were killed.[15] Peace often brings as many problems as war, not least the question of how to demobilize a large army and an even larger navy. Lord Liverpool and his ministers were keen that the expense of maintaining a now unnecessary army should be reduced as soon as possible and this required great tact, diplomacy and administrative skill from the commander-in-chief. The vast majority of army officers went on to half pay, while many of the rank and file joined the forces of the unemployed at a time when mechanization had reduced the demand for manual labour. In fact, the years immediately after the war were a time of dangerous popular unrest in Britain. In 1799 and 1800 the government passed very unpopular laws which forbade working men to threaten strike action and there was a widespread recognition that the parliamentary system was corrupt and out-of-date. There were too many constituencies in the south with hardly any voters, while in the north populous new industrial towns had grown up without any representation in Parliament.

The extremes of the French Revolution were very recent history, fuelling the radicalism of some activists, while at the same time increasing the anxiety of the government. In 1815 ministers introduced a law which fixed the price of corn at levels favourable to the landowner rather than the consumer and there were serious riots in London as a result. In November 1816 about 10,000 people assembled on Spa Fields in Islington to listen to demands by the radical orator Henry Hunt for parliamentary reform, and an even larger crowd met there again one month later. Extremist elements, led by Arthur Thistlewood, planned revolutionary schemes, such as the capture of the Tower of London and the Bank of England, but these were foiled by the authorities.

In August 1819 a vast crowd of between 60,000 and 80,000 people met in St Peter's Fields in Manchester, again to listen to Hunt, and on this occasion the local magistrates panicked and instructed the militia to arrest him and disperse the crowd. An ill-advised cavalry charge led to the deaths of fifteen people, with many hundreds injured. Nicknamed 'the Peterloo Massacre', this outrage inflamed public opinion, especially when the government passed the 'Six Acts' in December, which tightened up the rules on seditious publications and potentially dangerous meetings and gave magistrates increased powers to search individuals and property. All this provoked an extreme response from Arthur Thistlewood, who persuaded twenty-seven men to agree to arm themselves with pistols and grenades, burst into a dinner party attended by most members of the cabinet in London and kill the lot of them, then cut off their heads and stick them on Westminster Bridge. Fortunately, there were double agents among the plotters: the scheme was foiled by the Bow Street Runners, and Thistlewood and four others were hanged.

As commander-in-chief during these years York was well aware of the problems of keeping the peace and he became increasingly committed to charitable and philanthropic causes, which he hoped would reduce discontent. In the summer of 1812 a group of people had decided to set up a charity to raise money for the poor and an initial meeting for this purpose was held at the Freemasons' Hall in London. York was a hundred miles away at the time, but on being told about the impending meeting he hastened to London in order to chair it. As a result:

His presence essentially aided the benevolent purpose, and the contributions exceeded the most sanguine hopes of those who projected the scheme. On this occasion the Duke expressed himself highly gratified, in having been able to forward the humane project, adding that he should be at all times happy in lending his assistance towards promoting any benevolent design; and that for this purpose he would most readily obey any call made upon him to preside, in order to further the ends of charity.[16]

He was as good as his word in July 1816 when he presided over a meeting at the London Tavern, attended by his brothers the dukes of Kent and Cambridge, as well as by the Archbishop of Canterbury, the Chancellor of the Exchequer and many other prominent people. The purpose was again to raise money for charitable purposes, and eventually £35,000 was achieved, the prince regent giving £500 and York £300.[17]

In April 1818 Queen Charlotte and the Duke of York were present in the Egyptian Hall of the Mansion House, which was used as an examination room for about 700 boys and 300 girls from the London National Schools. The children sang a hymn together and recited part of the Anglican church service before splitting into separate classes, where they did exercises in spelling and arithmetic. In May that year York presided over another meeting, at the Freemasons' Tavern, called to raise more funds for the National Schools movement. This was already providing training for about 500 teachers and education for some 165,000 children across the country in 276 schools. The queen and the prince regent gave £500 each, while York gave 100 guineas, and £5,000 was raised altogether. A few days later York chaired the anniversary meeting of the Yorkshire Society for the maintenance, clothing and education of the children of poor people from that county who were resident in London. He also kept a steady eye, during these post-war years, on the progress of his Royal Military Asylum for orphaned children in Chelsea.[18]

There can be little doubt that by now Frederick was widely admired and respected, both in the army and among the general public. Captain Gronow, a young officer who met him on several occasions in his later years, described him in his memoirs as:

Without exception one of the finest men England could boast of. He stood about six foot, was rather stout, but well proportioned, his chest broad and his frame muscular, and his face bore the stamp of authority and every feature was handsome. His brow was full and prominent, the eye greenish, beaming with benevolence, and a noble forehead completed the picture.[19]

## The Tragedy of Princess Charlotte

As we have seen, the prince regent married reluctantly in 1795, largely because he had already contracted a secret, and illegal, marriage to Maria Fitzherbert. However, he was desperately in need of money and Pitt promised him a handsome parliamentary grant if he would marry a suitable princess and produce an heir. But Princess Caroline of Brunswick, the daughter of his father's elder sister, indiscreet, gauche and insensitive, was not the right woman for him, as he knew when he first met her. By then it was too late, as they had already been married by proxy. They slept together on their wedding night, 8 April, but little, if at all, thereafter: yet, to her amazement, Caroline quickly became pregnant. Her daughter, Charlotte Augusta, was born at Carlton House on 7 January 1796; although the prince was delighted, it did not change the way he felt about Caroline and in 1797 they agreed to live separately. Charlotte was placed in the care of a governess, with a separate household, although Caroline was allowed access to her.

Caroline lived in a number of houses around London, cultivated her own circle of friends and adopted a number of poor children, including a boy named William Austin. In 1806 her neighbours, Sir John and Lady Douglas, fell out with her and accused her of infidelity with several men (including George Canning) and claimed that Austin was her own son. A supposedly secret investigation by the prime minister, lord chancellor, lord chief justice and home secretary decided, after hearing the evidence, that there was no foundation for these allegations.

Despite this, George continued to exclude Caroline from the royal circle and restricted her access to their daughter, who grew up to be a spirited girl who was very fond of her grandfather, the king. Bored with life at Windsor and surrounded by her maiden aunts after the king's relapse, at the age of sixteen she naturally became attracted to young officers, in particular her first cousin, George FitzClarence, the acknowledged illegitimate son of her uncle William. He was quickly sent away to join his regiment, whereupon Charlotte began to take notice of a young cavalry officer, Lieutenant Charles Hesse. Born around 1791, he was allegedly the son of a Prussian merchant, although he had been educated in England. After his father had been ruined in the French war, he seems to have been befriended by the Duchess of York and in 1808 he was given a commission as a cornet in the 18th Light Dragoons by the duke.[20] This connection with the Yorks gave rise to rumours that he was in fact an illegitimate son of the duke, although Frederick never recognized him as such. Hesse was handsome and confident, though rather short, and over several weeks in 1812, in Windsor Great Park, a love affair blossomed:

Charlotte, driving in an open carriage with Hesse on horseback at her side, fell imperceptibly and delightfully in love. For six weeks Lady de Clifford [her governess] sat day after day and twice a day in the carriage with her charge, pretending not to notice what was going on. Notes, tokens, rings were exchanged, and she tried not to hear what the two voices were murmuring gently to each other. It was a wartime romance, precarious and therefore thrilling: at any moment, Hesse's regiment would be sent abroad, and Charlotte, like tens of thousands of other young women, would be left at home to mourn.[21]

Lady de Clifford eventually told Princess Caroline what was going on, but she was delighted, declaring that she was half in love with Hesse herself. She made it easy for the pair to meet in her apartments at Kensington Palace, even locking them in the same room together alone on one occasion. Fortunately, as Charlotte admitted later, Hesse restrained himself from taking advantage of her and in due course he was sent out with his regiment to the Peninsula.[22] But Charlotte had written him many indiscreet letters and given him trinkets, and she was worried that these might come to light, especially if he were to be killed in action.

The following year her father decided that Charlotte must marry and suggested William, the Hereditary Prince of Orange, some four years her senior. Exiled with his family from the Netherlands, he had fought as a colonel in the British army in the Peninsula, where he was popular with the soldiers, who, as we have seen, called him 'Slender Billy'. By 1813 his father had been restored as sovereign of the Netherlands and a marriage would be good for relations between the two countries. The prince arrived in England in the middle of December 1813 and went to see the regent at Windsor and the Yorks at Oatlands over the next two days, before being introduced to Charlotte at Carlton House. She found him to be very plain and very thin, although quite intelligent, but eventually decided that she could not spend half her life in the Netherlands. She refused to rush into marriage and little was done for several months, because the defeat of Napoleon became the great issue of the day. Moreover, she received conflicting advice; the Duke of York, of whom she was fond, urged her to marry Prince William, but she was told, mischievously, by her younger uncle the Whig Duke of Sussex, that York really wanted her out of the country so that he could be regent in the case of her father's death.[23]

Charlotte, whose affections had begun to rest elsewhere, finally refused to marry Orange when he said that her mother would not be welcome. The prince regent angrily confined her to Warwick House, her residence in London, but she defiantly ran into the street and took a cab to her mother's house in

Connaught Place. There York and others persuaded her to return home before the mob, with whom Charlotte was very popular, should take her side and attack the prince regent in Carlton House. Subsequently the Duke of Sussex asked Lord Liverpool in the House of Lords whether Charlotte was a prisoner in her own house and was summoned to Carlton House, where he had such a blazing row with his brother that they hardly spoke to one another again.[24] The regent's wife, meanwhile, admitted defeat, and made a life for herself, for the time being, in exile on Lake Como in Italy, where she became very close to a former servant, Bartolomeo Pergami, who was widely thought to be her lover.

Relations between Charlotte and her father continued to be strained, but eventually she persuaded him to allow her to marry Prince Leopold of Saxe-Coburg. In contrast to William of Orange, Leopold, aged twenty-six, was outstandingly handsome and had already fought with distinction in the Russian Imperial Army, where he held the rank of lieutenant general. On the other hand, he came from only a minor princely house in Germany and had little or no money. Nevertheless, they were a dazzling couple who received the adulation of the London crowds when they were married in the crimson drawing-room at Carlton House on 2 May 1816.

By courtesy of the Duke and Duchess of York, their honeymoon was spent at Oatlands, where they did not fail to notice the profusion of dogs and excessive smell of animals. The prince regent visited them there two days after the wedding and spent two hours describing details of 'every regiment under the sun', which, Charlotte made clear, 'is a great mark of the most perfect good humour'. A few weeks later Charlotte had a miscarriage and another in December, but her third pregnancy went the full term and indeed ominously beyond, because her labour lasted two days: she finally gave birth to a stillborn baby boy on 5 November 1817 and suffered a fatal haemorrhage herself a few hours later. For once, the royal family were united with the general public in their shock and grief. Henry Brougham wrote much later in his *Memoirs* that it would be difficult for people not alive at the time to believe how universal and how genuine the national sorrow was. 'It really was as if every household throughout Great Britain had lost a favourite child,' he declared.[25]

# Chapter Twelve

## George IV, 1820

The death of Princess Charlotte threw the long-term future of the monarchy into confusion. The prince regent renewed his attempts to divorce the exiled Princess Caroline, but divorce at that time was not possible without proof of adultery, which was lacking. Caroline was prepared to negotiate for the title of Duchess of Cornwall, with a suitable pension, but she was not prepared to admit adultery. The Duke of York was now the regent's heir, but he had no legitimate children; nor, very remarkably, did any of his four younger brothers. They had mistresses and illegitimate offspring, but no child who could legally succeed to the throne. As for Frederick's six sisters, only three married and none of them had children who survived infancy. The Duke of Kent, who had lived happily with a mistress for twenty-seven years, was prevailed upon to abandon her and marry Prince Leopold of Saxe-Coburg's recently widowed sister Victoria. Then in November Queen Charlotte died and York succeeded her as the legal guardian of his father, the king, for which task he was voted an allowance of £10,000 by Parliament. He took this duty seriously and often visited his father at Windsor, where, according to Roger Fulford, 'he sometimes watched the blind, bearded figure of his father in his gown of royal purple strumming tunelessly on a harpsichord or chattering of ancient troubles'.[1]

The marriage of the Duke of Kent quickly produced a daughter and on 24 June 1819 she was christened from a font of gold in Kensington Palace by the Archbishop of Canterbury. The prince regent and most of the royal family were present and it was York who pronounced the official names of the baby as Alexandrina Victoria. Sadly, babies born to the duchesses of Clarence and Cambridge did not survive long: moreover, the Duke of Kent himself, apparently the healthiest of men, who often boasted that he would outlive all his brothers, suffered suddenly from lung complications following a chill caught in Sidmouth, where he died on 22 January 1820.

In the same month George III began to decline in health and on the 20th York wrote to the regent: 'alas, upon going into the room yesterday, I never was more shocked than in perceiving the melancholy alteration which has taken place during the ten days that I have not seen him. The degree of weakness and languor in his looks and the emaciation of his face struck me more than I can describe.' On the 29th he wrote again: 'Dearest brother, it is my melancholy duty to inform you that it has pleased Providence to take to himself our beloved King and Father; the only immediate consolation under such a calamity is the almost conviction that his last moments were free from bodily suffering and mental distress. He expired at 38 minutes past 8 o'clock, pm.'[2]

With York and his brothers standing beside him, the new George IV was officially proclaimed king outside Carlton House on 31 January, the ceremony having been postponed for a day because 30 January was the anniversary of the execution of Charles I. On 1 February, however, George became seriously ill with something that seemed like pneumonia or pleurisy, and it was considered a real possibility that he might also die. Whig supporters such as Henry Brougham were seriously alarmed at the thought that York might now become king, because he would favour the Tories and never give them 'the least annoyance'. In fact, George did slowly recover, but he was not well enough to attend either his brother's funeral or his father's funeral in St George's Chapel, Windsor, on 16 February. The Duke of York acted as chief mourner on both occasions in his place.[3]

The opening months of the new reign were dominated by the problem of the king's estranged wife, who now claimed her full rights as queen. Popular opinion was strongly behind Caroline (whose true character was largely unknown to most people), largely because the king was not admired: everyone knew about his mistresses and considered that he was treating his lawful wife extremely badly. Convinced that there was enough evidence to prove her adultery, the government, under pressure from the king, introduced a 'Bill of Pains and Penalties' to Parliament, which, if passed, would have stripped Caroline of her title and rights as queen and legalized a divorce. Naturally, this was a sensation. Charles Greville wrote: 'No other subject is ever talked of ... If you meet a man in the street, he immediately asks you "Have you heard anything new about the Queen?" All people express themselves bored with the subject, yet none talk or think about any other ... Since I have been in the world I never remember any question which so exclusively occupied everybody's attention, and so completely absorbed men's thoughts.'[4]

The evidence was heard in the House of Lords from 17 August 1820 and all peers were required to attend, including the Duke of York. The streets outside Parliament were thronged with Londoners, who, in the custom of the day, made no secret of their feelings towards public figures. Even the Duke of Wellington, known to be a critic of the queen, was booed and hissed. However, according to the Russian ambassador's wife, the gossipy Princess Lieven, York was 'the idol of the mob; they are all for the Queen and for him. He frowns and does not bow, because they cheer him by the title of King'. Lord Fitzwilliam thought that York's popularity had never been higher and that 'he was huzzaed every step he took'. Another witness wrote that the duke 'was so pleased [at the calls of] "Long Live Frederick the 1st" – he bows and bows and rides along with his hat in his hands'.[5]

Caroline was brilliantly defended by Henry Brougham, even though many witnesses claimed to have seen her in compromising situations with Pergami. After many delays and postponements, a final vote was taken on the Third Reading of the Bill on 10 November, with York voting firmly with the 108 peers in favour, although 99 voted against. With such a slender majority in the Lords, ministers knew that the Bill was unlikely to pass in the Commons and informed the king that they would have to abandon it. George was extremely upset and apparently considered moving to Hanover and leaving England in the hands of the Duke of York. In London there were three days of popular celebrations, with fireworks, bonfires, dancing in the streets and parades. In an echo of the Clarke trial, Brougham became the hero of the hour, receiving the freedom of many cities and wallowing in popular acclaim.

Although not the ideal role model as a constitutional monarch, George IV was nevertheless an exceptionally talented and imaginative patron of the arts and he was determined to make his coronation ceremony the most splendid in history. He was also determined that the queen would not be part of it. Parliament voted nearly a quarter of a million pounds for the occasion and vast sums were spent transforming the interior of Westminster Hall for the coronation banquet and designing special furniture and royal robes. The king's train, for instance, was twenty-seven feet long and covered with stars and he wore a hat which boasted ostrich feathers and a heron's plume.

Despite being seriously overweight, George managed to convey the impression of great dignity, to the surprise of many of his critics. He had decided that all the official robes should be based on Elizabethan fashions and the Duke of York, in his costume, looked not unlike a latter-day Henry VIII, in white knee breeches, surcoat and ruff, all covered in a crimson cloak smothered in ermine. Not long afterwards the artist Thomas Phillips produced a magnificent full-length portrait of Frederick in these coronation robes, commissioned for the town hall in Liverpool and now to be seen in the Walker Art Gallery there. The coronation was held on 19 July 1821, a very hot day; the religious ceremony in the Abbey lasted five hours and the king enjoyed a very loyal response from the invited guests. According to the diarist Harriet Arbuthnot, George was received 'with the loudest cheers, which were repeated with increased vehemence when the crown was placed on his head, and particularly, when the Duke of York did homage and kissed him'.[6] Afterwards, a sumptuous coronation banquet, the last in British history, took place in Westminster Hall and York, together with all the other royal dukes, was served at table by Lord Denbigh, the premier earl of the kingdom.

The queen had been determined to attend, but in the intervening months her support among the mob had slowly dwindled, while the splendour of the coronation gave the king a new dignity and importance. When she presented herself at both Westminster Hall and the Abbey she was refused admittance by strong-arm men dressed as pages and was forced to make an undignified retreat. That night she attended a performance at Drury Lane and went home feeling unwell. Over the next three weeks her condition worsened and she died on 7 August, aged fifty-three. Rumours abounded about the cause of this sudden death – obstruction of the intestine? cancer? poison? Some of the support she had lost returned and the crowds turned ugly and had to be restrained as her coffin passed through London on its way to Harwich, from where it was transported for burial in Brunswick Cathedral.

The king was now a free man, but, far more sadly for him, so was the Duke of York, because he had been at his wife's side when she died, at the same age as Caroline, after what was described as 'a painful illness' at Oatlands on 6 August 1820, just as the 'trial' of the queen was about to begin. Frederica had asked to be buried in the chancel of the parish church of St Nicholas in Weybridge and the funeral duly took place there on Sunday, 13 August. Given her rank, she could have demanded a resting place of greater national importance but the request was consistent with her general lack of pretension and her charitable support for the locality, maintained over many years. Joseph Todd, the landlord of the Ship Inn at Weybridge began a collection for a memorial to her and a column which once stood at Seven Dials in London was purchased and suitably modified. It still stands and bears the inscription:

> This column was erected by the inhabitants of Weybridge and its vicinity on the 6th day of August, 1822, by voluntary contribution, in token of their sincere esteem and regard for her late Royal Highness, the most excellent and illustrious Frederica Charlotte Ulrica Catherina, Duchess of York, who resided for upwards of thirty years at Oatlands in this parish, exercising every Christian virtue, and died, universally regretted, on the 6th day of August 1820.[7]

Frederica's charity was extensive, and perhaps understandably for a childless woman it tended to focus on young people. According to one observer:

... the children of the neighbourhood were considered by her nearly as her own, being clothed and educated under her immediate supervision ... she every Sunday summoned them into her presence and administered cake and wine to the joyful and innocent troop with her own hands. As they grew up, apprentice premiums were allowed for them and even small marriage portions were awarded to the young women ... The old and sick were not forgotten.[8]

The Duke of York commissioned from the famous sculptor Francis Chantrey a very fine monument to his 'beloved and lamented consort', which was completed in 1823 and installed near Frederica's tomb in the old parish church. The monument features the duchess kneeling in prayer above a lengthy inscription which praises the 'simplicity of character and manners which distinguished her throughout her life and dictated in her last moments the wish to be buried in this church without pageantry or parade'. It also records Frederica's 'unaffected piety and her never failing benevolence manifested alike in acts of extensive charity and in judicious offices of personal kindness'. In 1846 an ambitious new High Church rector managed to persuade his congregation to agree to the building of a brand new church to Gothic Revival designs by J.L. Pearson (who was later the architect of Truro Cathedral). This was sited very close to the old church, which was demolished (despite the fact that it dated from Norman times) when the new one, dedicated to St James, was opened. As a result the fine tomb of Frederica, which had stood in the chancel of the old church, was left in the open air, where it is now part of the surrounding burial ground. The Chantrey memorial, fortunately, was carefully dismantled and replaced in a prominent position inside the bell tower of the new church, where it can be admired today.

It is sometimes stated that Frederick and his wife were 'separated' but this is not the case in any formal sense. The couple remained very fond of each other and officially lived a life together, although they were frequently apart. As commander-in-chief, the duke was often deskbound in Horse Guards or reviewing troops around the country while Frederica preferred to stay quietly on her own in the country. Even so, the duke often took his friends to Oatlands for an evening of cards. One of his guests, the diarist Thomas Raikes, wrote about Frederica's pet dogs: 'There were some twenty or thirty different sorts in the house; and many a morning have I, to my annoyance, been awakened from an incipient slumber, after a long sitting at whist, by the noisy pack rushing along the gallery next to my bedroom, at the call of old Dawe, the footman, to their morning meal.' In addition to the dogs, a contemporary print of the farmyard at Oatlands shows that there were also an ostrich, wallabies, exotic goats, wild and tame fowl and a pride of peacocks, while Raikes alleged that there were also monkeys and eagles. Frederica had each of her dogs buried under its own tombstone, creating an extensive 'pet cemetery'. After a visit to Oatlands in 1883, the historian Lord Macaulay described the cemetery as 'that most singular monument of human folly', going on to say: 'I can understand, however, that a sensible man may have a fondness for a dog. But sixty-four dogs! Why, it is hardly conceivable that there should be warm affection in any heart for sixty-four human beings.'[9]

## The Duchess of Rutland

Following the death of Princess Charlotte and her baby, George IV tried to persuade his brother Frederick to marry again, after he became a widower. In many ways this would have been the most sensible course because it was generally assumed, not least by Frederick himself, that he would be king one day. Throughout his life he had been fit and hearty, if a good deal overweight in later years, whereas his brother had suffered from endless ailments, was grossly fat and had nearly died in 1820. Frederick is widely quoted as having said, at the coronation of his brother, that his own coronation would be just as grand – no doubt a joke in dubious taste, as were many that passed between the two of them. If Frederick were to be king, he would need a queen and his brother produced a list of suitably royal candidates for him to consider. However, Frederick had recently developed a close attachment to a lady who, although high born, could not possibly become his wife because she was already very much married to the Duke of Rutland.

Elizabeth Howard, born in 1780, was a daughter of the Earl of Carlisle and she married John Manners, the fifth Duke of Rutland, in 1799. As a very young man, Frederick had considered marrying Mary, the dowager Duchess of Rutland, who was still very much alive and no doubt amused to see the duke now passionate about her daughter-in-law. Elizabeth bore her husband ten children, seven of whom survived, and the last two, both boys, were born in December 1818 and June 1820. The precise nature of the relationship between York and the duchess is difficult to define, but whatever it was it did not prevent a close friendship existing at the same time between York and Rutland. Elizabeth was a highly talented beauty with strong aesthetic interests which included architecture, interior design and painting. Soon after her marriage, a hugely ambitious rebuilding began of the Rutlands' main seat, Belvoir Castle, with James Wyatt as the architect, and under her supervision one of Britain's most spectacular mock castles was created, with sumptuously decorated and furnished rooms. Elizabeth also had practical interests in agriculture, ran a farm of 800 acres as well as tree plantations and received many accolades from agricultural societies.[10]

It was under the influence of Elizabeth Rutland that York embarked upon a project that, it must be said, was foolhardy. After Frederica's death he decided to sell the Oatlands estate, in an attempt to pay off his very considerable debts. The first sale, in 1822, did not go well and most of the lots failed to meet their reserve. The duke clearly allowed the house to be used for special functions because in 1823 a young socialite and dandy named Edward Hughes Ball, who had inherited a very large fortune, spent his honeymoon there. After this, Ball (soon nicknamed 'The Golden Ball') began to negotiate with York for the purchase of the estate, which, apart from the main house, consisted of about 3,512 acres and included the manors of Byfleet and Weybridge, Walton-on-Thames and Walton Leigh. There were numerous legal complications over titles of ownership but the process was complete by 1827.[11]

This sale should have gone a long way towards resolving the duke's financial problems, especially as in 1825 George IV helped him out with £50,000 from the revenues of the Kingdom of Hanover. But the duke, like many of his brothers, especially George IV, had a serious weakness where money was concerned. He was generous to a fault, so a lot of it went that way. He was also, as already noted, a lifelong gambler. This would not have been too much of a problem had he been a skilful card player, but he was not. He played for high stakes and cheerfully bore his frequent losses. Worse still, he kept a string of race horses, well known to be a ruinously expensive pastime that became highly fashionable while Frederick was a young man.

The St Leger was first run at Doncaster in 1776, the Oaks at Epsom in 1779 and the Derby the following year. After an interval of thirty years Newmarket joined the fashionable circuit with the 2,000 Guineas in 1809 and the 1,000 Guineas in 1814. The Prince of Wales had led the way as an enthusiast for the turf and between 1788 and 1791 his horses, based at Newmarket, won a remarkable 185 races. Then, in the latter year, George fell out with the Jockey Club and decided to sell his stud at Tattersall's. Prices ranged from 25 to 270 guineas and the main purchasers were Lord Grosvenor, the Duke of Bedford and the Duke of York. *The Times*, critical as usual, disapproved of York's purchases, taking the view that Frederick should have 'seen the imprudence of keeping up a very large turf establishment'.[12]

In many ways, York was rather successful as an owner. He won the Derby with 'Prince Leopold' in 1816 and again with 'Moses' in 1822, both trained by William Butler. He must have been fond of one of his horses, perhaps ironically named 'Banker', because there is a painting of it by Edwin Cooper, *c*. 1820, currently in the Royal Collection. The Duke of Rutland was also successful in the big races, winning the Oaks at Epsom in 1811 and 1814, and the 1,000 Guineas in 1816 and the 2,000 Guineas, both at Newmarket, in 1828. There was a cordial friendship between the two men, cemented by their interest in racing, and York was a frequent guest at the Rutlands' house at Cheveley, near Newmarket. However, there was never any question of the prize money covering the vast expense of maintaining York's large stud, with all its attendant expenses.

Without a wife and after the sale of Oatlands, York should have been able to live within his means in London. In 1802 he had moved to a smaller house in South Audley Street, having sold his Piccadilly mansion to Alexander Copland, a builder. Copland employed Henry Holland to convert it into prestigious chambers for bachelors, during the course of which a staircase, considered to have been one of the finest in London, was demolished. In due course the building was named The Albany in honour of the duke and it has proved a successful enterprise ever since. In 1807 the duke moved again, this time to the seventeenth-century Godolphin House in Stable Yard, close to St James's Palace and formerly the home of Charles James Fox.

In 1815 he took over a neighbouring building constructed around 1737 as a library for Queen Caroline and, together with the imaginative Duchess of Rutland, who had already worked on several schemes for the improvement of public monuments and parks in London, he conceived the amazing plan of demolishing both these houses and building himself a new 'York House', as a palace fit for the king he assumed he would one day be. As with his brother at Carlton House, he went ahead with this notion despite having no money, on the assumption that the government would eventually bail him out. First of all he appointed Robert Smirke as architect and then, persuaded by Elizabeth, he sacked him in favour of Benjamin Wyatt. Smirke was very angry because he had already drawn up the basic plans for the house, and there was a public row. Nevertheless, the duchess laid the foundation stone of the newly agreed scheme with due ceremony on 27 June 1825.[13]

Only a few months later, on 29 November 1825, this vivacious, intelligent and talented woman died suddenly at Belvoir at the age of forty-five, apparently from 'an obstruction of the bowels'. Three days before, she had been 'gay and cheerful in the midst of her family, and rode on horseback over the extensive farm and plantations'. Obituary notices, rightly remarking upon her virtues and accomplishments, included the fact that: 'She had also taken much pains in the formation of a plan for a royal palace, suited to a sovereign of the British empire, and which it was proposed to place in a situation uniting all the advantages of health, convenience and magnificence.'[14] York hastened to Belvoir to console Rutland and attend the funeral. They were both devastated:

Rutland, who died in 1857, never married again, while York began to suffer more seriously from excessive water under the skin, known as 'dropsy', a condition that had afflicted his mother and troubled most of his brothers.

## Catholic Emancipation

In 1825 the explosive issue of Catholic Emancipation came to the fore with the passing in the House of Commons of a Bill, proposed by the radical Sir Francis Burdett, to abolish many of the laws which restricted the liberties of Roman Catholics. This was in response to the formation in 1823 of the Catholic Association, an organization led by the Irish politician Daniel O'Connell and dedicated to the cause of Emancipation. The Bill passed the Commons by 248 votes to 227 and then came before the Lords. As we have seen, George III was resolutely opposed to any concessions to Catholics, on the grounds that he had sworn in his coronation oath to preserve the Protestant Church of England. Moreover, the House of Hanover only reigned in Britain because Parliament had declared the otherwise rightful Stuart heirs to be excluded because they were Roman Catholics. York considered it his duty to follow the line taken by his father, both for constitutional reasons and also because he was a faithful member of the Anglican Church. Sir Herbert Taylor, York's chief secretary and confidant in his later years, heard from Batchelor, the duke's valet, that:

> His Royal Highness, when he did not go to church, never missed devoting some time to his prayers, which he read to himself, in general early, that he might not be disturbed, but if disturbed in the morning, in the afternoon or evening: and that when travelling on a Sunday, he always took a Bible and Prayer Book inside the carriage, and was very particular in their being placed within his immediate reach; and that though he did not object to a travelling companion on other days, nothing annoyed him more than any one proposing to be his companion on a Sunday.[15]

Ahead of the debate on the Bill in the House of Lords, the Dean and Chapter of Windsor, who knew York well because of his association with Windsor as guardian to his father, asked whether he would present a petition from them to the Lords and this he readily agreed to do. On 25 April 1820 he rose from his seat in the Lords and said: 'My Lords, I hold in my hand a petition from the collegiate church of St George, Windsor, praying that no further concession may be made to the Roman Catholics.' He went on to remind the house that it was twenty-five years since Catholic Emancipation was first raised, and it had then seriously affected his father's mental stability and caused the resignation of Pitt, 'one of the ablest, wisest, and honestest ministers that this country ever had'. His own opposition to the measure had not changed, he said. Indeed, 'I have every year seen more reason to be satisfied with my decision ... The Roman Catholic will not allow the Church of England or Parliament to interfere with *his* church, and yet he requires you to allow him to interfere with your Church, and to legislate for it.'

York then told the House that, although he was speaking only in a personal capacity, he urged them to consider the dilemma faced by the king, because:

> By the coronation oath, the sovereign is bound to maintain the Church established, in her doctrine, discipline and rights, inviolate. An Act of Parliament may release future sovereigns and other men from this oath ... but can it release an individual who has already taken it? ... I feel very strongly on this whole subject; I cannot forget the deep interest which was taken upon it by one now no more ... I have been brought up from my early years in these principles; and from the time when I began to reason for myself, I have entertained them from conviction; and, in every situation in which I may be placed, I will maintain them. So help me God.[16]

The melodramatic conclusion to this speech, which was accompanied by the duke striking his breast with his right hand, together with the fact that he nearly broke down when speaking of his late father, produced a respectful silence in the Lords, even though many peers were Whigs. But the powerful pro-Emancipation lobby in the Commons, consisting of the Whigs, Radicals and Irish, were well aware that forthright opposition of this kind, coming from one who was the king's favourite and most influential brother, as well as the heir to the throne, could be a disaster for their cause. Scurrilous pamphlets, ridiculing and lampooning the duke and dragging up the old scandals, were rapidly printed and distributed, while Henry Brougham amused the Commons by pointing out that it seemed there was little hope for Roman Catholics, 'so help them God'.[17]

On the other hand, Protestants throughout the country were delighted and copies of the duke's speech were widely read, some of them 'printed in letters of gold on vellum and satin, splendidly ornamented'. The borough of Taunton petitioned the Lords in favour of York's 'manly, constitutional and decisive declaration', and while visiting the Rutlands at Cheveley Park, he received a deputation from the mayor and aldermen of Cambridge, presenting him with the freedom of the borough. Rutland, as high steward of the city, spoke on their behalf, praising York's 'many private virtues', the 'principles which have invariably actuated your public conduct', and especially his support for 'that glorious key-stone of our constitution, the Protestant ascendancy in Church and State'. Afterwards, the Rutlands entertained the mayor's party to 'an elegant and sumptuous collation', at which toasts were drunk to the duke and duchess, and to their young son and heir, the Marquess of Granby. The duchess replied on behalf of her boy as 'a delighted mother', and the deputation left, dazzled by the hospitality of their hosts, and the charm of the duchess. No doubt, like everyone else, they were very shocked to hear of her death only a few weeks later.[18]

The merchants of Dublin made York a freeman of their guild and asked him to sit for a portrait to hang in their hall, while the borough of Albrighton in Shropshire congratulated him on his defence of 'our Protestant constitution', ending 'Go on, then, royal Prince, like your venerated Sire, in the fearless discharge of your duty to God and your country.' He received another deputation, this time from leaders of the Protestant Union, praising him as 'the illustrious defender of their best rights, privileges and immunities, both civil and ecclesiastical', and presenting him with a loyal address 'printed in gold letters on vellum, ornamented by a rich border' and emblazoned with his royal arms. Early in 1826 he received another loyal declaration of Protestant thanks from the parishioners of Clerkenwell, which they modestly described as being in 'a remote part of the metropolis'.[19]

## Death and Funeral

For most of his life the Duke of York was famous for having the constitution of an ox: brimming with energy, capable of going nights without sleep, rising early, working hard all day and playing hard by night. But from about 1822 onwards he suffered from increasingly serious symptoms of what his contemporary biographer John Watkins called 'a spasmodic affection of such a nature that he could not lie down but at the imminent risk of suffocation'.[20] This was almost certainly excess fluid in the abdomen, which causes pain, bloating and breathing difficulties, and is caused by heart problems. When suffering from one of these attacks, Frederick could not lie down for fear of suffocating, and he often slept in an easy chair. On returning from Ascot on 9 June 1826 he had a major relapse in his house in Audley Street, after which he was more or less an invalid, receiving medical attention from Sir Henry Halford and Dr Macgregor. This did not mean that he released his hold on the reins of the Horse Guards: on the contrary, he continued to maintain a close watch on developments through his two chief officials, the adjutant general and the quartermaster general. He was closely involved with two main issues at this time: one was the sending of a British military expedition to Portugal and the other a restructuring of the pension arrangements for former army officers.

On 24 June he moved to the country air of Brompton Park, lent to him by a friend, where he called for his secretary, Lieutenant General Sir Herbert Taylor, and told him that he felt his condition was serious. He moved to the sea air of Brighton in August, where he felt somewhat better, and then made the five-and-a-half-hour journey to London on 26 August, staying in the Duke of Rutland's Arlington Street house. On the 27th the Bishop of London came quietly to administer the sacrament, as a precaution, and on 3 September the duke was 'tapped', an operation which removed excess fluid from the abdominal cavity. This painful procedure, which took away twelve pints of water, left him weak, and both his legs, especially the left, showed signs of gangrene. On 17 October, at Macgregor's request, the advice of the surgeon Sir Astley Cooper was sought. By now there was a general awareness that the duke was very seriously ill.

In November he decided to write an earnest memorandum to the prime minister, Lord Liverpool, warning him of the dangers of Catholic Emancipation and urging him to form a government composed only of ministers who would resist moves in that direction, although the details he suggested remained secret. Just before Christmas Sir Herbert Taylor told him that, in the opinion of the doctors, he had not long to live and on 27 December Sir Robert Peel visited him and told Taylor that he had been 'much shocked' by his appearance. The king, who had been a regular visitor during his brother's illness, also saw him on that day, bringing him a bowl of his favourite soup and finding him 'very weak and languid'.

On the 28th he was given the sacrament once more by the Bishop of London, this time formally robed for an official service, in the presence of the duke's favourite sister, Princess Sophia, although later that day Charles Greville looked in and found him 'very cheerful'. The following day he was well enough to conduct Horse Guards business with the adjutant general and quartermaster general, determined to fulfil his duties as commander-in-chief to the last. The king came again and spent an hour with him. It would be the last time he saw him alive. By the 30th the duke had weakened further but received visits from his brothers the dukes of Clarence and Sussex, as well as Princess Sophia. After this he sank gradually and he died, sitting in his large armchair and wearing a grey dressing-gown, at about 9.20 pm on 5 January 1827. He was sixty-three years old. Sir Herbert Taylor, who was in an upstairs room at the time, was called immediately:

I hastened down, but my dear master had expired before I could reach his room, and I had the comfort of learning that he had expired without any struggle or apparent pain. His countenance indeed confirmed this: it was as calm as possible and quite free from any distortion, indeed, it almost looked as if he had died with a smile upon it ... Such was the end of this amiable, kind and excellent man, after a long and painful struggle, borne with exemplary resolution and resignation.[21]

According to Robert Huish, writing in 1827: 'No political occurrence, since the death of Princess Charlotte and his late Majesty, created in this country a more general sympathy than the protracted sufferings and demise of the Duke of York.'[22]

On Wednesday, 17 January the duke's coffin was taken to St James's Palace, where it lay in state for the next two days in the royal apartments, attended by guards of honour from the Grenadiers, the Lancers and the Yeomen of the Guard. Many members of the public were admitted and filed past in silence, while large crowds gathered outside. On Saturday, 20 January a hearse, attended by squadrons of Life Guards and Lancers and followed by a lengthy procession of coaches containing members of the royal family and others, set out from St James's towards Hammersmith. Along the route they saw that 'the signs of many of the public houses were covered with crepe, and one of the signs had a flag suspended by a line across the street, in the centre of which was inscribed in large letters "Our Nation's Hope. The Father of the Army"'. As night fell, every fourth soldier carried a lighted torch, which made the procession even more impressive, and from Frogmore to Windsor Castle the road was lined with soldiers, many of them carrying torches. At nine o'clock the hearse arrived at St George's Chapel, where the funeral service took place in the presence of the Duke of Clarence, other members of the royal family and a large and distinguished congregation, after which the coffin was lowered into the royal vault.[23]

George IV was extremely upset by the death of Frederick, who was, after all, his younger brother. Charles Greville, whose diaries, highly critical of the king, caused outrage when they were published in Queen Victoria's reign, had to admit that George 'showed great feeling about his brother and exceeding kindness in providing for his servant ... he gave £6,000 to pay immediate expenses and took many of the old servants into his own service'. He also made sure that the coffin was placed as close as possible to that of George III in the vault.[24] The king did not attend the funeral on the advice of his doctors and, indeed, the long time spent waiting or standing in the unheated chapel on a bitterly cold night took its toll on many of the congregation. The dukes of Wellington, Sussex and Montrose caught severe colds, the Bishop of Lincoln died soon afterwards and George Canning, soon to become prime minister, contracted rheumatic fever and died a few months later.

It has to be said that the duke's financial affairs at his death were in serious disarray, as they had been during most of his life. Like his elder brother, he had no real grasp of the value of money or the need for a businesslike approach to it and he was not seriously embarrassed by being personally in debt. This is mysteriously inconsistent with his work at the Horse Guards, where he routinely demanded economy and efficient administration from his subordinates. In his will he appointed his friends Sir Herbert Taylor and Colonel Stephenson as executors and gave them the whole of his real and personal estate in trust to discharge all just claims and pay the residue, if any, to his sister, Princess Sophia. The duke's personal estate was valued at £180,000, the duty on which was remitted by the Treasury 'for the benefit of the creditors'.[25]

Unfortunately, his debts seem to have been in the region of £200,000, so a major selling campaign was urgently necessary. The government stepped in and paid off the mortgage on the site of York House and sold a 99-year lease on it to the Marquess of Stafford, soon to be the Duke of Sutherland and one of the richest men in England. Under his patronage, Benjamin Dean Wyatt built one of the most spectacular private palaces in London, with an interior considered to be the wonder of the age and which, as Stafford House, stood at the centre of London social life throughout the nineteenth century. In 1912 it was bought by the millionaire Sir William Lever, later Lord Leverhulme, who renamed it Lancaster House in honour of his native county; the following year he presented it to the nation as a place for hosting government functions and as an early home for the London Museum.[26]

The ongoing sale of what was left of land at Oatlands brought in some money and so did lesser sales of the duke's personal property. The chief item was his stud, which was sold at Tattersall's for £8,000 in February 1827, while his wines, china, linen and items of furniture fetched £6,000 at Christie's in the same month. In March came two further sales at Christie's of his silver and plate and then of jewellery and fire-arms. In April his fine Parisian furniture was auctioned and finally Sotheby's sold several thousand volumes of his library.[27] His debts were a matter of public knowledge and as the plans for his lofty memorial eventually became known, wits joked that he had to be placed so high to be out of reach of his creditors.

# The Column

On 23 January an order came from the Horse Guards in the king's name which praised the late Duke of York and 'the able administration of the command held by His Royal Highness for a long series of years, his assiduous attention to the welfare of the soldier, his unremitting exertions to inculcate the true principles of order and discipline, his discernment in bringing merit to the notice of the Crown, and the just impartiality with which he applied the honour of the service ...'. It went on to declare: 'The King feels, that under the present afflicting circumstances, His Majesty cannot more effectively supply the loss which the nation and the army have sustained, than by appointing to the chief command of His Majesty's forces, Field Marshal his Grace the Duke of Wellington, the great and distinguished general who has so often led the armies of the nation to victory and glory, and whose high military renown is blended with the history of Europe.'[28]

The day after York's death, the United Service Club in London proposed raising a subscription for a marble statue to be placed in the Club, an example soon followed by the Caledonian United Service Club in Edinburgh. The London club was founded in 1815 as a gentlemen's club for senior officers in the army and navy and its magnificent clubhouse was built by John Nash between 1826 and 1828, much the same time as Decimus Burton was building the Athenaeum Club (founded by the duke's admirer John Wilson Croker), more or less opposite to it, on Waterloo Place. The Scottish sculptor Thomas Campbell was given the United Service Club commission and he produced a very fine, slightly larger-than-life figure of the duke based to some extent, it would seem, on Thomas Phillips's 'coronation' portrait. It was placed in an imposing location, at the top of the double staircase in the main lobby. The club closed in 1976 but it was taken over by the Institute of Directors, and the duke's statue stands there still, casting its eye over the many people who climb day by day to the impressive rooms on the first floor.

According to a report in the *Courier* of 15 January 1827, 'the army, to a man, are panting for an opportunity to testify its respect and admiration towards the illustrious commander-in-chief' and on 9 February a meeting of the duke's friends took place at the Royal Union Association in London, where a major national monument was discussed.[29] On the 26th the Duke of Wellington chaired another meeting for this purpose at the Freemasons' Tavern, by which time £13,000 had already been voluntarily subscribed. In his opening speech Wellington endorsed the high praise already bestowed on York and declared that 'it is not extraordinary, it is not astonishing', that so many wished to raise a monument to his memory. He also emphasized York's concern for individuals, declaring that 'I never recommended any officer on any occasions for his exertions in the field to His Royal Highness, without that officer being in some way or other rewarded.'[30] At this meeting it was also claimed, perhaps questionably, that the duke's monument would be the first to be financed entirely from voluntary public subscription.[31]

By August 1829 a committee of nearly thirty prominent men had been appointed for the purpose of inviting the foremost British architects and sculptors to submit suitable plans for a monument in an open competition and it included the Archbishop of Canterbury, the bishops of London and Durham, the dukes of Wellington and Rutland, the marquesses of Anglesey and Londonderry (i.e. Castlereagh), and the painter, Sir Thomas Lawrence. The committee considered the possibility of a statue placed over the Whitehall entrance to Horse Guards but swung round to the idea of a column. Several notable architects and sculptors produced models and in December 1830 the committee chose the designs of Benjamin Dean Wyatt, York's architect for 'York House', who had produced plans for a Tuscan-style classical column, similar in design and size to Trajan's column in Rome and surmounted by a statue of the duke.

The most impressive memorial column in Britain at the time was Sir Christopher Wren's famous Monument in the City of London, raised to commemorate the Great Fire of 1666. More columns were erected in the following century, such as James Wyatt's memorial to Sir Watkin Williams Wynne, completed in 1790 on his estate in Denbighshire. After Nelson's death at Trafalgar, the hero was commemorated by a number of impressive columns, starting with one in Dublin in 1808 and another in Montreal, of all places, in 1809, as well as further examples in Birmingham (1809), Bridgetown, Barbados (1813), Edinburgh (1815) and Great Yarmouth (1819). In Shrewsbury the tallest Doric column in Britain was erected between 1814 and 1816 in honour of the local hero General Rowland Hill, one of Wellington's most trusted and successful subordinates, and plans were already afoot to construct a column in memory of Viscount Melville (formerly Henry Dundas) in Edinburgh. If he deserved such recognition, it might have been thought, the Duke of York certainly did.

The site eventually chosen was not without irony, as it was on the spot where Carlton House had until recently stood. Despite the vast expense that had been lavished on the building and furnishing of this palace for the Prince of Wales, and the many extravagant balls and entertainments that had been held there, it fell out of favour after George became king. It was looking tired and in any case its rooms were too small for entertainment on a kingly scale. The British royal family, George was aware, lived modestly by continental standards.

Britain had no Versailles, no Schönbrunn, no Potsdam, no Hermitage: even some of the minor European royal families inhabited finer palaces. George IV was determined to show the world that the nation that had emerged as one of its superpowers after 1815 could compete in all respects. Hence in the last ten years of his life he concentrated his attention on massive rebuilding programmes in London and at Windsor Castle.

The king's favourite architect was John Nash, born in 1752, the son of a Welsh industrial builder. After a shaky start in his profession, he had by 1806 established himself as a successful designer of classical town houses in London and 'picturesque' country houses, such as the imposing East Cowes Castle he built for himself on the Isle of Wight. He was a Whig in politics and a friend of Charles James Fox, who probably introduced him to the then Prince of Wales, who, so the gossips said, had an affair with his much younger wife. Ignoring Nash's dubious origins and social pretensions, the prince was convinced of his talent and commissioned him to recreate the Brighton Pavilion in its present, exotic, mock-Indian style.

After this, Nash worked with the prince on magnificent schemes for a 'Regent's Canal', a 'Regent's Park' and a number of fine squares and grand avenues, which were only partially realized with the eventual completion of Regent Street and Trafalgar Square. Carlton House was not included in the new designs and it was demolished between 1826 and 1829. In its place Nash built two terraces containing superior town houses and originally planned a fountain between them. Meanwhile the old Buckingham House was greatly enlarged and rebuilt by Nash after 1826, with many of the Carlton House items of furniture and paintings being moved to the now much grander 'Buckingham Palace'.

At the same time George IV employed his other favourite, the bluff Derbyshire architect Sir Jeffrey Wyatville, to create, as an alternative palace, the 'romanticized' Windsor Castle that essentially stands today. Among the Duke of York's effects discovered after his death was some fine needlework which had been done by Frederica, depicting elaborate flowers and foliage. This was sent to the furniture-making firm of Morel and Seddon, which created a sofa and six open armchairs which they upholstered with this needlework and then delivered to Windsor Castle, where they helped to furnish part of Wyatville's newly built apartments.[32] Inevitably the king was much criticized at the time because of the vast expense of all this regal building, but together with Nash and Wyattville he created iconic structures which became, over the years, inseparable features of 'Britishness'. In addition, George was very largely responsible for making the government acquire important picture collections as a core for the new National Gallery to be built on Trafalgar Square, and central to the design for this was the fine classical portico which had once graced the front of Carlton House.

George IV died in 1830, but by then he had done enough to ensure that an impressive memorial to Frederick would be built. Subscriptions quickly raised £25,000, augmented by officers and men in the armed forces, who, very willingly, it was alleged, had a day's pay docked for the purpose. The site chosen was the space previously earmarked for a fountain, between the two wings of Carlton House Terrace. This was a splendid location, appropriate because it enabled the statue of the duke to look across at Horse Guards, where he had spent so much of his useful working life, and because it created a fine focal point for any observer looking south from Piccadilly Circus, down Lower Regent Street. A Mr Nowell of Pimlico was engaged to build the column in not more than two years, for the sum of £15,760, 9 s 6 d; in fact, he finished it in twenty months.

The 'grand opening' of the Duke of York's column took place on 8 April 1834 at 11.00 am, by which time a considerable crowd had assembled. The column itself had been completed by the end of 1832, but it was almost impossible to see because of the scaffolding that surrounded it and as yet it lacked the crowning glory of the duke's statue. This had been delayed because the chosen sculptor, Sir Richard Westmacott, had originally been commissioned to create a statue twelve feet high, but then the committee changed its collective mind and asked him to make it closer to fourteen feet tall, which, he complained, meant that he had to destroy what he had already done and start again.[33] The completed statue, encased in oil-cloth, lay on a wagon nearby, ready to be lifted into position. According to the *Morning Post*:

> Several thick ropes were attached to the middle of [the statue] and at about 11.00 am the workmen commenced raising it. In consequence of its immense weight (upwards of seven tons) the greatest care and caution were necessary to prevent any accident, and upwards of an hour was occupied in raising it little more than ten feet. It reached the top at about five o'clock in the afternoon.[34]

The column stands 123ft 6in high and the statue is a further 13ft 9in tall, making a total of 137ft 3in (or 155ft 3in from below the 'Duke of York's steps' on the Mall). The column is made of Aberdeenshire granite in three colours: light grey for the pedestal, a bluer grey for the base of the shaft and red Peterhead granite for the rest of the pillar. It is hollow and contains a winding staircase leading to an observation platform, from which, before access was closed, it was possible to see the Surrey hills on a clear day.

The *Mechanics' Magazine*, reprinting an article by J. Robertson in the *Architectural Magazine*, described the finished work enthusiastically, arguing that it should be:

> ... looked upon as an undertaking of no ordinary merit; for whether we consider the peculiarity of the artificial foundation, the successful mode of forming the casing or wall of the staircase, the steps and the newel all in one piece, the difficulty of procuring [granite] blocks large enough for this purpose from Scotland, and that of finding vessels with hatchways sufficiently large to admit these blocks into their holds, the hardness of granite to work with the chisel, and the many other contingent circumstances, we must look upon this monument as a great and magnificent work.[35]

The column's designer, Benjamin Dean Wyatt, was the son of the famous late-Georgian architect James Wyatt, who died in 1813. As a young man, Benjamin worked for Richard Wellesley in India and then became private secretary to Arthur Wellesley in Dublin. He came to prominence as an architect with his rebuilding of Drury Lane Theatre in 1812, after a fire, and Wellington, who was offered a town and a country residence by a grateful nation, employed Wyatt to draw up new schemes for Stratfield Saye in Hampshire, which were never implemented, and for Apsley House in London, which were. Wyatt was also the Duchess of Rutland's preferred architect at Belvoir Castle, responsible for most of the grand interiors, and, as we have seen, he began work on York House about 1825. He was probably encouraged to put in designs for the York memorial by Wellington and Rutland, who were both members of the selection committee.

The creator of the duke's statue, Richard Westmacott, was by this time the most highly regarded sculptor in Britain; when he died in 1856, the *Gentleman's Magazine* described St Paul's Cathedral as 'a sort of gallery of the works of Sir Richard Westmacott'. His sculptures also adorn the Marble Arch, as well as the pediment of the National Gallery. It seems that he had envisaged the statue looking north towards Regent Street, but Wellington thought otherwise and a piece in *The Times* reported that he 'held it a point of propriety that the commander-in-chief should face the Horse Guards'. He had a word in the ear of William IV, who made it known that this was also his wish.[36]

Soon after the completion of the York monument, the *Saturday Magazine* wrote:

> The Duke is represented, as he should be, in the modern costume, with a cuirass and military boots. Over his left shoulder is thrown an ample mantle,

on which is emblazoned the Order of the Garter. The weight of the figure is about seven tons. It is cast hollow, gradually varying in its thickness from the lower part; and at a mean, may be taken at three-fourths of an inch. Though not cast entirely in one jet, but in separate pieces, the parts are so thoroughly amalgamated by bringing the separate portions of metal together into fusion, that they not only form one mass, but even the discerning eye of the artist himself, when the metal is cleaned off, is unable to discover the junction. This latter process, known only to the moderns, and we believe, exclusively to this country, is as important as it is curious. It reduces the risk in casting, for in case of failure in a single jet, it is necessary to reconstruct the whole mould.

The article goes on to say that the duke merited such a monument because:

He conferred extraordinary benefits on the army, and therefore the country. With the heroic story of Britain's victories, under her matchless Wellington, the name of the Duke of York is inseparably connected. To recount all the advantages rendered by the Duke of York, in his official capacity, it would be necessary to go through many particulars connected with points of discipline; regulations concerning military schools, personal attention to the conduct of individuals, the enforcement of order and punctuality. It is indeed allowed, even by those who as impartial chroniclers have deemed it just to touch upon his faults, that as a public man, he identified himself with the welfare of the service; and by unceasing diligence in his situation, gave to the common soldier comfort and respectability. It is not too much to say that his exertions contributed towards forming those armies that trampled down our country's enemies, while by their state of discipline, a point to which he had directed his great care, they generally gained the good will even of foreign lands.[37]

To those who might have wondered then (and those who continue to wonder now) why the duke deserved so prominent a memorial in the heart of London, this contemporary answer is as good as any. In the autumn of 2014, in good time for the 200th anniversary of Waterloo, repairs were undertaken to the column and the statue was cleaned, so that it looked again much as it would have done in 1834.

The Caledonian United Service Club's enthusiasm for a memorial honouring the duke in Edinburgh emphasizes that he was as highly esteemed in Scotland as in England, and in due course Thomas Campbell, who had come second to Westmacott in the competition for the statue on the London column, was commissioned to produce a suitable statue to be placed in a very prominent position on the Esplanade outside Edinburgh Castle. Campbell was born in Edinburgh in 1790 and his artistic talent was spotted by a deputy governor of the Bank of Scotland, who paid for him to study at the Royal Academy Schools in London and then to set up a studio in Rome. In due course the Duke of Devonshire gave Campbell's reputation a boost by becoming his patron and recommending him to many members of the aristocracy. Campbell's impressive statue of the Duke of York was finished in 1837 and, like the one he completed for the United Service Club, it was influenced by the Thomas Phillips portrait of 1823. The duke is again presented in ceremonial dress with knee-breeches, this time holding a hefty field-marshal's baton in his right hand. In 1950 the first of the annual Edinburgh tattoos took place on the Esplanade, staged very close to the statue and exhibiting the kind of military drill and manoeuvres of which the duke would doubtless have been proud.

## Reputations

Prince Frederick, Duke of York and Albany, was clearly a likeable person. He was his father's favourite son and the Prince of Wales's favourite brother, and as a rule he remained on excellent terms with his other brothers and sisters. The only difficulty he experienced in this regard was in his role as commander-in-chief, where duty demanded that he refuse important military commands to both the Prince of Wales and the Duke of Kent, which caused friction with both brothers for a time. Charles Greville, York's contemporary, clearly regarded him as a real gentleman, and the historian Roger Fulford described him as 'manly, gentle and unintellectual – three qualities which were truly English'.[38] Women found him very attractive and, as his letters showed, he was tender and affectionate towards the loves of his life, as long as they remained loyal to him. He was also generous to those in need and gave much of his time and energy to charitable causes, especially those concerned with education.

Regarding York's record as a field commander, Sir John Fortescue, the eminent historian of the British army, was predominantly critical but both Colonel Alfred Burne and Professor Richard Glover, two more recent military historians who had access to important additional material unavailable to Fortescue, pursue the thesis that, in the campaigns of 1793–1795, the British forces were badly equipped and organized by a government whose war aims were far from clear. Working with coalition allies, the government regarded York's royal status as a distinct advantage but, aware of his comparative youth and inexperience, they gave him more the appearance rather than the reality of command. Nevertheless, he was personally responsible for successes at

Famars, Valenciennes, Linselles, Vaux, Le Cateau and Villems, while the retreat from Dunkirk resulted from lack of reinforcements and the non-arrival of a siege train rather than from serious mistakes on York's part. Many superficial accounts blame him for losing the battle of Turcoing, but, as has been shown, this was a battle lost by his coalition allies, not by him.

As for the Helder campaign, York was personally in command for barely six weeks, during which time he achieved some successes but was badly let down by his Russian allies and hindered by the caution of General Abercromby, whose advice York had undertaken to heed. Beyond this, it must be wondered whether the aims of the Helder campaign were realistic, given the strength, enthusiasm and sheer numbers of the French Revolutionary armies. It was all very well for people at home to expect the French to be trounced, as so often in the past, but the fact was that the British army, though much improved by York's reforms, was at this stage still small, compared with a revitalized enemy invigorated with revolutionary zeal.

York's royal status and high social profile made his shortcomings as a commander all the more vulnerable to public criticism, while as a committed Tory he was a target for the Whig opposition, who used his perceived failures to weaken support for the government. Moreover, the fact that he was well known to be a womanizer, a heavy drinker and a gambler was a drawback, even though these weaknesses were shared by many men in the fashionable world of the time. No one, for instance, could have been more famous for his womanizing and infidelity than Admiral Nelson, while British popular culture then and now has tended, if anything, to admire the hard drinker. Add to this a strong current of radical and even republican sentiment among the political and vocal classes, the licence permitted in those days to caricaturists and newspaper writers, and the activities of a rowdy London 'mob' and the caricatures of York and other members of the royal family are readily explained.

Yet, as a very young man, York was a sensible and highly valued representative of his father in Hanover and the courts of Germany, where he was popular and respected, while there can be absolutely no doubt about his outstanding achievements as commander-in-chief. He twice received the formal thanks of Parliament for his work at the Horse Guards, while his memorial literally placed him on a lofty pedestal – the only member of the British royal family to be so honoured. The military historians Fortescue, Burne and Glover have all enthusiastically endorsed the contemporary view that York made an enormous contribution to Britain's success in the French wars as a result of the many reforms in the army introduced while he was commander-in-chief, and Wellington himself put on record his own recognition of this. Although at first

York was no great admirer of the young Arthur Wellesley, he came to recognize his exceptional talents as a field commander and gave him full support. At regimental dinners after 1815 the names of the Duke of York and the Duke of Wellington would appear level, entwined in laurel leaves, and when York died in 1827 medals were struck commemorating his richly deserved reputation as 'The Soldier's Friend'.[39]

Frederick had five brothers and in Victorian times it became fashionable to regard these 'royal dukes' as reprehensible buffoons, a view resulting largely from the stricter code of morality that by then governed public life, at least on the surface, and also the publication of the scurrilous diaries of Charles Greville after 1874. In fact, three of the brothers became kings whose record is not entirely unimpressive. George IV as regent presided over the defeat of Napoleonic France and the emergence of a Britain stronger than ever before, while as King he was a spectacular patron of the arts. William IV (formerly the Duke of Clarence) performed his duty as a constitutional monarch in supporting the Great Reform Bill of 1832, while the Duke of Cumberland succeeded to the throne of Hanover in 1837 because of the Salic Law which barred his niece Queen Victoria from reigning there, and he died in 1851 much respected by the Hanoverians as the 'Father of his Country'.

The Duke of Cambridge, a successful soldier, was effectively in charge of Hanover from 1813 to 1837, although the Duke of Kent had a less commendable career as Governor of Gibraltar, where his rule gave rise to mutiny. The irony was that he, unlike many of his brothers, disapproved of alcohol and punished its use in the ranks with excessive severity. The Duke of Sussex, the only one of the brothers who did not serve in the armed forces, was nevertheless respected as a person of liberal political inclinations and a supporter of many charities. Except for him, all York's brothers were appointed field marshals, or (in the case of the Duke of Clarence) lord high admiral, although none of them could compare with York in military service or in his contribution to the development of the army.

As for York's sisters, the eldest, Charlotte, became Queen of Württemburg, Elizabeth married the Landgrave of Hesse-Homburg, and Mary married her cousin the Duke of Gloucester. None of them had surviving issue. Amelia died young and Augusta and Sophia, Frederick's favourite sister, all died elderly spinsters, victims of the difficulty of finding a husband of suitable status and of their mother's need for companionship. Although court gossips spread rumours about both Amelia and Sophia, there is no proof that they ever took lovers or had illicit children and, unlike their brothers, they were spared the attentions of the scurrilous press.[40]

## The Nursery Rhyme

In the twenty-first century the nursery rhyme and song 'The Grand Old Duke of York', or alternatively 'The Noble' or 'The Brave Duke of York', is far more popular and famous in the English-speaking world than it has ever been, thanks largely to the internet, where animated cartoons with musical accompaniment abound on 'YouTube' and elsewhere. The catchy tune and amusing narrative, together with the opportunities it gives for accompanying actions – such as standing up and sitting down at the appropriate times – make it an ideal nursery rhyme and it also became very popular among the scouting community as a fireside community song:

> Oh, the Grand Old Duke of York,
> He had ten thousand men,
> He marched them up to the top of the hill,
> And he marched them down again.
> And when they were up, they were up,
> And when they were down, they were down,
> And when they were only half-way up,
> They were neither up nor down.

The issues are whether the duke in question was Frederick, Duke of York and Albany, and what might be the event commemorated in the rhyme.

In 1609, after many years of war, Spain was forced to make peace with England and also her rebellious provinces in the Netherlands, largely because they had both been supported by France under the able warrior-king, Henry IV. However, in 1610 Henry planned another attack on Spain and her ally, the Holy Roman Emperor, after a dispute over the succession to the strategically important duchy of Cleves-Jülich. Henry made alliances with German and Italian princes, raised an army of 40,000 men and in May 1610 declared his queen regent of France and prepared to lead his army into the Rhineland. At this point he was assassinated in Paris and the whole scheme came to nothing. According to Professor Hugh Trevor-Roper, Henry's death 'was an incomparable service to Spain [which] afterwards counted it as one of the saving miracles of the House of Habsburg. For, in effect, for the next decade it destroyed the new power of France which, during the last decade, had forced Spain into retreat in Europe.'[41]

According to Iona and Peter Opie, the editors of the second edition of *The Oxford Dictionary of Nursery Rhymes*, published in 1997, the British historian James Howell, later historiographer royal, wrote in May 1620 a letter to his friend, Sir James Crofts, concerning this episode, in which he said: 'France, as all Christendom besides, was in a profound peace … when Henry the fourth fell upon some great martial design, the bottom whereof is not known to this day … he levied a huge army of forty thousand men, whence came the song *The King of France with forty thousand men*'. Sung to a version of the old French air 'le petit tambour', the words are quoted in a manuscript (MS Sloane, no. 1489) dated about 1630, as being:

> The King of France and four thousand men
> They drew their swords and put them up again.

In a news sheet of 1642, titled *Pigges Corantoe or Newes from the North*, the refrain had become:

> The King of France with forty thousand men
> Went up a hill and so came down again.[42]

The writers of *Pigges Corantoe* suggested that the song had been popularized by Richard Tarlton, Queen Elizabeth I's favourite jester. However, he died in 1588 and if James Howell is correct, the source cannot lie with him. At any rate, for some reason this jingle caught on in England during the seventeenth century and with varying words it became a well-known popular rhyme. In 1842 four versions of it were identified by the antiquarian James Orchard Halliwell, who included them in his compilation *The Nursery Rhymes of England*, commenting that the reference to a hill was 'perhaps a parody on the popular epigram of Jack and Jill …'.[43] Halliwell made no mention of a 'Grand Old Duke of York' variation and this is significant, because had one been current in Britain as a nursery rhyme in 1842, he would surely have known about it and also had some idea about the military episode to which it referred.

Only at the end of the century do we find specific references to the Duke of York verses. In 1892, in his *English Folk-Rhymes*, G.F. Northall tells us that: 'In Warwickshire juveniles say:

> Oh the mighty King of France (or Duke of York)
> With his twenty thousand men
> He marched them up a very high hill
> And he marched them down again, etc.'[44]

The eight-line Duke of York version did at last appear in *A Dictionary of British Folklore*, edited by the antiquarian and folklorist Sir George Laurence Gomme in 1894, and it also featured in *Mother Goose* of 1913, Arthur Rackham's very influential compilation of around a hundred of the most popular nursery rhymes in Britain, illustrated by himself.[45] Hence we are led to the likelihood that the York version emerged as a nursery rhyme, based on the much older 'King of France' model, only during the second half of the nineteenth century. If this is the case, there is no real need to look for an actual hill relevant to a Duke of York because this was likely to have been a metaphorical concept (possibly following the 'Jack and Jill' rhyme) which was part of the earlier verses.

So, which Duke of York could these Victorian children have been singing about? For the reasons given, it is very unlikely to have been (as is sometimes suggested) Richard, Duke of York, at the battle of Wakefield in 1460, during the Wars of the Roses. This battle took place at nearby Sandal Magna, where the rebel Duke of York had a well-fortified castle standing on the top of Sandal Hill. He and his army were safely positioned there, although surrounded by Lancastrian opponents led by King Henry VI's wife, Queen Margaret. For reasons that are not clear, York chose to bring his troops down from safety, as a result of which his army was attacked and defeated and he himself was killed.

There is an oral tradition, propagated by a local pub, the Durham Ox at Crayke, that the prominent hill there played a part in this event but Crayke is forty miles away from Sandal and it is unlikely that there is any connection. Another unlikely suggestion is that the rhyme refers to King James II (formerly Duke of York), who, when faced with the invasion of William of Orange in 1688, marched troops to Salisbury Plain, only to retreat in the face of the advancing enemy. But why would Victorian children have been encouraged to sing about either of these two historical figures?

So we come to Prince Frederick. As has been indicated in the text, there were two occasions in his career as a field commander which offer possible scenarios for a military reverse relevant to the rhyme. The first was at the battle of Turcoing in May 1794 when, acting under the orders of his far more numerous coalition allies, Frederick had a small force of about ten thousand troops under his command. To support his allies, he ordered his men to advance from the so-called 'heights' near Roubaix, but in fact they were not needed and returned to the same position without seeing any action. Some accounts portray Turcoing as a disastrous defeat for York, but in fact it was nothing of the kind and he was congratulated by his allies for this prudent manoeuvre, through which casualties were avoided.

The second incident was in the Helder campaign at the battle of Bergen in September 1799 when another ten thousand soldiers under Abercromby were recalled by York, contributing to a tactical defeat. This time he was in full

command, and must take responsibility for the decision. This event gave rise
only a few weeks later to the publication of an ironically critical poem, which
referred specifically to 'ten thousand troops' who were ordered into battle and
then recalled, although there is no mention of a hill of any sort.

In both these cases, ten thousand men were involved, although only at
Roubaix was there a 'hill'– in fact, only a mild eminence. Also, the troops in
both cases set out on a mission and were then recalled, having achieved little.
The fact that the Bergen incident led to a published poem on the subject
suggests that it might have become a focus for the duke's critics at the time;
moreover York was in sole command on this occasion and not acting under
pressure from his allies. On the other hand, the Bergen incident was far from
crucial in the wider scheme of things and cannot in any way be considered a
serious military reverse.

Alfred Burne, in his military biography of the duke, published in 1949,
does not regard any aspect of Frederick's military career as being deserving of
a 'libellous lampoon' such as the nursery rhyme might be, if interpreted as a
criticism. He wrote:

> I have been at some pains to discover the origin of this jingle, and to locate
> the hill, if such exists. I have failed. The name of the author seems to be
> 'sunk without a trace'. As for the hill, Mount Cassel in Belgium is sometimes
> pointed to as the spot, but there can be no substance in this; the nearest the
> duke ever got to Mount Cassel was over ten miles away.[46]

So there is very little compelling evidence for a military event involving a hill
in the duke's career which was so absurd and unsuccessful as to have given rise
to the jingle. Moreover, as already mentioned, it does not seem that the rhyme
was current during his lifetime. There is no reference to it in the biographies
produced by Robert Huish and John Watkins in 1827, the year of York's death,
nor does it seem that marching up and down a hill was made the subject of a
caricature by Gillray or Rowlandson or anyone else, which it surely would have
been had it been a popular joke at the time. During the Mary Anne Clarke
scandal, for instance, there was plenty of scope for the suggestion that the
Grand Old Duke of York had 'had ten thousand women'.

It should also be remembered that, although Frederick did not cover himself
in glory in his days as a young field commander, his subsequent achievements as
commander-in-chief over a period of thirty years were easily enough to eclipse
any criticisms of his earlier military career. Here was the man who reformed
the army beyond recognition, who improved the lot of the common soldier
to the point where he was hailed as 'The Soldier's Friend', who shared with

Wellington some of the acclaim for success in the Peninsula and at Waterloo, who twice received grateful addresses from Parliament. He died a popular hero, commemorated by impressive memorials in both London and Edinburgh which were very promptly funded by volunteers and well-wishers.

Perhaps, then, it is the duke's achievements and not his failures that are commemorated in the nursery rhyme, and we should look for a suitable origin elsewhere. In the town of Woodbridge in Suffolk there is an oral tradition that this was the place where troops marched up and down as part of their training. As we have seen, the duke, as commander-in-chief, was responsible for the defence of the south coast, where a chain of Martello towers was constructed on the coast from Kent to Suffolk. One of the most vulnerable points was the River Deben and in 1803 a garrison of five thousand Light Dragoons was accommodated in a barracks on top of Drybridge Hill near Woodbridge, and remained there until 1814, no doubt marching up and down the hill from the barracks to the town on many occasions. The duke made a number of recorded inspections of the garrison from 1803 onwards and in 1811, together with the prince regent and the dukes of Cumberland and Cambridge, he reviewed ten thousand troops on Rushmere Heath near Ipswich.[47]

Given that the result of all this training was the defeat of Napoleonic France and the emergence of a triumphant Britain, it is possible that a jingoistic, patriotic rhyme, based on the already existing 'King of France' song, gradually emerged which actually celebrated the duke's role as someone who made a major contribution to victory. The accolades 'Grand Old Duke of York' or 'Noble Duke of York' might not be cynical epithets, therefore, but genuine compliments. During the reign of Queen Victoria, who as a little girl had fond memories of her uncle Frederick, the rhyme would have grown in popularity. Would Victorian and Edwardian nannies have chosen to propagate a rhyme which demeaned the British empire and a prominent member of the royal family? After the First World War, when militarism became unpopular and when few people knew much about this Duke of York, the rhyme was perhaps increasingly seen as a critical parody, a view that strengthened during the rest of the century, along with the 'Oh What a Lovely War' mentality that blamed the alleged incompetence of Haig and his generals for the huge casualties of 1914–1918.

In the absence of clear evidence about the author of the Duke of York verses and his or her motives, we are in the realm of guesswork here, but if an unproductive military episode is still demanded as the origin of the nursery rhyme, the best bet is the retreat at the battle of Bergen, even though it was a relatively minor incident and there was certainly no hill. However, the argument for the rhyme as a posthumous celebration of the duke and a victorious Britain seems increasingly far more convincing. Finally, there is always the possibility that because 'Duke of York' fitted more neatly into existing rhymes about the 'King of France' than, say, 'Duke of Marlborough' or 'Duke of Wellington', his name was adopted by camp-fire singers, drummer-boys or nannies who might well have known very little about him.

## Epilogue

The Duke of Wellington served as commander-in-chief for only a year because in January 1828 he resigned the post on being appointed prime minister. He was succeeded at Horse Guards by General Rowland (Lord) Hill, an extremely popular and successful field commander who had served with distinction under Wellington in the Peninsula and at Waterloo. He was MP for Shrewsbury and so well thought-of there that between 1814 and 1816 a memorial column 133ft 6in high was erected in his honour, with a 17ft statue of him standing on top, the whole edifice mounted on a pedestal guarded by four stone lions. Although it cost a lot less than York's memorial (about £6,000), it was bigger, and indeed larger than the column eventually erected in Trafalgar Square between 1840 and 1843 in honour of Nelson. 'Daddy Hill', as he was known because of his famous concern for the welfare of his soldiers, remained in post until his death in 1842, after which Wellington, relieved of his political duties, returned to Horse Guards from 1842 until his death ten years later.[48]

There had been no great move towards innovation or reform since York's death in 1827 and Wellington's successor, Field Marshal Lord Hardinge, had to deal with heavy criticisms of the army and its performance in the Crimean War from 1853 to 1856, the year in which he died. He was replaced by Prince George, Duke of Cambridge, the Duke of York's nephew and first cousin of Queen Victoria. Born in 1819, he was only thirty-seven when appointed, although he had held important commands in the Crimea. He remained in the post until 1895 and he is widely blamed by historians for reactionary and unimaginative policies that hampered the development of the army along the modern lines favoured on the continent, especially in Germany. He was frequently at loggerheads with politicians and the succession of reforms in the army initiated by the Gladstone administration between 1868 and 1874 were mostly achieved without his full cooperation. The secretary of state for war, Edward Cardwell, made many changes, including the abolition of flogging and what was left of the practice of purchasing commissions, and he also introduced shorter periods of service. Moreover, the UK was divided into sixty-six regimental districts, based on county boundaries. Regiments usually had three battalions, one serving abroad, one training at home and one of militia.

After the duke's retirement, his successor Sir Garnet Wolseley, an experienced commander, had to deal with many problems encountered in the Second Boer War, which began in 1899. He retired in the following year and his successor, Lord Roberts, was the last holder of the post of commander-in-chief, which was abolished in 1904 and replaced with the post of chief of the general staff and then chief of the imperial general staff from 1909. The army headquarters had moved from Horse Guards in 1858 to Cumberland House in Pall Mall and in 1906 it transferred to a new 'War Office' building in Whitehall, ready to face what turned out to be the unimagined horrors of twentieth-century warfare.

# Appendix

## The Subsequent Career of Duellist Colonel Charles Lennox

The Duke of York's duelling adversary in 1789 was in fact the great-grandson of King Charles II because the two dukedoms of Richmond and Lennox were created for Charles Lennox (b. 1672), the illegitimate son of Charles II and his French mistress, Louise, Duchess of Portsmouth, from whose family Lennox later inherited in addition the dukedom of Aubigny in France. Both he and his son, the second duke, were enthusiastic players of cricket, which they helped to establish as a popular game in England. The third duke (whose sister Lady Sarah Lennox the young George III had considered marrying) was a soldier and politician who served as Master-General of the Ordnance from 1782 to 1795 and in retirement established a racecourse at Goodwood, his house in Sussex. He had no legitimate children, so his heir was his nephew Charles (b. 1764), who, as we have seen, was given a commission in the Coldstream Guards and famously fought a duel with his commanding officer, the Duke of York, in May 1789. After this, Lennox's brother officers passed a resolution that he had 'behaved with courage, but from the peculiarity of the circumstances, not with judgement', and he left the Guards for the 35th regiment of foot in Edinburgh. Before arriving, however, he fought another duel, in July 1789, with the writer Theophilus Swift, who had published a critical account of Lennox's role in the York duel. This time, Lennox's aim was better and Swift was hit in the body, although not fatally.

As a very able cricketer, in the family tradition, Lennox played the game with his men in Edinburgh and was very popular with them. Later in 1789 he married Lady Charlotte Gordon, a daughter of the fourth Duke of Gordon, with whom he had seven sons and seven daughters. She, by all accounts, was very snobbish, being 'excessively proud and disdainful of persons of inferior rank'. She is also said to have 'ruined her husband by gambling'. In 1790 he became MP for Sussex but subsequently went out with his regiment to the West Indies, where in 1794 he survived an outbreak of yellow fever which took a heavy toll on both officers and men. He succeeded his uncle as Duke of Richmond, Duke of Lennox and Duke of Aubigny in 1806, and he was Lord

Lieutenant of Ireland from 1807 to 1813. In 1815, with the rank of full general, he was in command of a reserve force charged with defending Brussels from possible French attack, and it was in his rented house in Brussels that he and his wife gave the famous ball on the eve of the battles at Ligny and Quatre Bras. In 1818 Richmond was appointed Governor-in-Chief of British North America and embarked on an extensive tour of Canada. The following year he was bitten by a pet fox, eventually died in agony from rabies in August and was buried in the Anglican cathedral in Quebec. Richmond County in Nova Scotia is named after him, as is the town of Richmond, Ontario.[1]

## The Duke of York's Alleged Illegitimate Children

The best known of the Duke of York's alleged illegitimate children is Captain Charles Hesse (c. 1791–1832), who appears in the text as the young officer who had a serious affair with Princess Charlotte of Wales. The person who let this particular cat out of the bag was Captain Charles Gronow (1794–1865), Old Etonian, Guards officer and popular dandy, who wrote some reminiscences which give colourful insights into high society life at the time. Of Hesse he wrote:

> One of my most intimate friends was the late Captain Hesse, generally believed to be a son of the Duke of York, by a German lady of rank. . . . Hesse, in early youth, lived with the Duke and Duchess of York; he was treated in such a manner by them as to indicate an interest in him by their Royal Highnesses which could scarcely be attributed to ordinary regard, and was gazetted a cornet in the 18th Hussars at seventeen years of age. Shortly afterwards, he went to Spain, and was present in all the battles in which his regiment was engaged, receiving a severe wound in the wrist at the battle of Vitoria. When this became known in England, a royal lady [Princess Charlotte] wrote to Lord Wellington, requesting that he might be carefully attended to, and, at the same time, a watch, with her portrait, was forwarded, which was delivered to the wounded Hussar by Lord Wellington himself. When he had sufficiently recovered, Hesse returned to England, and passed much of his time at Oatlands, the residence of the Duchess of York; he was also honoured with the confidence of the Princess Charlotte and her mother, Queen Caroline.

Gronow then describes how the prince regent asked him to return Princess Charlotte's watch and letters, and concludes:

Hesse's life was full of singular incidents. He was a great friend of the Queen of Naples, grandmother of the ex-sovereign of the Two Sicilies; in fact, so notorious was that liaison, that Hesse was eventually expelled from Naples under an escort of gendarmes. He was engaged in several affairs of honour, in which he always displayed the utmost courage; and his romantic career terminated by his being killed in a duel by Count L[eon], natural son of the first Napoleon. He died, as he had lived, beloved by his friends, and leaving behind him little but his name and the kind thoughts of those who survived him.[2]

The letters of Lady Blessington give us a few more details. It seems that Hesse went to Naples in the first instance as equerry to the Princess of Wales, that he fought and was wounded at Waterloo, and that he married Mary Elizabeth Chambre in 1825. His death in 1832 came as a result of a duel with Count Leon after a dispute over a card game.

The most authoritative investigator into the illegitimate offspring of royal personages is Antony J. Camp, an experienced professional genealogist, who in 2007 privately published a 446-page book entitled *Royal Mistresses and Bastards: Fact and Fiction 1714–1936*. He carefully considers the evidence for all those who have been mentioned as mistresses or illegitimate children of the Duke of York and comes to the conclusion that there is no certain evidence to prove that Hesse was Frederick's son. He seems to have been the protégé of a Prussian nobleman, the Margrave of Anspach, and his wife – both of whom were well known to Frederica – and his father may have been a Prussian merchant.

However, Camp is prepared to authenticate the claim that Frederick had two children by Ann Hart, or Vandiest, with whom he had a liaison between 1799 and 1802. The children were called Frederick George Vandiest (1800–1848) and Louisa Ann Vandiest (1802–1890). It seems that they were both adopted by Ann Hart's partner George Vandiest, and that Frederick married Sophie Cheesewright in 1824. They lived in Stockwell, Surrey, and Frederick was appointed 'one of the Gentlemen of His Majesty's Most Honourable Privy Chamber in Ordinary' in January 1833, according to the *Court Journal*, which would suggest that William IV was aware of the connection between Vandiest and his late brother. Louisa Vandiest married a Scotsman, Charles Crokat, in 1820, by whom she had three girls (one named Frederica) and a son, named Charles Frederick.

Antony Camp considers many others who have been claimed as illegitimate children of the duke, but he regards none of them as beyond doubt. In the 'uncertain' category he places Frederic James Lamb (b. 1781), the son of Lady Melbourne, as well as John Molloy (b. 1789), John Stilwell (b. 1790s) and Richard Lifford (1793–1794) and their unknown mothers. In the 'fiction' category come the claims of Agnes Gibbes and her son George Nathaniel Gibbes (1786–1787); George Clarke, the son of the famous Mary Anne Clarke; Ellen, her daughter, who married into the du Maurier family; and Eleanor White, the daughter of Mrs Mary White (b. 1817). Altogether, Camp investigates twenty-two women whose names have been 'linked' with the Duke of York, a number which seems quite modest compared with the seventy-five women associated with his elder brother.[3]

## Portraits of the Duke and Duchess of York

Unfortunately it has not been possible to include a large number of illustrations in this book, but many of the portraits of the duke can be viewed online at various websites. The most accessible is on Google under 'Images for Frederick Duke of York', but the online catalogues of the Royal Collection and the National Portrait Gallery can also be consulted, as well as others. One of the earliest and most splendid portraits is the full-length image painted by Sir Joshua Reynolds in 1788, soon after Frederick returned from Germany, which is in the Royal Collection at Buckingham Palace. He is portrayed as a fine young man of about twenty-five, wearing the robes of the Order of the Garter and looking every inch a prince, though certainly not a bishop. Another portrait, of similar date, is one by the American painter Mather Brown of the duke in uniform, currently hanging in the National Trust Collection at Waddesdon Manor, Bucks.

A miniature by William Grimaldi, painted a year or two later than the Reynolds portrait, makes Frederick look, if anything, rather younger and a touch effeminate, which cannot be true to life. Again the duke is in Garter robes and it is possible that Grimaldi used Reynolds' big picture as a template. Born near London in 1751 to an Italian father and English mother, Grimaldi trained as a miniaturist and came to the notice of Reynolds, who recommended him to the Prince of Wales and to Frederick. For the prince Grimaldi painted a miniature of Maria Fitzherbert, and for the duke he painted this miniature, which Frederick obviously liked because he gave it to Frederica on their marriage in 1791. Grimaldi was appointed enamel painter to Frederick in 1790, to Frederica in 1791 and to the Prince of Wales in 1804.

Shortly after their marriage Frederick commissioned portraits of himself and Frederica from the well-known society painter John Hoppner and some authorities regard these as among the best paintings Hoppner ever produced. Frederick is portrayed in military uniform, standing in front of a rearing horse which is being restrained by a trooper. The portrait of Frederica sets her in a garden, in the company of three young ladies and – most important of all – with a little white pet dog, which looks at her adoringly. These portraits were probably done in 1791 and Hoppner produced a second portrait of Frederick in 1794 based very much on the 1791 image, but portraying him this time as commander of the British forces in the Netherlands. All these paintings are in private collections, but on public view in the Holburne Museum in Bath is a miniature by John Bogle, painted around 1793, which presents probably a very accurate image of Frederick, in uniform and with the Garter ribbon across his chest, looking dignified and very much aware of the military responsibilities he bore at that time.

The next important full-length portrait was painted by Sir William Beechey in 1807 and it shows the duke, by then aged forty-four, in a relaxed pose in uniform as commander-in-chief. According to Alfred Burne, it was painted for the duke's recently founded Asylum in Chelsea and it now hangs in pride of place at the Duke of York's Royal Military School in Dover. After the victory at Waterloo Sir Thomas Lawrence painted a full-length formal portrait in 1816 with the duke in contemporary uniform and dramatically cloaked in his dark blue Garter robes. This is part of the Royal Collection and hangs in the Waterloo Chamber in Windsor Castle. As has been noted in the text, at the coronation of George IV in 1821 the duke wore robes which were reminiscent of the Tudor style, appearing in a silken doublet and knee breeches, and he was painted in this magnificent get-up in 1823 by Thomas Phillips. The portrait went initially to Liverpool's Town Hall and is now in the City's Walker Art Gallery. As has been suggested in the text, Thomas Campbell probably based his two statues of the duke on this picture.

In 1822 Sir Thomas Lawrence produced a more informal head-and-shoulders portrait of the duke in civilian dress. One version of this was auctioned in London at Sotheby's in 2004 and another at Christie's in 2007. Several other artists subsequently copied or engraved what was evidently a popular image (*see* dust jacket). In 1826 Andrew Geddes produced a full-length portrait for the Duke and Duchess of Rutland, which hangs in Belvoir Castle, and one of the last images was a portrait completed by James Lonsdale in 1827 showing the duke in Masonic regalia, which hangs in Mark Masons' Hall near St James's Palace in London. There are many other likenesses of the duke and a few more of the duchess, but these are arguably the most important and the best.

## Gillray and Rowlandson Caricatures of the Duke

A number of factors combined to make the reign of George III a perfect environment for the flourishing of political caricatures. Perhaps most important was the re-emergence of two political parties, which meant that there was generally an active and vociferous opposition to the individuals in power. Then the American and French Revolutions encouraged anti-monarchical sentiment, while the constitutional nature of the king's role made it difficult for him to suppress critical publications. Other individuals lampooned by the newspapers could resort to the law courts but this was an expensive business and many instead attempted to bribe journalists to keep quiet. Advances in the technology of printing made good-quality caricatures viable and print-shops and publishing firms sprang up in London and elsewhere to distribute them, while the 'coffee-house' culture of the time meant that there was a suitable arena for people to have a good laugh over the latest productions. Two artists in particular, James Gillray and Thomas Rowlandson, made the best of these opportunities and became the leading caricaturists of their day.

James Gillray (1756–1815) was born in London, the son of a Scottish soldier who became a Chelsea pensioner. He began as a letter-engraver and then studied at the Royal Academy, where he paid the fees by selling caricatures, almost all etched, some with aquatint. He was responsible for at least a thousand caricatures, and probably many more, and his attitude was generally anti-French while politically he favoured neither Whigs nor Tories but regarded both as fair game. For most of his life he lived with Hannah Humphrey, a publisher and print-seller in Mayfair, and he began to show signs of madness in 1811, dying four years later.

Thomas Rowlandson (1756–1827) was the son of a bankrupt textile merchant and began drawing talented sketches in the margins of his school books in London when he was ten years old. At sixteen he studied at a drawing academy in Paris before enlisting as a student at the Royal Academy in London, where he remained for six years. Then he inherited the considerable sum of £7,000 from an aunt, but seems to have blown it all on dissipation and the gaming table. So he had to draw caricatures for a living and teamed up with the art publisher Rudolph Ackerman. His drawings were done with a pen in outline and then gently washed with colour, after which they were etched on copper and then aquatinted. In general he was less concerned with politics than Gillray and tended to concentrate on social life and fashion. He died unmarried in his London lodgings in 1827, a few weeks after the Duke of York.

The National Portrait Gallery holds many caricatures featuring the duke and they can be easily viewed on their online catalogue. One of Gillray's first depictions of Frederick, published on 15 May 1789, was deeply scandalous because it showed him, in a night-shirt, getting into bed with Sarah, Countess of Tyrconnell, while her husband quietly leaves the room, saying 'A good night to your Royal Highness . . . I'll be back to breakfast . . .'. A few days later

Frederick fought his famous duel with Colonel Lennox, and Gillray produced two further drawings, both flattering to York and portraying him as, basically, a brave lad. The first depicts him as 'Brunswick Triumphant', a manly prize-fighter, stripped to the waist, and in the second the duel is described as a contest between 'a prince and a poltro[o]n'.

Gillray welcomed the marriage between Frederick and Frederica, producing a cartoon that showed 'the soldier's return, or rare news for old England', and another in which Frederick presents his new wife, who carries an abundance of gold coins about her person, to the king and queen, who are delighted – more about the money, by implication, than the wife. Gillray was probably not aware that the match did not come with great riches. He also produced a number of other drawings reflecting the positive reaction to the wedding in London society and made fun of the duchess's little feet in a cartoon that placed her husband's big feet together on a bed between his wife's open legs and dainty shoes.

After Frederick had left to take up his command in the Netherlands, Gillray produced an irreverent drawing of the 'Fatigues of the campaign in Flanders', which, of course, shows the duke, with a portly girl on his knee, carousing at a table next to William V of Orange, who is shown to be ugly and fat, and belching. In February 1794 Gillray compared York's return to London with Rabelais' 'Gargantua and Pantagruel', showing York, whose campaign had gone quite well so far, offering his father the keys to Paris, which of course was premature, to say the least.

The Mary Anne Clarke scandal provided plenty of scope for the caricaturists, and the Royal Collection holds several of Thomas Rowlandson's prints about it. There is one of 'Samson asleep on the lap of Delilah', another of the duke on his knees before a whale which had been sensationally caught off Gravesend, imploring it to divert popular interest away from the Clarke trial, another celebrating the vote which technically acquitted him of blame, and another, entitled, 'The resignation, or John Bull overwhelmed with grief'. Here the duke says to John Bull, who is in tears, 'Goodbye Johnny – I am going to resign – but don't take it so much to heart, perhaps I may very soon come back again,' to which John Bull replies, 'O Dunna, dunna go, it will break my heart to part with you – you be such a desperate moral character!!'

A more hard-hitting scenario, entitled 'The York Auctioneer and his Clark, or a new way to pay old debts', has the duke auctioning a captain's commission for 700 guineas and a bishopric for 1,000, while a black servant in the audience thanks his master for making him a captain. Meanwhile, Mary Anne, brandishing a quill pen, writes down all the successful bids. The inference that the duke was selling commissions via his mistress in order to pay off his debts (which were well known to be considerable) no doubt accurately reflected the beliefs of those who doubted York's honesty.[4]

However, compared with the sometimes scathing attacks on his elder brother and many politicians, the duke escaped comparatively lightly at the hands of both Gillray and Rowlandson. As the war against Napoleonic France became more of a national threat, the caricaturists in any case became more patriotic, and with military success in the Peninsula and finally at Waterloo, York moved out of reach of the critics. As emphasized in the text, there seem to be no contemporary caricatures which refer to a 'Grand Old Duke of York' and this is powerful evidence that this epithet might well have become attached to the duke some considerable time after his death.

## Subsequent History of the Duke's Country Homes

As we have seen, Frederick's house and estate at Allerton Mauleverer were sold to Colonel Thomas Thornton in 1791. In 1805 they were sold again, to Charles, the seventeenth Baron Stourton, who ran a Roman Catholic mission there and built a chapel in 1807. This was enlarged by his son in 1837 and again when his grandson pulled down most of the house built for the duke and created a gothic revival mock-castle between 1848 and 1854 to designs by the architect Charles Martin. During the Second World War the castle was the headquarters of No. 6 Group of the Royal Canadian Air Force and upon the death in 1965 of the twenty-second Baron Stourton (who also held many other ancient baronies) a three-day sale disposed of most of the contents. The castle was then rented to religious organizations until 1983, when, as it was in a very poor state of repair, the twenty-fourth Lord Stourton sold it to an American businessman, Dr Gerard Arthur Rolph, who was interested in preserving it as part of English and world heritage. He set up a charitable foundation for this purpose in 1986, which has succeeded in restoring the castle and its 43.5 hectares of garden and parkland to their former Victorian glory. It is currently open to the general public as a 'stately home' and venue for weddings and other functions.[5]

The Oatlands estate, finally purchased by Edward Hughes Ball in 1827 after years of legal disputes, remained in his ownership only until 1846 because he was a gambler on a heroic scale, allegedly losing £45,000 in one night, and he was forced gradually to sell parts of the estate. In 1846 what remained was divided into many lots and it took four sales to dispose of them. The mansion itself and several other lots were purchased by James Peppercorne, who lived there with his family for some time. By about 1856 he had set up the South Western Hotel Company and he employed Thomas Henry Wyatt to remodel the house, with a new entrance front, and it opened as a high-class hotel in 1858, patronized by Emile Zola, Anthony Trollope and Edward Lear, among many other celebrities. In 1916 the hotel was requisitioned by the war office and most of the furniture was sold. Early in 1917 wounded soldiers were moved there from the New Zealand Military Hospital in Walton, but the hotel reopened after the war, when it was bought by North Hotels. Since then various additions have been made under a number of owners and in 2011 Oatlands Investments Limited inaugurated a thorough refurbishment. Today Oatlands Park is an impressive hotel in a spectacular setting, but there is little or no trace of the house inhabited by the Duke and Duchess of York. Even Frederica's pets' cemetery has been built over, although some of the headstones were rescued and have been laid out on the front lawn.[6]

## The Duke of York's Royal Military School

After the duke's death in 1827 his asylum in Chelsea went through a number of significant changes. Although at the height of the Napoleonic War it had as many as 1,500 pupils, the number fell drastically in peacetime, down to a total of 357 in 1836. Between 1816 and 1840 the asylum also had a branch in Southampton, which provided schooling for about 400 children of both sexes until 1823, when the boys were transferred to Chelsea. The girls stayed on at Southampton until falling numbers brought about closure in 1840. After that date the number of girls in Chelsea was wound down, so that by 1846 the asylum was an all-male institution.

In that year, as a result of changing times and changing needs, the decision was taken to set up at the asylum a training school for military schoolmasters, who were professional teachers seconded to regiments to educate soldiers and also their children. This was a scheme intended to tackle one of Victorian Britain's most pressing problems – poor educational provision for the masses. Ironically, the teacher-training school followed the French model of the 'Normal School' and involved the replacement of military personnel at the asylum with civilians. There was also a 'Modern School' at the asylum which continued to provide general education for boys from a military background.

In 1892 the asylum was renamed the Duke of York's Royal Military School, and after various plans to demolish the building and move it to a more spacious location, a fine 150-acre campus was eventually provided on the Kentish cliffs close to Dover Castle, and the school moved there in 1909 as a boys' boarding school with strong army associations. On this site a newly built central structure with a lofty clock tower was flanked by a crescent of boarding houses and an impressive chapel, all set in extensive grounds suitable for parades and military manoeuvres. Meanwhile the original building in Chelsea became the

Duke of York's Barracks until 2003, when it was sold to the Cadogan estate. The surrounding area was developed as the 'Duke of York's Square', with the Saatchi Modern Art Gallery housed in the main building, encircled by an extensive complex of shops and restaurants.

During the First World War the boys at Dover were moved to accommodation in Hutton, near Brentwood in Essex, while their school became a transit camp for troops crossing to the western front. When the Republic of Ireland was established in 1922, the Royal Hibernian Military School was moved from Dublin to Shorncliffe Barracks near Folkestone, and in 1924 its boys merged with the Duke of York's pupils. During the Second World War the school once again became a transit camp and the boys and staff were evacuated to a hotel in Braunton, North Devon. After the war the school developed its academic side more strongly, with civilian teachers outnumbering the military, although the boys still wore uniform and were subject to firm discipline. In 1994 girls were admitted, and in 1999 a civilian headmaster succeeded many military predecessors.

In September 2010 the school made the important transition from being an independent school funded by the ministry of defence to an academy. Public funding of £25 million was provided to increase the number of pupils from about 400 to 700 or more, and some redundant buildings were demolished and new facilities constructed in an ambitious modernization scheme. The Duke of York's Royal Military School now describes itself as an 'Academy with Military Traditions' and with its splendid, renovated site and excellent facilities it seems well set to meet the needs of pupils who would benefit from a boarding education. Moreover, it continues to perpetuate and honour the name and memory of its founder. Pupils at the school have been known as 'Dukies' for generations and once a year the school parades for 'Grand Day', which has its origins in ceremonial inspections held at the school in Chelsea by the Duke of York.[7]

## Places and Titles

There are a number of foreign locations, mostly in Canada, which have been named in honour of Prince Frederick. In 1784 New Brunswick in Canada became a separate province from Nova Scotia and in 1785 its capital was named Fredericton and the surrounding area was known as York County. In 1792 another York County was named after Frederick in Ontario and in 1793 a new 'Fort York' was established there on the site of the former French 'Fort Toronto'. Renamed 'York', it became the capital of Upper Canada in 1796, and it was designated a city and renamed Toronto in 1834, becoming the capital of Ontario in 1867. The boundaries of the Ontario York County changed over the years, becoming the York Regional Municipality in 1971. In 1799 'Fort Frederick' was constructed near what became Port Elizabeth in South Africa to defend the harbour from possible French attack, and it survives as a small but well-preserved historical relic. 'Duke of York Bay' in northern Canada was named after Frederick by the explorer, Admiral Sir William Parry, who sailed into the bay on 16 August 1821, the duke's birthday, while on his second voyage in search of a northwest passage from the Atlantic to the Pacific.

Because Frederick had no legitimate children, his titles became extinct on his death. The tradition of bestowing the dukedom of York on second sons was maintained and in two cases during the twentieth century the second son succeeded to the throne. In 1892 Queen Victoria granted the dukedom of York (although not Albany) to the Prince of Wales's son, Prince George, who became King George V in 1910. He created Prince Albert, his second son, Duke of York in 1920 and he succeeded as George VI in 1936 after the abdication of his elder brother. His daughter Queen Elizabeth II gave the title to her second son, Prince Andrew, in 1986.

As for the Albany dukedom, this was bestowed by Queen Victoria on her fourth son, Prince Leopold, in 1881. He suffered from haemophilia and died at the age of thirty, just before the birth of his only son, Charles Edward, who succeeded him as Duke of Albany. In 1900 he reluctantly inherited the sovereign German dukedom of Saxe-Coburg-Gotha and had little choice but to side with Germany in 1914. After the fall of the Kaiser in 1918, a revolution deposed Charles Edward as sovereign of Saxe-Coburg and Saxe subsequently joined Thuringia while Coburg became part of Bavaria. In 1919, because he had opposed Britain in wartime, he was also stripped of the dukedom of Albany and his other British peerages by Order in Council. In the 1930s Charles Edward supported Hitler and the Nazi Party and his three sons fought for the German army in the Second World War. He died in 1954 and has been succeeded as head of the family by his son Prince Friedrich Josias and his grandson Prince Andreas.

## Charles Greville and the Yorks

Charles Cavendish Fulke Greville (1794–1865) was an aristocrat whose mother was the eldest daughter of the third Duke of Portland, Whig prime minister from 1807 to 1809, while his father was a cousin of the Earl of Warwick. He was a page of honour to George III and went to school at Eton before moving on to Oxford. He left the university when he was nineteen, before taking his degree, in order to become private secretary to Earl Bathurst, the secretary for war and the colonies. At the age of twenty he began to note down scraps in a journal, and in 1818 he began to write in greater detail. Among his first major entries is a lengthy one for 15 August 1818 which describes the regular house parties given by the Yorks at Oatlands over weekends in the summer, especially during the Egham races. Greville was barely twenty-four at the time and one wonders why he had become a favoured member of the Yorks' circle. The duke may have known him as a page to the king or as secretary to Bathurst and perhaps above all as a keen racegoer. Perhaps it was the duchess, whom Greville describes as 'clever and well-informed', who enjoyed his company, because it was she who sent out the invitations.

The circle of house guests was usually much the same and included the dashing regency beau Lord Alvanley, the Culling-Smiths, Lord Lauderdale, the Marquess of Worcester and his wife, Lord Erskine, and others. As soon as dinner was over the duke would sit down to play whist, for high or low stakes as his opponent preferred, and he would carry on until everyone had had enough. The duchess was not in the best of health, suffered from insomnia, rested on a couch fully dressed rather than going to bed and asked people to read to her when she could not sleep. Greville had a high regard for her and wrote at her death 'She is deeply regretted by her husband, her friends and her servants. Probably no person in such a situation was more really liked'. (14.7.1820)

In 1821 Greville was appointed clerk of the council in ordinary, which gave him a central role in the administration of the privy council for nearly forty years. In his journal he often wrote very critically about George IV and William IV, revealing a remarkable contempt for them and considering them not a little mad. York, however, he definitely liked. Conceding that he was no intellectual and was perhaps too easily amused by bawdy jokes, he nevertheless thought that York was loved and respected because 'he has a justness of understanding, which enables him to avoid the errors into which most of his brothers have fallen. . . . He is the only one of the princes who has the feelings of an English gentleman, his amiable disposition and excellent temper have conciliated for him the esteem and respect of all parties, and he has endeared himself to his friends by the warmth and steadiness of his attachments and from the implicit confidence they have in his truth, straightforwardness and sincerity'. (15.8.1818)

Also in 1821 York asked Greville to take over the management of his racing stud, which Greville was thrilled to do, and it was under his supervision that the duke's horse 'Moses' won the Derby in 1822. York clearly liked and trusted Greville, and he would often gabble away confidences as they rode to the races – about Lennox and the duel, about squabbles with his elder brother and also about the Duke of Wellington. According to Greville, York did not 'deny his military talents, but he thinks he is false and ungrateful, that he never gave sufficient credit to his officers, and that he was unwilling to put forward men of talent who might be in a situation to claim some share of the credit . . .' As for Waterloo, York 'attributes in great measure the success of that day to Lord Anglesea, who, he says, was hardly mentioned, and that in the coldest terms, in the duke's dispatch'. (24.6.1821) Greville was in the London house when York died and wrote 'I have been the minister and associate of his pleasures and amusements for some years. I have lived in his intimacy and experienced his kindness, and am glad that I was present on this last sad occasion . . .' (5.1.1827)

Greville himself died in 1865, by which time his memoirs had grown to a great length. He entrusted them to his friend Henry Reeve who edited them and in 1874 published the first three volumes, covering the years 1817 to 1837. Queen Victoria was outraged by the disrespectful tone of many passages, and copies had to be recalled and expurgated. Two further volumes appeared in 1885 and the last two in 1887. In recent times the diaries have been digitalized by Project Gutenberg and they can be very easily accessed and read online by searching, for instance, 'Greville Memoirs, Gutenberg'. It should be mentioned that nowhere in his journal does Greville make even the slightest reference to a 'Grand Old Duke', ten thousand men, or a hill, which lends weight to the argument that the nursery rhyme was not current during York's lifetime and probably evolved towards the end of the century.

# References

## Chapter One

1. Brooke, *King George III*, p. 15.
2. *Ibid.*, pp. 16, 22.
3. *Ibid.*, pp. 80–4.
4. Burne, *The Noble Duke of York*, p. 17. Burne blames the confusion on Frederick's original *DNB* entry, which provides the additional name.
5. Watkins, *A Biographical Memoir of Frederick, Duke of York and Albany*, pp. 4, 5.
6. *Ibid.*, p. 8.
7. Brooke, p. 266.
8. Hadlow, *The Strangest Family*, pp. 208, 210.
9. Watkins, p. 19.
10. Hibbert, *George IV, Prince of Wales*, (hereafter GPW), p. 7.
11. Watkins, p. 21.
12. Burne, p. 19.
13. Fulford, *Royal Dukes*, p. 22.
14. Burne, pp. 18, 19.

## Chapter Two

1. Smith, *George IV*, p. 13.
2. Fulford, p. 53.
3. Watkins, p. 25.
4. Aspinall (ed.), *The Later Correspondence of George III*, (hereafter LC), vol. V, pp. 682, 699.
5. *Ibid.*, p. 676.
6. *Ibid.*, p. 679.
7. *Ibid.*, p. 689.
8. Burne, p. 22.
9. Aspinall, LC, vol. V, p. 704.
10. Aspinall, LC, vol. I, p. 68.
11. *Ibid.*, pp. 69, 73.
12. *Ibid.*, pp. 102, 103.
13. *Ibid.*
14. Burne, p. 23.
15. Aspinall, LC, vol. I, p. 115.
16. *Ibid.*, pp. 128, 129.

17. *Ibid.*, pp. 132, 133.
18. Watkins, p. 30; Fulford, p. 56.
19. Aspinall, LC, vol. I, pp. 152, 153.
20. Burne, pp. 19, 24, 25.
21. Aspinall, LC, vol. I, p. 240.
22. Fulford, p. 282.
23. Aspinall, LC, vol. I, p. 256.
24. Huish, *Authentic Memoir of his late Royal Highness Frederick, Duke of York and Albany*, p. 8.
25. Burne, pp. 20, 33; Watkins, p. 27.
26. Aspinall, LC, vol. I, n., p. 17.

# Chapter Three

1. Fulford, p. 56.
2. Watkins, p. 37.
3. Foreman, *Georgiana, Duchess of Devonshire*, p. 79.
4. Gristwood, *Perdita, Royal Mistress, Writer, Romantic*, pp. 139, 140.
5. Smith, p. 21.
6. Hibbert, GPW, p. 23.
7. Smith, p. 22 and n.
8. Burne, p. 22.
9. *Ibid.*
10. *Ibid.*, pp. 21, 22.
11. Smith, pp. 26–30.
12. *Ibid.*, p. 35.
13. Fulford, p. 38.
14. See www. allertoncastle.co.uk/history.
15. Fulford, p. 60.
16. Marsh, *The Clubs of London*, p. 87.
17. Brooke, p. 327; Watkins, p. 46.
18. Watkins, p. 54.
19. Burne, p. 31.
20. Sir Gilbert to Lady Elliott, quoted in Smith, p. 56.
21. Burne, p. 227; Watkins, p. 72.
22. Hibbert, GPW, p. 111.
23. Fulford, p. 90.
24. Burne, p. 27.
25. Smith, pp. 57, 58.
26. *Ibid.*, p. 58.
27. For the whole story, see Ida Macalpine and Richard Hunter, *George III and the Mad Business*, Allen Lane, 1969.

## Chapter Four

1. Burne, pp. 28–32. Lennox succeeded his uncle as the fourth Duke of Richmond in 1806, and was Lord Lieutenant of Ireland from 1807 to 1813. It was his wife who gave the famous ball just before the battle of Waterloo. In 1818 he became Governor General of British North America but died in Canada the following year of rabies, after being bitten by a fox. He was a keen cricketer and, with Lord Winchilsea, guaranteed any losses Thomas Lord might have made in opening his first cricket ground in 1787.
2. Watkins, p. 66.
3. Hibbert, GPW, p. 101.
4. Watkins, p. 74.
5. Aspinall, LC, vol. I, p. 417.
6. *Ibid.*, n., p. 545.
7. *Ibid.*, pp. 496, 497.
8. *Ibid.*, p. 530.
9. *Ibid.*, p. 534.
10. *Ibid.*, pp. 545, 547.
11. Burne, p. 33.
12. Aspinall, LC, vol. I, p. xx.
13. Watkins, pp. 82, 83.
14. See Oatlands Heritage Group website, at www.oatlands-heritage.org.
15. Hibbert, GPW, p. 123.
16. *Ibid.*, p. 125.
17. Watkins, p. 84.
18. *Ibid.*, p. 85.
19. *Ibid.*, pp. 86–90.
20. Hibbert, GPW, p. 129.
21. Huish, p. 2; Aspinall, LC, vol. 1, p. xx.
22. Fulford, pp. 62, 90.
23. Aspinall, LC, vol. I p. 609.

## Chapter Five

1. Hague, *William Pitt the Younger*, p. 335.
2. Fortescue, *British Campaigns in Flanders, 1690–1794*, (hereafter BCF), p. 179.
3. Schama, *Patriots and Liberators*, p. 56.
4. Watkins, p. 100.
5. Fortescue, BCF, p. 180; Burne, pp. 35–8.
6. Fulford, p. 64.
7. Burne, p. 39.
8. Fortescue, BCF, pp. 185, 186.
9. Aspinall, LC, vol. II, p. 31.
10. Burne, p. 46.
11. *Ibid.*, p. 49.
12. *Ibid.*, p. 57.
13. Aspinall, LC, vol. II, n. p. 901 and following.

14. Burne, p. 64.
15. *Ibid.*, p. 67.
16. *Ibid.*, p. 70.
17. *Ibid.*
18. *Ibid.*, pp. 73–8.
19. *Ibid.*, p. 80; *Oxford Dictionary of National Biography*, vol. 33, p. 384.
20. Burne, p. 94.
21. *Ibid.*, pp. 100, 101.
22. *Ibid.*, p. 110.
23. *Ibid.*, p. 116.

## Chapter Six

1. Hague, p. 341.
2. *Ibid.*, p. 347.
3. Fortescue, BCF, p. 278.
4. Burne, p. 124.
5. *Ibid.*, p. 132.
6. *Ibid.*
7. *Ibid.*, p. 136.
8. Glover, *Peninsular Preparation*, (hereafter PP), p. 3.
9. Burne, pp. 14, 15.
10. *Ibid.*, pp. 157, 158.
11. *Ibid.*, p. 163.
12. *Ibid.*, p. 164.
13. *Ibid.*, p. 165.
14. *Ibid.*, p. 190.
15. *Ibid.*, p. 203.
16. Watkins, p. 128.
17. Fortescue, BCF, p. 391.
18. *Ibid.*, p. 397.
19. Glover, *Britain at Bay*, (hereafter BB), pp. 38, 39.

## Chapter Seven

1. Aspinall, LC, vol. II, p. 298.
2. Burne, p. 228.
3. *Ibid.*, p. 235.
4. Glover, PP, p. 121.
5. *Ibid.*, p. 122.
6. *Ibid.*
7. *Ibid.*, p. 179.
8. Watkins, pp. 153, 154.
9. *Ibid.*, pp. 155–6.
10. Fulford, p. 63.

11. Hague, pp. 400–7.
12. Watkins, p. 156.
13. *Ibid.*, p. 158.
14. Burne, p. 239.

## Chapter Eight

1. Burne, p. 259.
2. *Ibid.*, p. 260.
3. Schama, pp. 393, 394.
4. Ibid., p. 395.
5. Burne, p. 269.
6. Burne, p. 272.
7. *Ibid.*, pp. 271, 272.
8. *Ibid.*, pp. 272, 273.
9. *Ibid.*, p. 275.
10. *Ibid.*, pp. 276, 277.
11. *Ibid.*, pp. 280, 281.
12. *Ibid.*, pp. 284, 285.
13. Fulford, p. 72.
14. Hague, p. 449.
15. Glover, BB, p. 39.

## Chapter Nine

1. Watkins, p. 188.
2. *Ibid.*, pp. 189, 190.
3. Brooke, p. 315.
4. Glover, PP, p. 194.
5. *Ibid.*, pp. 198, 199.
6. *Ibid.*, pp. 201–5.
7. *Ibid.*, pp. 205–10.
8. For detailed information about what became of the Duke of York's Royal Military School, see A.W. Cockerill's extensive archive online by searching A W Cockerill Duke of York.
9. Hague, p. 493.
10. Watkins, pp. 202–8.
11. Glover, PP, p. 31.
12. *Ibid.*, p. 57.
13. *Ibid.*, p. 33.
14. *Ibid.*, p. 127.
15. *Ibid.*, p. 128.
16. Hague, p. 577.
17. Glover, BB, p. 143.
18. Longford, *Wellington, The Years of the Sword*, p. 38.
19. Holmes, *Wellington, The Iron Duke*, (hereafter WID), pp. 121, 122.

20. *Ibid.*, pp. 93, 109.
21. Muir, *Wellington, the Path to Victory*, p. 171.
22. Muir, *Britain and the Defeat of Napoleon*, illustration on p. 45.
23. David, *All the King's Men*, p. 396.

## Chapter Ten

1. Fulford, p. 75.
2. Berry, *By Royal Appointment*, pp. 48, 49; Fulford, p. 75 and illustration between pp. 96/7.
3. Burne, pp. 289, 290.
4. *Ibid.*, pp. 292, 293.
5. Gurwood, *The Speeches of the Duke of Wellington in Parliament*, vol. I, pp. 47, 49.
6. Burne, pp. 295, 296.
7. *Ibid.*, pp. 299, 300.
8. *Ibid.*, p. 301.
9. Berry, p. 143.
10. *Ibid.*, p. 133.
11. Gurwood, vol. I, pp. 65, 67.
12. Longford, pp. 169, 170.
13. Burne, pp. 304, 305.
14. *Ibid.*, p. 317.
15. *Ibid.*, p. 319.
16. Berry, pp. 181, 182.
17. *Ibid.*, p. 216.
18. *Ibid.*, p. 217.

## Chapter Eleven

1. Fulford, pp. 83, 84.
2. *Ibid.*, p. 83.
3. *Ibid.*
4. Knight, *Britain against Napoleon. The Organization of Victory, 1793–1815*, p. 206.
5. Burne, pp. 322, 323.
6. Glover, PP, pp. 159, 160.
7. Fulford, p. 87.
8. Watkins, p. 231.
9. *Ibid.*, p. 232.
10. Burne, p. 324.
11. Watkins, p. 233.
12. Hamilton-Williams, *Waterloo: New Perspectives*, p. 75.
13. Holmes, WID, pp. 252, 254. Statistics concerning the size and composition of the armies at Waterloo (which vary a good deal from one authority to another) are taken from Bernard Cornwell, *Waterloo*, pp. 34–6, 38.
14. Watkins, p. 234.
15. See A.W. Cockerill archive as in Chapter 9, note 8, under 'Early History, 1803–1892'.

16. Watkins, p. 236.
17. *Ibid.*, p. 235.
18. *Ibid.*, p. 237.
19. Quoted in Burne, p. 327.
20. *Reminiscences of Captain Gronow*, project Gutenberg translation online, under 'Captain Hesse, formerly of the 18th Hussars'.
21. Holme, pp. 107, 108.
22. *Ibid.*, pp. 108, 109.
23. *Ibid.*, p. 137.
24. Fulford, p. 254.
25. Smith, pp. 164, 165.

## Chapter Twelve

1. Fulford, p. 91.
2. Brooke, p. 386.
3. Hibbert, *George IV, Regent and King*, (hereafter GRK), pp. 145, 146.
4. *Ibid.*, p. 157.
5. *Ibid.*, p. 162.
6. Smith, p. 189.
7. See Oatlands Heritage Group website (hereafter OHGW) at www.oatlands-heritage.org.
8. Foster, *A Companion and Key to the History of England* (OHGW).
9. *The Graphic*, 31.3.1883 (OHGW).
10. *Monthly Magazine and British Register 1826* (hereafter MMBR), p. 102.
11. OHGW.
12. Hibbert, GPW, p. 110n.
13. Pearce, *London's Mansions*, p. 197.
14. MMBR, p. 102.
15. Watkins, p. 272.
16. *Ibid.*, p. 255.
17. Fulford, p. 95.
18. Watkins, pp. 255–8.
19. *Ibid.*, pp. 258–65.
20. *Ibid.*, p. 265.
21. *Ibid.*, p. 282.
22. Huish, p. 1.
23. Watkins, pp. 287–90.
24. Hibbert, GRK, p. 283.
25. Watkins, p. 308.
26. Pearce, p. 197.
27. Watkins, pp. 308–10.
28. *Ibid.*, p. 292.
29. Ward-Jackson, *Public Sculpture of Historic Westminster*, p. 386.
30. Watkins, p. 293.
31. Ward-Jackson, p. 387.
32. See Royal Collection website at www.royalcollection.org.uk.

33. Ward-Jackson, p. 388.
34. Burne, p. 333.
35. *Mechanics' Magazine, Museum, Register, Journal and Gazette*, no. 574, 9 August 1834, pp. 305–11.
36. Ward-Jackson, p. 388.
37. *The Saturday Magazine*, 10 May 1834, p. 178.
38. Fulford, p. 100.
39. Longford, p. 346.
40. Fulford, pp. 39, 40.
41. *New Cambridge Modern History*, vol. IV, pp. 267, 268.
42. Opie and Opie (eds), *The Oxford Dictionary of Nursery Rhymes*, (hereafter ODNR), pp. 206, 207. The manuscript c. 1630 is MS Sloane, 1489.
43. Halliwell, *The Nursery Rhymes of England*, part one, numbers VI, VIII, IX.
44. Northall, *English Folk-Rhymes*, pp. 98, 99.
45. Opie and Opie, ODNR, pp. 522, 523.
46. Burne, p. 14.
47. Woodbridge Conservation Area Appraisal Supplementary Planning Document, July 2011, p. 10; Louis Musgrove in the *Ipswich Society Newsletter*, issue 183, April 2011.
48. Newman and Pevsner, *The Buildings of England, Shropshire*, pp. 578, 579.

## Appendix

1. *Oxford Dictionary of National Biography*, vol. 33, pp. 365, 366.
2. *Reminiscences of Captain Gronow*, Project Gutenberg transcription online under 'Captain Hesse, formerly of the 18th Hussars'.
3. Anthony Camp, *Royal Mistresses and Bastards, Fact and Fiction, 1714–1936*, published by the author, 2007. See summary on his website at anthonyjcamp.com.
4. Thanks to Robert Harding for showing me his copy of this caricature, apparently signed 'I Spy I'.
5. See Allerton Castle website at www.allertoncastle.co.uk/historyhtml.
6. See Oatlands Park Hotel website at http://oatlandsparkhotel.com/hotel/history.
7. See A.W. Cockerill archive as in Chapter Nine, note 8, and Lorraine Sencile at doverhistorian.com/2014/01/13.

# Sources

## Published Letters

A. Aspinall (ed.), *The later Correspondence of George III, 1783–1810*, 5 vols, Cambridge, 1962–1970

*The Correspondence of George, Prince of Wales, 1770–1812*, 8 vols, Cassell, 1963–1971

*The Letters of King George IV, 1812–1830*, 3 vols, Cambridge, 1938

## Published Diaries and Speeches

Creevey, T., *The Creevey Papers*, 2 vols, ed. Sir Herbert Maxwell, 1903

Croker, J.W., *The Correspondence and Diaries of the Late Rt Hon John Wilson Croker*, 3 vols, ed. L.J. Jennings, 1884

Greville, C.C.F., *The Greville Diary*, 2 vols, ed. P.W. Wilson, 1927

Gurwood, J., *The Speeches of the Duke of Wellington in Parliament*, vol. 1, John Murray, London, 1854

## Contemporary Articles

'Annual Register', 1827
    *Historical Memoir of Frederick, Duke of York* (anon)
    *Memorandum of the last illness and death of the Duke of York* (by Sir Herbert Taylor)
    *Character of the Duke of York* (by Sir Walter Scott)
Mechanics' Magazine, no. 574, August 1834
    *A Descriptive Account of the Duke of York's Monument*

## Studies of the Duke of York's Life or Military Career

Burne, Alfred, *The Noble Duke of York*, Staples Press, 1949

Fortescue, Sir John, *British Campaigns in Flanders, 1690–1794*, Macmillan, 1918

——, *A History of the British Army*, vol. IV, part II, 1789–1801

Fulford, Roger, *Royal Dukes*, Fontana revised edition, 1973

Glover, Richard, *Peninsula Preparation, The Reform of the British Army, 1795–1809*, Cambridge, 1963

——, *Britain at Bay, Defence against Bonaparte, 1803–1814*, George Allen & Unwin, 1973

Huish, R., *Authentic Memoir of his late Royal Highness Frederick, Duke of York and Albany*, London, 1827

Taylor, Lieutenant General Sir Herbert, *Journal of the last Illness and Death of His Royal Highness*, London, 1827

Watkins, John, *A Biographical Memoir of Frederick, Duke of York and Albany*, 1827, General Books OCR edition, 2009


## Other Publications

Berry, Paul, *By Royal Appointment*, Femina, 1970

Brooke, John, *King George III*, Constable, 1972

Clarke, Mary Anne, *The Rival Princes*, etc., David Longworth, New York, 1810

Cornwell, Bernard, *Waterloo*, William Collins, 2015

David, Saul, *All the King's Men*, Penguin, 2013

du Maurier, Daphne, *Mary Anne*, Arrow Books, 1954

Foreman, Amanda, *Georgiana, Duchess of Devonshire*, HarperCollins, 1998

Forster, Margaret, *Daphne du Maurier*, Chatto & Windus, 1993

Gristwood, Sarah, *Perdita, Royal Mistress, Writer, Romantic*, Bantam, 2005

Hadlow, Janice, *The Strangest Family*, Collins, 2014

Hague, William, *William Pitt the Younger*, Harper Perennial, 2005

Halliwell, James Orchard, *The Nursery Rhymes of England*, Frederick Warne & Co., London and New York, 1886

Hamilton-Williams, David, *Waterloo; New Perspectives*, BCA/Cassell, 1993

Hibbert, Christopher, *George IV, Prince of Wales*, Longman, 1972

——, *George IV, Regent and King*, Allen Lane, 1975

Holme, Thea, *Caroline, A Biography of Caroline of Brunswick*, Hamish Hamilton, 1979

Holmes, Richard, *Wellington, The Iron Duke*, HarperCollins, 1996

——, *Redcoat, The British Soldier in the Age of Sword and Musket*, HarperCollins, 2001

Knight, Roger, *Britain against Napoleon, The Organization of Victory, 1793–1815*, Allen Lane, 2013

Lambert, Andrew, *The Challenge, Britain against America in the Naval War of 1812*, Faber & Faber, 2012

Longford, Elizabeth, *Wellington, The Years of the Sword*, Weidenfeld & Nicholson, 1969

Marsh, Charles, *The Clubs of London*, etc. vol. I, 1828

Muir, Rory, *Britain and the Defeat of Napoleon, 1807–1815*, Yale, 1996

——, *Wellington, the Path to Victory 1769–1814*, Yale, 2013

Nairn, Ian and Pevsner, Nikolaus, *The Buildings of England: Surrey*, second edition, revised, Penguin, 1982

Northall, G.F., *English Folk-Rhymes*, Kegan Paul, London, 1892

Opie, Iona and Peter (eds), *The Oxford Dictionary of Nursery Rhymes*, Oxford, second edition, 1997

Pearce, David, *London's Mansions*, Batsford, 1986

Schama, Simon, *Patriots and Liberators, Revolution in the Netherlands, 1780–1813*, Fontana, 1992

Smith, E.A., *George IV*, Yale University Press, 1999

Thompson, Andrew C., *George II*, Yale University Press, 2011

Trevor-Roper, Hugh, 'Spain and Europe 1598–1621', Chapter IV of *The New Cambridge Modern History*, vol. IV, Cambridge, 1970

Van der Kiste, John, *George III's Children*, Sutton Publishing, 1992

Ward-Jackson, Philip, *Public Sculpture of Historic Westminster*, Liverpool University Press, 2011

# Index